Sharīʿa in Africa Today

Islam in Africa

The titles published in this series are listed at brill.com/isaf

VOLUME 15

Sharīʿa in Africa Today

Reactions and Responses

Edited by

John Chesworth and Franz Kogelmann

BRILL

LEIDEN • BOSTON
2014

Library of Congress Cataloging-in-Publication Data

Sharia in Africa today : reactions and responses / edited by John Chesworth & Franz Kogelmann.
pages cm — (Islam in Africa ; v. 15)
Includes bibliographical references and index.
ISBN 978-90-04-25054-3 (hardback : alk. paper) — ISBN 978-90-04-26212-6 (e-book : alk. paper)
1. Islamic law—Africa. 2. Islamic courts—Africa. I. Chesworth, John. II. Kogelmann, Franz.

KBP64.S43 2014
340.5'9096—dc23

2013033032

This publication has been typeset in the multilingual "Brill" typeface. With over 5,100 characters covering Latin, IPA, Greek, and Cyrillic, this typeface is especially suitable for use in the humanities. For more information, please see www.brill.com/brill-typeface.

ISBN 978-90-04-25054-3 (hardback)
ISBN 978-90-04-26212-6 (e-book)

This book is printed on acid-free paper.

FSC www.fsc.org MIX Paper from responsible sources FSC® C109576

Printed by Printforce, the Netherlands

CONTENTS

LIST OF MAPS

ACKNOWLEDGEMENTS

We thank all those who have been involved in the project, 'Sharīʿa Debates and Their Perception by Christians and Muslims in Selected African Countries'.

We acknowledge the generous support for the project of the Volkswagen Foundation and the "Knowledge for Tomorrow" initiative.

We are grateful for the support of:

- Senior Staff Professor Kurt Beck and Professor Ulrich Berner, University of Bayreuth, and Professor Frieder Ludwig, now at Fachhochschule für Interkulterelle Theologie, Hermannsburg;
- Dr. Philip Ostien and Dr. Sati Fwatshak, who were country co-ordinators in Nigeria, together with Dr. Jamila Nasir from the University of Jos, Nigeria; Professor Esther Mombo, St. Paul's University, Kenya; country co-ordinator for Sudan, Associate Professor Osman Muhammad Osman Ali, University of Khartoum, Sudan;

We are grateful:

- for the involvement in the planning stages of Associate Professor Shamil Jeppie, University of Cape Town and Dr. Abdulkadir Hashim Abdulkadir, formerly at University of Zanzibar, now at University of Nairobi, Kenya;
- for those who were involved in introducing new methodologies to the Junior Scholars: Professor Gabriele Cappai, Dr. Katharina Hofer and Dr. Asonzeh Ukah;
- to Ahmad Elhassab Umar Elhassab and Mohamed Hamed Mohamed Ahmed who also participated in the project.

Finally we would like to appreciate the support and patience of our wives Phyll and Brigitte.

TECHNICAL NOTE

Non-English words are italicised; the transliteration of Arabic words follows that used in the *Encyclopedia of the Qur'ān* edited by Jane Dammen McAuliffe (Brill, 2001–2006).

The meanings of non-English words are given in parentheses following their first appearance, e.g. *ribā* (Arab.: interest).

All quotations from the Qur'ān use Abdel Haleem's *The Qur'an* (Oxford University Press, 2004), with the reference being given using the name of the sūra, with the number in parentheses, e.g. *al-Nūr* (24):31.

Quotations from the Bible use the *New Revised Standard Version*, (Oxford University Press, 1995), with the reference being given using the name of the book, with chapter and verse, e.g. Matthew 5:25.

All dates are cited according to the "Common Era" (C.E.), numerically equivalent to the Christian A.D.

PREFACE

This book originated in a research project "*Sharīʿa* Debates and Their Perception by Christians and Muslims in Selected African Countries" in which a group of African junior scholars at different stages of their academic careers were invited to participate. This research project was financed for three years (2006–2009) by Volkswagen Foundation under the funding initiative "Knowledge for Tomorrow—Co-operative Research Projects in Sub-Saharan Africa". Most of the research and writing sponsored by the project has been done by these African junior scholars, who include both Muslims and Christians. They have been closely supervised, assisted and evaluated by a group of senior scholars with a view to their proper training, their exposure to current ideas, methodologies, and milieus, and the enhancement of their formal academic qualifications.

The research here being reported on developed from a previous joint research project on the current *sharīʿa* debate in Nigeria, "The *sharīʿa* Debate and the Shaping of Muslim and Christian Identities in Northern Nigeria". This was also funded by Volkswagen Foundation and organized by the Universities of Jos, Nigeria, and Bayreuth, Germany, in 2002/2004. At an early stage of that research project it became obvious that the *sharīʿa* debate in Nigeria is not a single and locally-restricted phenomenon. In many other African countries with a Muslim population, heated public debates on certain aspects of Islamic law, and/or the relationship of Islam or religion in general and the state, are nowadays an important part of daily political life. Thus, a preliminary workshop was held in Limuru, Kenya, in July 2004, where the basic idea for the new research project was to develop new theoretical bases and research methods to examine this current phenomenon in a series of African countries. To reach this objective it was first of all necessary to get a general idea of these recent developments. Thus the organizers, John Chesworth, St. Paul's United Theological College (now St. Paul's University), Limuru, and Franz Kogelmann, University of Bayreuth, invited mainly junior scholars, both Muslims and Christians, from Austria, Germany, Kenya, the Netherlands, Nigeria, Rwanda, South Africa, Sudan, Tanzania, Uganda and the USA to attend the workshop. Keeping in mind that debates on Islamic law are not limited to sub-Saharan countries in Africa, the organizers also invited scholars from Egypt, Iran and Malaysia to attend. Due to the multi-disciplinary and international backgrounds of the participants, fruitful discussions took place and the first results of cross-fertilisation appeared. The workshop in Limuru gave the junior scholars the opportunity to establish new academic networks (south-south and north-south) and was also successful in taking first steps across the existing academic divides. One of the most important outcomes of the workshop was the insight that the quality of our understanding of the current *sharīʿa* debates in sub-Saharan Africa and their side-effects on society was highly unsatisfactory.

The University of Bayreuth worked in partnership with St. Paul's University, Limuru, Kenya; with the University of Jos, Plateau State, Nigeria and with the University of Khartoum, Sudan. Initially, the University of Cape Town, South Africa and the University of Zanzibar were also partners, but withdrew when no suitable junior scholars were proposed.

Following the Limuru workshop in 2004, a successful funding proposal was made to Volkswagen Foundation for a project called *Sharīʿa Debates and Their Perception by Christians and Muslims in Selected African Countries*. From late 2005, the selection of a group of junior scholars from the different countries began. The successful candidates were at various stages of post-graduate work; four were completing their MA research, four were working on their doctorates and three were conducting post-doctoral research. Four of the junior scholars were Christians and seven were Muslims; four were women and seven were men. They came from a variety of disciplines, Anthropology, Economics, Politics, Religious Studies and Theology.

They all met in Bayreuth for three months in the summer of 2006, where they trained in a variety of research methods in social science and learned about working on multi-disciplinary research. As a group we met with them on several occasions in Limuru, Kenya; Shendi, Sudan; Bamako, Mali; Jos, Nigeria and Kisumu, Kenya as well as for a further two months in Bayreuth during the summer of 2007.

Map 1 Map of Africa: Showing countries covered in the book

CHAPTER ONE

INTRODUCTION

John Chesworth and Franz Kogelmann

All over the world, in recent years, there has been a resurgence of religion in the public sphere. In many sub-Saharan African countries this has manifested itself most noticeably in claims by Muslims for increased recognition of Islamic religious symbols within political and civil spaces hitherto dominated by 'Western' systems, and especially for the implementation, in some form or other, of the sacred law of Islam, the *sharīʿa*. These Muslim claims, different in their character and scope from country to country, have sparked off intense debates in all the countries where they have been made.

Unfortunately, the quality of our understanding of these recent and important developments, and of where they are leading, is highly unsatisfactory. General introductions in Islamic law are available,[1] the role of Islam in African constitutionalism is discussed,[2] and the influence of Islamic law in Africa on the eve of colonial rule is also well described.[3] However, country specific studies focused on sub-Saharan Africa and based on empirical research are relatively scarce.

For Sudan, Fluehr-Lobban tried to survey the history and to detail the practice of Islamic law during the second half of the 1980s.[4] Her findings are partly based on field-work on the day-to-day working of the *sharīʿa* in Khartoum. A far more in-depth study, but lacking empirical research, is Layish and Warburg's book on the *sharīʿa* in Sudan under Numayrī.[5]

---

[1] Schacht, J., *An Introduction to Islamic Law*, Oxford: Clarendon Press, 1964; Doi, A. R. I., *Sharīʿah: The Islamic Law*, London: TaHa Publishers Ltd. 1984; Vikør, K. S., *Between God and the Sultan*, London: Hurst & Company, 2005; Hallaq, W. B., *A History of Islamic Legal Theories. An Introduction to Sunnī uṣūl al-fiqh*, Cambridge: Cambridge University Press (CUP), 1997; Hallaq, W. B., *The Origins and Evolution of Islamic Law,* Cambridge: CUP, 2005; Hallaq, W. B., *Sharīʿa—Theory—Practice—Transformations*, Cambridge: CUP, 2009a; Hallaq, W. B., *An Introduction to Islamic Law*, Cambridge: CUP, 2009b.

[2] an-Na'im, A. A., *African Constitutionalism and the Role of Islam.* Philadelphia, Pa.: University of Pennsylvania Press, 2006.

[3] Anderson, J. N. D., *Islamic Law in Africa*, London: Frank Cass & Co., 1970.

[4] Fluehr-Lobban, C., *Islamic law and society in the Sudan*, London etc.: Frank Cass, 1987.

[5] Layish, A. and G. R. Warburg, *The Reinstatement of Islamic Law in Sudan under Numayrī. An evaluation of a legal experiment in the light of its historical context, methodology, and repercussions*, Leiden: Brill, 2002.

Important as these two studies are, as well as others in this field,[6] they do not take into consideration the period after the Comprehensive Peace Agreement of 2005.

There are polemical articles, both Muslim and Christian, written about Nigeria post-1999, when the wave of re-implementation of Islamic law in the northern part of the country commenced, but also serious academic studies on this phenomenon.[7] For any future research on the re-implementation of Islamic law in Northern Nigeria, Ostien's five volume sourcebook on *sharīʿa* implementation in Northern Nigeria since 1999 will be indispensable.[8] However, certain aspects of the so-called *sharīʿa* project, such as its influence on education in northern Nigeria, are not covered. Studies on the impact of Islamic law on the Muslim community of Yorubaland in south-western Nigeria are almost non-existent.[9]

For East Africa, the situation is much the same. The practice of Islamic law in Zanzibar and the coastal strip of Kenya and mainland Tanzania is well-covered by the publications of Hashim, Hirsch, Stiles and Stockreiter.[10]

---

[6] See: Köndgen, O., *Das islamisierte Strafrecht des Sudan. Von seiner Einführung 1983 bis Juli 1992*, Hamburg: Mitteilungen des Deutschen Orient-Instituts 43, 1992; Köndgen, O., 'Sharia and national law in the Sudan', in *Sharia Incorporated. A Comparative Overview of the Legal Systems of Twelve Muslim Countries in Past and Present*, Otto, J. M. (ed.), Leiden: Leiden Univ. Press, 2010, pages: 181–230; Sidahmed, A., *Politics and Islam in Contemporary Sudan*, London: Routledge, 1997; El-Affendi, A., *Turabi's Revolution. Islam and Power in Sudan*, London: Grey Seal, 1991; Nageeb, S. A., *New Spaces and Old Frontiers. Women, Social Spaces and Islamization in Sudan*, Lanham: Lexington Books, 2004.

[7] Ostien, P. and A. Dekker, 'Sharia and national law in Nigeria', in *Sharia Incorporated*, Otto, J. M. (ed.), Leiden: Leiden University Press, 2010, pages 553–612; Weimann, G. J., *Islamic Criminal Law in Northern Nigeria*, Amsterdam: Amsterdam University Press, 2010; Ostien, P., 'Divine Law and Local Custom in Northern Nigerian Zina Trials', *Die Welt des Islams* 49. 3–4, 2009, pages 429–465; Ostien, P., 'Islamic Law and Muslim Governance in Northern Nigeria: Crimes Against Life, Limb and Property in *Shariʿa* Judicial Practice,' *Islamic Law and Society* 17, 3, 2010; Ludwig, F., 'Christian-Muslim Relations in Northern Nigeria since the Introduction of Shariʿah in 1999', *Journal of the American Academy of Religion* 76, 2008, pages 602–637; Christelow, A., 'Persistence and Transformation in the Politics of Shariʿa, Nigeria, 1947–2003: In Search of an Explanatory Framework', in *Muslim Family Law in sub-Saharan Africa. Colonial Legacies and Post-colonial Challenges*, S. Jeppie, E. Moosa & R. L. Roberts (eds.), Amsterdam: Amsterdam University Press, 2010, pages 247–272.

[8] Ostien, P., *Sharia Implementation in Northern Nigeria 1999–2006: A Sourcebook, 5 volumes*, Ibadan: Spectrum Books Ltd., 2007 (http://www.sharia-in-africa.net/pages/publications/sharia-implementation-in-northern-nigeria.php).

[9] See Makinde and Ostien's recent article: Makinde, Abdul-Fatah 'Kola, Ostien, Philip, Legal Pluralism in Colonial Lagos: The 1894 Petition of the Lagos Muslims to their British Colonial Masters, *Die Welt des Islams* 52:1, 2012, pages 51–68.

[10] Hashim, A., 'Coping with Conflicts: Colonial Policy towards Muslim Personal Law in Kenya and Post-Colonial Court Practice', in S. Jeppie, E. Moosa & R. L. Roberts (eds.), 2010, pages 221–245; Hirsch, S. F., 'State Intervention in Muslim Family Law in Kenya and

However, the hinterland and the current political context are mostly neglected.[11]

Thus, there is some scholarly literature on various *sharīʿa* debates in sub-Saharan Africa, but its coverage is in many cases patchy. The studies contributing to this literature tend to be mono-disciplinary, often uninformed by history, and, a very serious problem from African points of view, are mostly done by foreigners whose approach and perspective is different from African Muslims, and also from African Christians.

The present book takes up that challenge with an examination of various aspects of *sharīʿa* debates in sub-Saharan Africa, carried out by Africans, both Muslims and Christians.

The contributors to this book have sought to explore the impact of *sharīʿa* debates on Christian-Muslim relations in their own countries. They have done this by mapping the reactions and responses to *sharīʿa* debates in various communities, finding various levels of understanding and misunderstanding therein.

The countries involved in the research all have prior experience of *sharīʿa* for historical reasons in that, prior to European colonisation, they were either colonised by Muslim powers, for example the Coastal Strip of

Tanzania: Applications of the Gender Concept', in S. Jeppie, E. Moosa & R. L. Roberts (eds.), op. cit., pages 305–329; Hirsch, S. F., *Pronouncing and Persevering: Gender and Discourses of Disputing in African Islamic Court*', Chicago and London: University of Chicago Press, 1998; Hirsch, S. F., 'Kadhi's Courts as Complex Sites of Resistance: The State, Islam, and Gender in Postcolonial Kenya', in *Contested States: Law, Hegemony, and Resistance*, M. Lazarus-Black & S. F. Hirsch (eds.), New York: Routledge, 1994, pages: 207–230; Stiles, Erin E., *An Islamic Court in Context: An Ethnographic Study of Judicial Reasoning*, London: Palgrave Macmillan, 2009; Stiles, Erin E., 'Broken Edda and Marital Mistakes: Two Recent Disputes from an Islamic Court in Zanzibar', in *Dispensing Justice in Islam: Qadis and their Judgments*, Masud, M. K., R. Peters & D. S. Powers (eds.), Leiden: Brill, 2006, pages: 95–116; Stiles, Erin E., 'There is No Stranger to Marriage Here!' Muslim Women and Divorce in Rural Zanzibar', *Africa: Journal of the International Africa Institute*, 75, 4, 2005, pages: 582–598; Stiles, Erin E., 'When is a Divorce a Divorce? Determining Intention in Zanzibar's Islamic Courts', *Ethnology*, 42, 4, 2003, pages: 273–288; Stockreiter, E., 'Child Marriage and Domestic Violence: Islamic and Colonial Discourses on Gender Relations and Female Status in Zanzibar, 1900–1950s', in *Domestic Violence and the Law in Colonial and Postcolonial Africa*, Burrill, E. S., R. L. Roberts, & E. Thornberry (eds.) Athens, OH: Ohio University Press, 2010, pages 138–158; Stockreiter, E., *Tying and untying the knot: Kadhi's courts and the negotiation of social status in Zanzibar, 1900–63*, unpublished PhD thesis SOAS, University of London, 2008; Stockreiter, E., 'Islamisches Recht und sozialer Wandel: Die Kadhi-Gerichte von Malindi, Kenya, und Zanzibar, Tanzania', *Stichproben. Wiener Zeitschrift für kritische Afrikastudien* 2/3, 2002, pages 35–61.

[11] Exceptions are this short article: Hashim, A., 'Muslim State Relations in Kenya after the Referendum on the Constitution', in *AASR Bulletin* 24, November 2005, pages 21–27; and, more recently, Tayob, A. & J. Wandera (eds.), *Constitutional Review in Kenya and Kadhis Courts*, Cape Town: Centre for Contemporary Islam, University of Cape Town, 2011.

East Africa and Sudan, or were independent Muslim states, for example the Sokoto Caliphate in what is now Northern Nigeria.

The four countries where research has been carried out were chosen because they are all impacted by *sharīʿa* to a greater or lesser extent and they all have significant numbers of both Muslims and Christians in their populations.

The countries are not alphabetically or geographically presented, but are ordered from the perspective of the level of *sharīʿa* present in the country. We therefore begin with the total *sharīʿa* of the Sudan, where the September Laws were introduced by the Numayrī regime in 1983. We then move to Nigeria and the re-implementation, from 1999, of Islamic penal law in most of the states of Northern Nigeria, flanked by other measures to Islamize society. Then on to Kenya where the place of Kadhi's Courts in the Constitution was one of the factors leading to the rejection of the proposed Constitution in 2005. Finally we move to Tanzania where Kadhi's Courts were abolished on the mainland after independence and where there are now calls for their re-introduction.

Since the implementation of the September laws of 1983, Sudan has been a *sharīʿa* state. Islamic laws, including the application of corporal punishments, have been imposed on all Sudanese regardless of their religious affiliation. After the Comprehensive Peace Agreement of 2005 the situation changed fundamentally: Southern Sudan is exempted from *sharīʿa* and Khartoum as the capital of the state enjoys a special status. Even the states of Northern Sudan traditionally inhabited by a Muslim majority mostly stopped applying Islamic criminal law. The Sudanese junior scholars have been researching the impact of these changes on public life from different angles. They took especial note of the changes brought about by the Comprehensive Peace Agreement (2005) between the Khartoum government and the South, leading to the creation of a new state, South Sudan, in 2011.

Osman Mohamed Osman Ali was the project's country co-ordinator for Sudan. He is assistant professor of anthropology at the Department of Sociology and Social Anthropology at the University of Khartoum. In his contribution to this book he offers in a nutshell the results of his PhD thesis "The Dynamics of Interpretation of Textual Islam in Northern Sudan: Case Study among the Rural and Urban Population of Shendi Province". He did extensive field work on multicultural and multiethnic communities in the southern part of the River Nile State. He identified four subcultures in Shendi Province: Shendi town itself, the villages south and north of

Shendi town, and nomads' camps. To a varying extent in each, there are within these subcultures five active Sunni Muslim groups: the Republican Brothers, the Sufis, the Anṣār al-Mahdī (Arab. followers of the Guided One, i.e. members of a religious movement associated with the teachings of Muḥammad Aḥmad, the self-proclaimed mahdī of the 19th century), the Anṣār al-Sunna (Arab. followers of the *sunna*, i.e. those who call for the revival of the traditions of the Prophet Muḥammad), and the Islamic Movement. His chapter "*sharīʿa* and Reality": A Domain of Contest among Sunni Muslims in Shendi Province, Northern Sudan" shows that *sharīʿa* is not a monolithic entity. In fact it is a body of transmitted knowledge from which the actors draw different conclusions. It is shaped and appropriated according to their own perspectives.

Salma Mohamed Abdalla, a political scientist from the University of Khartoum and nowadays a PhD candidate at Bayreuth International School of African Studies in Germany (BIGSAS), researched "Christian-Muslim Relations among the Internally Displaced Persons (IDPs) in Khartoum: The Case of Mandela and Wad al-Bashīr Camps". Her research is based on field-work administered in these two IDP camps. The primary data of her research was collected using the methods of individual interviews, group discussions and focus group discussions. Her research questions were centred around the behaviour and attitudes of members of the IDP communities regarding inter-faith dialogue in daily life, on the one hand, and examining the political structure and the role of the state in Christian-Muslim relations on the other hand. Whereas problems do not occur in the day to day interactions of members of different religious groups, the research revealed issues of conflict at the level of the state. Many Christians see public order as a critical issue in Christian-Muslim relationships in the camps. Both religious groups agree on conflicts between Christians and the state.

In Nigeria, *sharīʿa* debates have a long tradition. The debate on the new Nigerian constitution during the second half of the 1970s inspired the first 'Grand Debate' on the future role of Islamic law in the Federal Republic of Nigeria. It was only after the return to democracy in 1999 that twelve states of Northern Nigeria started to re-implement 'full-*sharīʿa*' i.e. all aspects of Islamic law in personal and in criminal matters. The South West of Nigeria is inhabited by about 40–50 per cent Muslims, but Islamic law was never part of the official jurisdiction there. Nevertheless there is a tendency by certain Muslims to organize independent *sharīʿa* panels.

After Abdul-Fatah Makinde, a lecturer in Islamic studies, had submitted his PhD thesis "The Institution of Sharīʿah in Oyo and Osun States, Nigeria, 1890–2005" at the University of Ibadan, he focused his research on independent *sharīʿa* panels in the South West of Nigeria. Makinde arranged interviews with religious leaders and government officials. These show that there are Muslims in this region of Nigeria who demand that the government legislate for the establishment of Islamic jurisprudence in civil matters. Neither the state nor the Christian population seem to be happy with a formal state-sanctioned implementation of *sharīʿa* courts in South West Nigeria. Christians regard *sharīʿa* as the religious law of the Muslims, a private matter, hence the government's involvement is seen as superfluous. Government officials on the other hand show certain reservations and do not see the political necessity to act.

The education of Muslim women in Northern Nigeria is the topic of Chikas Danfulani's research. In her PhD project "The Re-Implementation of Sharia in Northern Nigeria and the Education of Muslim Women 1999–2007"[12] she shows how some Muslims in Northern Nigeria conceptualise education. The research is based on in-depth interviews conducted in Northern Nigeria with Muslim educators, professionals and policymakers in five states. Her results clearly show that there is in most cases a gap between the literature and the reality in the field. Even if there is a strong debate over the educational status of women in Northern Nigeria, very few states that have re-implemented *sharīʿa* have so far introduced new programmes on female education.

The Muslim population of Northern Nigeria is not a monolithic block. Various Sufi brotherhoods still have a great influence in this region. Whereas the time immediately before and after independence was characterised by a struggle between the two dominating *turuq,* Tijāniyya and Qādiriyya, since the 1970s there have been frequent violent clashes between Sufis and members of a reform Islam movement, the Yan Izala. Ramzi Ben Amara, who is trained in religious studies, worked on "The Development of the Izala Movement in Nigeria: Its Split, Relationship to Sufis and Perception of Sharia Implementation". His research was conducted through a series of interviews with adherents, supporters and opponents of the movement in a number of the Northern states of Nigeria.

[12] Danfulani, Chikas, 'The Re-implementation of Sharia in Northern Nigeria and the Education of Muslim Women 1999–2007', University of Bayreuth, 2012, available as an e-thesis via http://opus.ub.uni-bayreuth.de/opus4–ubbayreuth/frontdoor/index/index/docId/1134.

However, since the re-implementation of *sharīʿa* in Northern Nigeria, most of the inter-Muslim conflicts seem to be settled. Consequently most Muslim organizations gather under the banner of *sharīʿa*. Moreover the Izala movement claims to be the driving force behind the re-implementation. Part of the success of the Izala movement is its ability to involve Muslim women by educational programmes.

In East Africa Islam has been present since the 10th century. When the Sultanate of Zanzibar became a British protectorate in 1890, the Ten-Mile strip on the Mainland was ceded to British Imperial East Africa and Deutsch-Ostafrika with an agreement that Kadhi's Courts should continue to operate in this area, which was populated mainly by Muslims. As a result of the negotiations leading to independence, the future Prime Ministers of Kenya and Tanganyika agreed to continue the treaty of 1890. However, following independence changes were made.

In Kenya, Kadhi's Courts are an integral part of the national legal system and were established in every province of Kenya. Their jurisdiction is strictly restricted to Muslim personal law and nobody seemed to take serious offence at their existence until the Constitution of Kenya Review Commission published the so-called Bomas Draft Constitution in 2004. The amendment of the position of the Kadhi's Courts in the new constitution has sparked off a heated public debate.

In his MA thesis "Debates on Kadhi's Courts and Christian-Muslim Relations: A Case Study of Isiolo Town", Halkano Abdi Wario, a student in religious studies from Moi University, Eldoret, Kenya, examined how the debates on Kadhi's Courts had impacted Christian-Muslim relationships in a town of Northern Kenya with an ethnically and religiously-mixed population. The Kadhi's Courts issue acted as a focus for the tensions in the town and had implications for Christian-Muslim relations in the area. Wario's research is a multi-disciplinary study with in-depth interviews with community leaders and group interviews with 'focus groups' representing different communities. A specific focus of the research was the ways in which civic society groups prepared people for the constitutional referendum in November 2005. A number of thematic issues and emergent trends were revealed through the research. While most Muslims emphasize the courts' role and call for its improvement, most Christians cite the courts' illegitimacy due to the secular nature of the state. The debate about the courts was interpreted in terms of a majority-minority struggle to influence policy formulation in the country, accompanied by fears and suspicions. Furthermore, the debate linked past conflicts with present concerns—pointing to the question: Who owns Isiolo?

In addition to finalising her PhD on "Islam and Divination Among the Swahili of Kenya Coast" at Maseno University, Kenya, Esha Faki Mwinyihaji also researched "The *sharīʿa* and Muslim Women's Participation in the Public Sphere". Her method was to use in-depth interviews with members of the Swahili community. These were mainly women, in particular Swahili women who had become involved in politics and had stood for office at local and national levels, but she also included some male community leaders in her interviews. Various elements emerged that have prevented Swahili Muslim women's involvement in the public sphere, such as widespread ignorance of general and public affairs or the lack of access to the financial means needed for political mobilization. Customs such as early marriage, or the assumption that women cannot lead men, are also obstacles inhibiting Swahili women from organizing themselves. Furthermore, the idea of the empowerment of women among the Swahili is being questioned on Islamic doctrinal and cultural grounds. Swahili Muslim women are facing traditional interpretations of religious scripts that have for centuries reinforced patriarchal structures. They are faced with religious authorities who do not guide them but rule them, as well as by deeply rooted values of their culture.

The day to day practice of Kadhi's courts on the shores of Lake Victoria is the topic of Rebecca Osiro's PhD research "Women's Views on the Role of Kadhi's Courts: A Case Study of Kendu Bay, Kenya". Osiro holds an M.A. in Islam and Christian-Muslim Relations from St. Paul's University in Limuru. Her research has been conducted through interviews with the community, as well as by following cases through the Kadhi's Courts' system. An important part of the project was the examination of various Islamic legal practices and how they are understood and followed in the local context. The research also highlighted the fact that many of the women who have become Muslims on marriage are ignorant of their rights, both under Islamic and civil law. So, if a case comes to court, the Kadhi often cannot act because the lack of documents means that the validity of a marriage cannot be proved. Another phenomenon, which is also observable in many other Muslim communities, is that locally-embedded traditions are followed even when at odds with Islamic practice. The women interviewed supported the view that Kadhi's courts should be entrenched into the constitution and demanded more courts of this kind in Kenya.

The two parts which form the United Republic of Tanzania handle the *sharīʿa* question differently. At independence Zanzibar retained a legal structure with both State Courts and Islamic Courts. However, on the mainland, the Kadhi's Courts were abolished. The provisions of the

Uniform Marriage Act 1971 were regarded by the government as covering all the aspects of *sharīʿa* that were the remit of the Kadhi's Courts. Members of the different religious groups of mainland Tanzania have, most of the time, co-existed peacefully since independence, although some violent clashes have occurred since the 1990s. In the late 1990s, requests to re-establish Kadhi's Courts again surfaced in mainland Tanzania.

For his PhD project, William Kopwe, who holds an M.A. in Islam and Christian-Muslim Relations from St. Paul's University, Limuru, did research on "The Prospects and Problems of *Sharīʿa* Implementation on the Tanzanian Mainland". Through a series of interviews, the views of different sections of society concerning the prospects and problems of *sharīʿa* implementation on the Tanzanian mainland were explored. The research is about the social challenges posed to and by *sharīʿa* implementation on the Tanzanian mainland. Two major concepts, 'social' and 'challenge', are fundamental to this study. Three areas: legal pluralism, religious pluralism and state secularity are included in the term 'social'. The term 'challenge' is a two-fold concept. The first aspect is the whole matter of the legal and constitutional provisions for *sharīʿa* implementation in the country. The possibilities of, and hindrance to, *sharīʿa* implementation in the country in accordance with the country's constitution and legal system are examined. The second aspect of 'challenge' is the exploration of the impact of *sharīʿa* implementation on Christian-Muslim relations in the country with regard to the religio socio political heterogeneity of the country. The research shows that there is fear that the Kadhi's Courts will have a divisive effect on Christian-Muslim relations. It also demonstrates that there is general ignorance about what *sharīʿa* is and what the functions of the Kadhi's Courts are. The demand for Kadhi's Courts has created mutual suspicions between Christians and Muslims and raised fears that the re-establishment of Kadhi's Courts heralds the start of a move to create Tanzania into an Islamic state.

The second study on *sharīʿa* and its accompanying debates in Tanzania is very different. Bernadin Mfumbusa, who holds a PhD in mass communications from the Gregoriana in Rome and since 2011 has been Bishop of Kondoa, Tanzania, focused his research "*Sharīʿa* Debates and the National Consensus in Tanzania" on grassroots *sharīʿa* debates and their impact on the national consensus. His research concerns the profile of religion in Tanzanian public life. A series of thirty in-depth interviews were conducted with Muslims and Christians in the community, together with observation. Kondoa, a small town in Dodoma Region in central Tanzania, was selected for the case study largely because it is a microcosm of the country: multi-ethnic, multi-racial and multi-religious. Although people have lived there in relative peace and harmony since independence, signs of radicalization along religious lines are now apparent. Over the last two decades there has been a discernible shift in the trend of debates, from the pre-occupation in the pre-1985 period with the relationship between *ujamaa* (African socialism) and religion, or between religion and state, to the marginalization and victimization rhetoric which has taken on Muslim versus non-Muslim nuances in the post-1985 period. The research also shows that that the extent of conflict among Christians and Muslims has often been exaggerated. It also found that ethnic bonds transcend religious affiliations. In spite of generally peaceable relations in Kondoa, two areas of tension were found: one that was recognised as specifically causing tensions between Muslims and Christians was the impact of Christian NGOs on the Muslim way of life. The research documented the activities of one group, Compassion International, which on arrival linked itself to several churches in Kondoa and offered educational scholarships to Muslim children. Acceptance of the scholarship involved attendance at Bible Classes. The second area of tension is amongst Muslims themselves and results from the presence of new attitudes emanating from some Muslim youth who have been trained outside the country and are introducing different interpretations of Islam. This group of Muslim youths has formed the Ansaar Sunni, who are "Wahhabi" in temperament and cause tensions with older Muslims in the community who continue to adhere to the Shāfiʿī Madhhab.

The variety of research topics discussed in the different chapters reveals the range of reactions and responses to *sharīʿa* debates encountered in sub-Saharan Africa. Together, these pieces of research inform the continuing discourse of religious identities as Muslims and Christians seek ways of co-existing in the nation-states studied.

PART ONE

SUDAN: "TOTAL *SHARĪʿA*"

Map 2 Map of Sudan: Showing principal places referred to in Part One

CHAPTER TWO

"*SHARĪʿA* AND REALITY": A DOMAIN OF CONTEST AMONG SUNNI MUSLIMS IN THE DISTRICT OF SHENDI, NORTHERN SUDAN

Osman Mohamed Osman Ali

Introduction

This chapter examines the way in which some Muslim groups in Northern Sudan take opposite sides over the issues of *sharīʿa* and reality. It considers the Muslim diversity in Northern Sudan to be an argument that any attempt to implement the *sharīʿa* will be fraught with conflict. This premise is supported by field data from the urban and rural communities of the District of Shendi (Arab.: *muḥāfaẓat Shandī*),[1] which represents the southern part of the River Nile State (*wilāyat nahr al-Nīl*), on the eastern bank of the Nile. These communities are multicultural, multiethnic and inclusive of some Muslim and Christian religious groups.[2] The existence of Shendi town in between the villages of the north and the south, the natural environment, the economic activities, the kinship ties, and other aspects, all distinguish four subcultures in the District of Shendi: that of Shendi town, villages north of Shendi town, villages south of Shendi town, and nomads' camps. The Muslim groups (i.e., the Republican Brothers, the Sufis, the Anṣār al-Mahdī, the Anṣār al-Sunna, and the Islamic Movement), which are all Sunni, are found here and there within these subcultures, including both males and females in their memberships.[3] As there were no other Muslim groups in this region during the time of the research, the discussions in this chapter are restricted to these groups. Dividing the Muslims into these groups in the District of Shendi has been in response to their self-identification, as the boundaries among these groups are clear in the

---

[1] Fieldwork for collecting these data was done in 2002 and then updated in 2008, just before writing and finalising this chapter.

[2] Ali, O. M. O., 'Death-related Beliefs and Practices, an Area of Conflict in a Multicultural Community: Rural Shendi', M.Sc Thesis, University of Khartoum, 1994, pages 1–2.

[3] Ali, O. M. O., 'The Dynamics of Interpretation of Textual Islam in Northern Sudan: Case Study among the Rural and Urban Population of Shendi Province', Ph.D. Thesis, University of Khartoum, 2004, pages 202–203.

region. Importantly, as expressed by many Sufi informants, there are no essential differences among the various Sufi orders as regarding their teachings and cardinal rituals. They all adhere to both the Islamic *sharīʿa* and voluntary or optional religious services, and follow the same one path that is believed to lead to the Prophet Muḥammad, and ultimately, God. Even in their literature, the Sufi Sheikhs constantly urge their followers to assist and show respect and love to the followers of all the Sufi orders. For these reasons, all the Sufi groups have good, friendly relations with each other and cooperate in their religious activities and festivals. Building upon this, the Sufis are taken as a homogenous group in this chapter. Also, the Anṣār al-Mahdī feel an intimate relationship between the Sufi and Mahdist schools of thought. They utter not a single criticism against the Sufis. They respect the Sufis and think of them as following the right way, as they do. However, they state that the *imām al-mahdī* had been a Sufi disciple for a long time before he declared the Mahdiship. He presented his own legal rules and judgements only after that declaration. He then invited Sufis who were his contemporaries (including the Sufi Sheikhs) to follow him and criticized many of their manners of conduct, which he considered as not conforming to the Islamic religion. It is only for these reasons that the Anṣār al-Mahdī regard themselves as distinct from the Sufis who are presently existing in the District of Shendi, as do the Sufis in their feelings towards the Anṣār al-Mahdī.

The District of Shendi, due to the above considerations and for other reasons, is worthy of being described as a miniature representation of Northern Sudan. That is to say, this chapter deals with the philosophical underpinnings of the above-mentioned Sunni Muslim groups in the District of Shendi, but of course this has implications for the whole of Northern Sudan. Historically speaking, in the centuries known in Europe as the Middle Ages, the northern region of Sudan was divided into three kingdoms: Nobatia, Makuria and Alodia. Between these kingdoms and the Red Sea lay the Beja country.[4] The introduction of Christianity into these kingdoms in the sixth century marked a new era. Christianity was adopted to such an extent that it became the state religion.[5] With the fall of Egypt into the hands of the Muslims, preparations began for the conquest of Sudan. By 652 Islamic forces invaded Makuria, the northern kingdom, which defeated the invaders decisively and for six centuries thereafter was able to impose its own

[4] Hasan, Yusuf Fadl, 'The Penetration of Islam in the Eastern Sudan', in *Islam in Tropical Africa*, Lewis, I. M. (ed.), London: Oxford University Press, 1966, pages 144–159, (page 144).

[5] Hasan, 1966, pages 144–145.

terms upon relations with the Muslim world. The Muslim forces, then, turned their acquisitive attentions eastward towards the Beja. Raids were undertaken to impose tribute upon nearby chiefs and open their country to Muslim traders. In years to come, many immigrant Arabs would be absorbed into the northern Beja lineages, creating mixed-descent communities that were recognized as the first Beja Muslims.[6] After a time, many Arabs drifted towards Alodia, the southern kingdom, which by the twelfth century began to break up.[7] Then, hostilities between Makuria and Muslims began to erupt. In 1276 an Islamic force conquered Makuria and, under the terms of settlement, its people were allowed to keep their religion as protected persons under *sharīʿa* and were to be governed via a puppet king chosen by the conquerors. In 1324 Muslims seized the throne from the old dynasty.[8] Over the next few centuries, renewed centripetal social forces restored royal rule to the Nile and introduced a form of state government to the western highlands. Thenceforth, the Sudanese kingdoms were lands of Islam.[9]

It was the influence of traders and Muslim holy men that finally won the victory for Islamic culture in Northern Sudan. The holy men transmitted the version of Islam known as Sufism. The more charismatic of them bonded with their followers into orders (Arab.: *ṭarīqa* / *ṭuruq*). The coming of the *ṭuruq* into Northern Sudan can be divided into two stages. The first, which may be dated from about the 16th century, began with the recruitment of some holy men into the decentralized "ancient" *ṭuruq*, the Qādiriyya and the Shādhiliyya. The second stage took place in the 18th and 19th centuries when the country came to be dominated by a number of centralized reformist *ṭuruq*, namely, the Sammāniyya, the Khatmiyya, the Idrīsiyya and the Tijāniyya.[10] In 1881, a Sufi leader by the name Muḥammad Aḥmad proclaimed his mission as *imām al-mahdī* (Arab.: divinely guided leader). He called upon people to fight against the Turks who, because of their impiety and oppression, were unbelievers. By the time of his death in 1885, the Mahdist forces controlled most of northern Sudan and began to establish a centralized state based on principles of rule defined

---

6 Spaulding, Jay, 'Precolonial Islam in Eastern Sudan', in *The History of Islam in Africa*, Levtzion, Nehemia & Pouwels, Randall L. (eds.), Oxford: James Currey Ltd, 2000, pages 117–118.

7 Hasan, 1966, page 151.

8 Spaulding, 2000, pages 118–119.

9 Spaulding, 2000, pages 119–120.

10 Karrar, A. S., *The Sufi Brotherhoods in the Sudan*, London: Hurst & Company, 1992, pages 1, 20.

by *al-mahdī*. The followers of *al-mahdī*, the Anṣār al-Mahdī, did not disappear when the Anglo-Egyptian army conquered the Mahdist state in 1898–99. In the 20th century, they emerged as the largest organized group in Sudan.[11] One important new element in Sudan was the emergence of a significant Islamic grouping: the Muslim Brotherhood (Arab.: al-Ikhwān al-Muslimūn), which began as a student organization in the 1940s and had some following among urban intellectuals and professionals.[12] One more Muslim group in Sudan was the Republican Brothers (Arab.: al-Ikhwān al-Jumhūriyyūn), which was founded by Maḥmūd Muḥammad Ṭaha in 1945. The Republican Brothers aim at constructing a new civilization that is based on the Qurʾān.[13] The different Muslim groups, except the Sufis, consider the Republican Brothers as the most genuine Sufi group in Northern Sudan. A recent Muslim group in Northern Sudan is Anṣār al-Sunna, which calls for the revival of the traditions of the Prophet Muḥammad. Their simple version of Islam is akin to that of the Wahhābiyya, the influential followers of the dominant religious doctrine in Saudi Arabia.[14]

It is worth mentioning here that the word 'reality' is used in the present chapter with two different meanings. The first meaning refers to the 'inner, hidden reality', the synonym of the transcendental world, which consists of everything that some people assume to exist independent of and beyond their experiences, as maintained in the Sufis' arguments in the coming few pages. In short, it is whatever is deduced from observations and cannot be directly perceived. The second meaning of reality is simply the realm of undeniable facts, which exist in the manifest world. It is whatever is experienced as physical. This second meaning is used in dealing with the adaptability of *sharīʿa* to the recurrent developments in the manifest world. So, the first meaning of reality becomes clearer as it is contrasted with its second meaning from which alone it is inferred.

It should be made clear in this introduction that the chapter makes one central point, which is amply bolstered by empirical research and which can be stressed: the *sharīʿa* is not a monolithic entity, but is a body of knowledge

---

[11] Voll, J. O., 'The Eastern Sudan, 1822 to the Present', in *The History of Islam in Africa*, Levtzion, Nehemia & Pouwels, Randall L. (eds.), Oxford: James Currey Ltd., 2000, pages 153–155.

[12] Voll, 2000, pages 161, 163–164.

[13] Ṣāliḥ ʿAbd al-Qādir Ṣāliḥ al-Shaykh, *Al-munaẓẓama al-siyāsa al-waḥīda alatī lahā athar ʿalā al-waḥda al-waṭanīya fiʾl-sūdān* [The One Single Political Organization and its Impact on the National Unity in Sudan], npd, 1997, pages 27–29.

[14] Human Rights Watch 'Behind the Red Line: Political Repression in the Sudan', www.hrw.org/legacy/reports/1996/Sudan.htm (accessed: 27.07.2004).

from which different actors draw in different ways, i.e., it is shaped and appropriated according to the perspectives of the relevant groups.

Background of the Followers of the Muslim Groups in the District of Shendi

The nomads live along *khūr*s and *wādīs*,[15] which are found throughout the region away from the Nile and where the soil tends to be of loose mud and is fertile for grazing, rain-fed cultivation and the growth of large clumps of thorn-bushes (almost all of which are species of acacia). At the beginning of the rainy season many nomads move eastwards beyond Kassala State boundary for water and grass. Villagers, who are mostly farmers, live along the Nile in areas north and south of Shendi town. Cultivation is the most-practised occupation in the villages, followed by grazing and then all the other occupations (i.e., trade, railway-worker, etc.). The population of Shendi town engages in much more widely diversified occupations.

The ethnic origins of the majority of the inhabitants of the District of Shendi are peculiar to those people stretching out into the area between the Southern boundary of the Central Nilotic Sudan and the Mediterranean Sea, in addition to Eastern Sudan. Observably, Shendi town is a mosaic of blocks inhabited by people of different ethnic origins, from all parts of Sudan and from African and Asian countries. About 60% of these ethnic groups have representation in the rural areas. Also, the town population includes a fair number of Copts, who constitute one of the Christian groups in the region. The majority of the ethnic groups in the rural communities are from Northern and Central Nilotic Sudan. People from Southern and Western Sudan do not constitute major groups in any of these communities though their numbers are remarkable in Shendi town. Those from Eastern Sudan appear as major groups only at the nomads' camps and the villages north of Shendi town. The traditionally indigenous population of the District of Shendi (the Jʿalīyyīn) still exist as major groups in both village and nomadic areas. In the villages south of Shendi town is found a major group tracing its descent from the Egyptians (i.e., the Muwalladīn). There are major groups who trace their descent back to dead holy men in the villages north and south of Shendi town. Most of the ethnic groups that exist in the villages north of Shendi town are open to each other in

[15] A *khūr* is a watercourse, usually dry, except during the rainy season; a *wādī* is a watercourse which is usually dry, except during the rainy season, but wider than the *khūr*.

terms of marriage, as are most of the ethnic groups in the villages south of Shendi town. Marital relations between the populations of the North and the South of the Nile area are rare, and, when found, they appear to be indirect and via few widely spread ethnic groups. All the nomadic ethnic groups are open to each other in terms of marriage and in turn have links with the ethnic groups along the Nile.

The link between the rural population and Shendi town has been developed partially because the town provides them with services including administration, education, health, marketing, business, finance, communication and transport. Shendi town is closely tied to the surrounding rural areas via a bus-network. The District of Shendi as a whole is connected with the National Capital (Khartoum), Atbara, Al-Damar, Gedaref, New Halfa and Kassala, also through the bus service. These internal and external networks are able to function because of the existence of a number of paved and unpaved routes. Besides these, there is a newly-built bridge connecting the District of Shendi with the District of al-Matamma on the western bank of the Nile. In addition, the railway lines pass through the area from the South to the North.

As to basic and higher secondary education, it is observed that an acute shortage in the educational services reveals itself in the rural residential areas. Such an observation becomes more marked at the nomads' camps. At all educational levels, males and females have equal opportunities as far as the number of schools available to each gender is concerned. A point applicable to both sexes is that the higher the educational level the lesser will be the chances for many of them to continue their education. This is mainly due to the small number of higher secondary schools. For the same reason, boys and girls from rural areas are enrolled in the higher secondary schools in Shendi town. Adults' education is limited to women's guidance and to Shendi town and villages (particularly north of Shendi town). Such a kind of adults' education is intended to provide women (usually ten to thirty years old) with information on writing and reading, handicrafts and domestic economy.

The Sufi orders (i.e., the Khatmiyya, the Tijāniyya, the Qādiriyya, the Sammāniyya, etc.) dominate the majority of the rural areas in the District of Shendi. They dominate approximately 77% of the villages north of Shendi town and 92% of those of the south. As far as the nomads are concerned, the Sufis predominate in approximately 68% of the camps. Next to the Sufi orders come the Anṣār al-Mahdī representing 20% and 2% of the villages north and south of Shendi town, respectively. Also, they are the main group in about 32% of the nomads' camps. The Anṣār al-Sunna comprise about 3% of the villages north of Shendi town and 6% of those of the south. It is remarkable that, though the Anṣār al-Sunna are a relatively new Muslim group in the area, its adherents are increasing at the expense of the traditional Sufis and the Anṣār al-Mahdī. But none of the nomads' camps is dominated by the Anṣār al-Sunna. The reason for this may be due to intact beliefs of the Sufi and Anṣār al-Mahdī doctrines among the nomads who have also remained away from the external agents of socio-cultural change. Again, the spread of education among the nomads in the District of Shendi has been very slow. Even the Sufi and Anṣār al-Mahdī leaders exploit this situation to build resistance against the penetration of the Anṣār al-Sunna into the nomadic areas. However, few young nomads join the Anṣār al-Sunna. Some of those who do are reprimanded or even beaten so as to encourage them to retreat from the Anṣār al-Sunna doctrine. Even more harshly, certain families may disassociate themselves from their youngsters who insist on continuing as Anṣār al-Sunna. In Shendi town, we find adherents to all these Muslim groups, as well as to the Republican Brothers, amongst the Muslim population. The distribution of these Muslim groups in the District of Shendi may be an attribute of historical factors. The degree of dominance of each Muslim group coincides with the time of its emergence in the region. In other words, the older the group is, the more dominant are its adherents. The Sufi orders have been in existence since the beginning of the Islamization of the Shendi population. The Anṣār al-Mahdī cropped up during the Mahdist Regime. The Anṣār al-Sunna date their appearance as an organized group in Shendi to the late 1970s. Large Christian groups are found residing with the Muslim urban population.

Sharīʿa *as Divine Blueprint*

It is commonly argued, particularly among the Sufis, the Anṣār al-Mahdī, the Anṣār al-Sunna, and the members of the Islamic Movement in the District of Shendi, that the Islamic *sharīʿa* is a system of thought and organization that is always characterized by its availability to human beings, mainly because it is from the presence of Allāh[16] and, therefore, inclusive, and free of any deficiency. To these Muslim groups, Allāh projected the *sharīʿa* for all human beings, and therefore it is inclusive of all things that could bring about happiness to them. One can find in the *sharīʿa* the best

[16] The name 'Allāh' is used for God in the Islamic religion and in the communities under study.

planning for even the smallest or largest element in all aspects of social life. It is stressed that no-one is more knowledgeable about Allāh's creation than Allāh. To Ernest Gellner, this is a model which is available in writing, and equally available to all literate men, and to all those willing to heed literate men. This model holds that Islam is a distinctive historical totality, which organizes various aspects of social life. It maintains that a set of rules, which are to be implemented throughout social life, exists, eternal, divinely ordained, and independent of the will of men, which defines the proper ordering of society.[17]

Building upon the above arguments, the Sufis, the Anṣār al-Mahdī, the Anṣār al-Sunna, and the members of the Islamic Movement in the District of Shendi refuse the adoption of democracy, communism, socialism and capitalism in constructing any Islamic state. They consider the trend that rejects Islam as the base of the political and other practices in a state, and restricts it only within the places of worship, as an attempt to destroy the Islamic religion. This is mainly because the historical literature lets it be seen that Islam flourished only after it had been enacted as both religion and state. Moreover, these urban, villagers and nomad Muslim groups argue that the communists, the socialists, the capitalists, and others who are also bearers of systems of thought and organization, which human beings reached through their own experiences, presented ideas that Islam preceded in time with more perfect ones. Because of this belief, these Muslim groups feel in no need of such man-made ideas or systems of thought and organization. As such they declare that communism, socialism and capitalism have brought nothing new or better to the benefit of human beings. They put it the other way round, saying that Islam was communicated to human beings by Allāh who created them and who is the most knowledgeable about their own various affairs; whilst communism, socialism, capitalism, democracy, etc., are just human references that should not be looked at with favour, whatever level of development they reach.

The members of the Islamic Movement, the Anṣār al-Sunna, and the Anṣār al-Mahdī in the urban, village and nomadic areas of the District of Shendi think that, in any Islamic state, all *sharīʿa* laws should be implemented over all fields of life in a given society without the omission of a single point. As an exception, the Anṣār al-Sunna in the villages south of

[17] Gellner, Ernest, *Muslim Society*, Cambridge: Cambridge University Press, 1981, pages 1–2.

Shendi town restrict the government's efforts in this implementation to what they call 'the general *sharīʿa*' that deals only with social facts outside the domestic sphere. They assert that a Muslim government is not concerned with what they call 'the private *sharīʿa*', which deals with facts within the domestic domain.

The Adaptability of Sharīʿa

As to how they deal with the Islamic texts, the Anṣār al-Mahdī in the villages and nomads' camps of the District of Shendi resort to the *ḥadīth* text:

> Allah said: '... and My slave keeps on coming closer to Me through performing Nawafil (praying or doing extra deeds besides what is obligatory) till I love him, so I become his sense of hearing with which he hears, and his sense of sight with which he sees, and his hand with which he grips, and his leg with which he walks.'[18]

They understand by this text that whenever a person penetrates deeply into the practice of his religion, his religious knowledge deepens, as Allāh drops good (the faith) into his heart and presents him with extraordinary senses of hearing, sight, etc. Only then detailed perfect religious knowledge will be bestowed upon that person from the presence of Allāh. He could then see even what will happen in the future. Accordingly, these village and nomad Anṣār al-Mahdī think of two levels of interpretation of the Qurʾānic and *ḥadīth* texts: the esoteric and the exoteric. They consider the esoteric exposition of the hidden meanings of the texts (i.e., *taʾwīl*), which they associate only with the higher degrees of religious understanding and wide-ranging knowledge, to be better and more perfect than the exoteric interpretations. However, they point out the necessity of taking the recent scientific and technological developments in the ever-changing world into consideration, in the interpretations of the Islamic texts. They see the necessity of renewing (or modernizing) the Islamic religious teachings, in order to cope with such developments. Here, they cite one of *imām al-mahdī*'s sayings: "All that have been brought by the Qurʾān are on our heads; all that have been brought by the *ḥadīth* are on our shoulders; but all that have been brought by the Prophet's Companions or the Scholars of Jurisprudence are questionable, for we are men just like them: We can

---

[18] Ṣaḥīḥ al-Bukhārī, volume 8, book 76, number 509, see: http://www.usc.edu/schools/college/crcc/engagement/resources/texts/muslim/hadith/bukhari.

also derive qualified judgements". In effect, *imām al-mahdī* tried to derive judgements and to renew the Islamic religious teachings. Nonetheless, the Anṣār al-Mahdī stipulate that the renewal of the Islamic religion should fall in with the Qurʾān, the *sunna* and the sayings of *al-salaf al-ṣāliḥ* (Arab.: the worthy ancestors of Islam, the venerable forefathers).[19] They present an example of such updated interpretations of the Islamic texts. They state that people in the recent past used to explain *sūrat Luqmān* (31): 34:

> Knowledge of the Hour [of Resurrection] belongs to God; it is He who sends down the relieving rain and He who knows what is hidden in the womb. No soul knows what it will reap tomorrow, and no soul knows in what land it will die; it is God who is all knowing and all aware.

as meaning that no one could, for example, know whether a foetus is male or female other than Allāh. Given the fact that science and technology are now able to show the sex of a foetus after it reaches the fourth month of its age, this Qurʾānic text could now be understood as that Allāh knows whether a foetus is male or female even before its mother becomes pregnant.

The supporters of the Islamic Movement bring forward the *ḥadīth* text:

> On the day he returned from the Battle of Ahzab, the Messenger of Allah (may peace be upon him) made for us an announcement that nobody would say his Zuhr prayer but in the quarters of Banu Quraiza. (Some) people, being afraid that the time for prayer would expire, said their prayers before reaching the street of Banu Quraiza. The others said: We will not say our prayer except where the Messenger of Allah (may peace be upon him) has ordered us to say it even if the time expires. (When he learned of the difference in the view of the two groups of the people, the Messenger of Allah (may peace be upon him) did not blame anyone from the two groups.[20]

Such an admission, to the supporters of the Islamic Movement, took into account that some people deal only with the manifest meanings of texts, while others look into the reasons behind these texts and into their latent meanings. So, they have concluded that the *sharīʿa* allows any interpretation of the Islamic texts.

The members of the Islamic Movement do not restrict themselves to the outer or the inner meanings of Islamic texts, or to a particular doctrine.

---

19 As will be mentioned frequently, later in this chapter, all Muslim groups in the District of Shendi use the Arabic phrase, *al-salaf al-ṣāliḥ* to mean the Prophet's Companions, their successors, and the successors of their successors.

20 Ṣaḥīḥ al-Muslim, book 19, number 4374, see: http://www.usc.edu/schools/college/crcc/engagement/resources/texts/muslim/hadith/muslim/019.smt.html.

However, they lay out the various issues for consultation, and what the scholars (*ʿulamāʾ*) recommend, they take as the right opinion. They take into consideration both the understanding of *al-salaf al-ṣāliḥ* and recent developments that were previously unknown—in the financial, the criminal and other aspects of social life. For example, no views are to be found in the Qurʾān and the *ḥadīth* in respect of stealing in a big commercial house that is watched by a closed television network, or of blood groups that are identified by modern laboratories. Such new developments create the need for giving free play to the *ijtihād* (Arab.: deriving qualified up-to-date judgements) and to rational thinking. The members of the Islamic Movement argue that the Islamic jurisprudence, which was written 700 years ago, did not imagine the problems that have resulted from the recent great scientific developments and the modern way of life, and did not face issues similar to those of the present.

These proponents of the Islamic Movement implicitly think about modernizing the *sharīʿa* to make it cope with the many developments that have taken place in all aspects of modern life. They see great differences between the human beings of the 7th century and those of the present time, as to the complexity of their life, knowledge, technology, etc. They seem to have the opinion that the conventional *sharīʿa* could not stand up to the changes in current human society, and that the Muslims should therefore derive up-to-date qualified judgements. The members of the Islamic Movement state that it is as if they are living between two men: the first one knows well the *sharīʿa* in the texts, but does not know the society; the second one knows well the society, but does not know the *sharīʿa*. The former represents those Muslims who studied the old books of Islamic jurisprudence, but were ignorant of many developments of the modern age, i.e. they live out of their age. Consequently, they seek the application of the Islamic laws as they are. The latter stands for those Muslims who studied the Western culture, but were ignorant of the *sharīʿa*, and as a result they became consciously or unconsciously secular. Finally, the members of the Islamic Movement intend to deal with these challenges by studying the *sharīʿa* while living in the modern society, to live in their age. They have begun treating the new issues accordingly. In other words, Muslims should comprehend both *sharīʿa* and modern society, and the Qurʾān and the *ḥadīth* should be treated as suitable everywhere and at any time.

The Anṣār al-Sunna in Shendi town and villages north and south of it are in an exactly contrary position to the above opinions. They claim that they understand the Islamic texts only "as understood by *al-salaf al-ṣāliḥ*". They mean by *al-salaf al-ṣāliḥ* the Prophet's Companions, their successors, and the successors of their successors according to the *ḥadīth* text: "It was asked from Allah's Apostle (may peace be upon him) who amongst the people were the best. He said: (People) of my generation, then those next to them, then those next to them . . .".[21] *Al-salaf al-ṣāliḥ* are taken as models of human behaviour and belief for the Muslims, so that to follow them is like following the Prophet Muḥammad. The phrase "as understood by *al-salaf al-ṣāliḥ*" points at guarding against one's own attempts to interpret the Qurʾānic and *ḥadīth* texts, and instead points to sticking to the understanding of the Companions, their successors, and the successors of their successors up to the four Scholars of Jurisprudence (Imām Ibn Ḥanbal, Imām Mālik, Imām al-Shāfiʿī and Imām Abū Hanīfa). Importantly, the Anṣār al-Sunna take Ibn Ḥanbal as their Imām insofar as he laid down the legal school according to which they now live. *Al-salaf al-ṣāliḥ*, to them, means the people who become a model in deeds and understanding. For the Anṣār al-Sunna, their creed is based on the genuine beliefs that *al-salaf al-ṣāliḥ* stood for in their understanding of the Islamic religion. These beliefs are thought to be inherent in the Qurʾān and the *ḥadīth* and detailed by the scholars. The Anṣār al-Sunna say that they depend on the true *ḥadīth* and the plain Qurʾānic verses, as they consider them as the original Islamic texts. They even look at the *ḥadīth* as being elucidative of the Qurʾān and circumstantial to the Qurʾānic judgements, i.e. it could restrict the absolutes, unbind the restricted, make exceptions of rules, generalize the specifications, or specify the generalities. Not only this, but also some *ḥadīth* are thought to abrogate some Qurʾānic texts. When the Qurʾān is absolute or generalizing as to the referents, the *ḥadīth* texts come to be restrictive or particularizing, respectively. An instance is the absolutistic *sūrat al-Māʾida* (5): 38: "Cut off the hands of thieves, whether they are man or woman, as punishment for what they have done—a deterrent from God: God is almighty and wise". This Qurʾānic verse orders the thief's hand to be cut off, but it does not specify what amount of stolen property renders such cutting to be appropriate or from where to cut along the arm from shoulder to hand. A *ḥadīth* answers such questions, as the Prophet Muḥammad said: "Allah's Messenger (may peace be upon him) cut off the hand of a thief for a quarter of a dinar and upwards"[22] and he used to cut at the hand joint.

[21] Ṣaḥīḥ al-Muslim, book 31, number 6151, see: http://www.usc.edu/schools/college/crcc/engagement/resources/texts/muslim/hadith/muslim/031.smt.html.

[22] Ṣaḥīḥ al-Muslim, book 17, number 4175, see: http://www.usc.edu/schools/college/crcc/engagement/resources/texts/muslim/hadith/muslim/017.smt.html.

To the Anṣār al-Sunna in the urban and village communities in the District of Shendi, *ijtihād* should act only where there is no single Qurʾānic or *ḥadīth* text. They state that to derive a judgement when there is text could lead to a great deviation from the right course. Also, it should only be used by the legal scholars who know its tools and operate as the so-called absolute *mujtahidūn* who are able to Islamise, demonstrate and apply the rules.

The Anṣār al-Sunna in the District of Shendi hold the opinion that those who propose the re-fashioning of the Islamic teachings so as to cope with the recent developments in the world cannot bring even a single legal evidence to support their argument or pursuit, simply because nothing in Islam could be re-fashioned, i.e. all the Islamic teachings suit everywhere and every age. They even think that it is not allowable to transgress the apparent usages and meanings of words in the Qurʾān and the *ḥadīth*, since scholarly people lay it down that because the texts are sacred, one should not transgress the bounds of words. To them, the esoteric exposition of the hidden meaning (*taʾwīl*) leads to stray beliefs and practices.

Dale Eickelman repeatedly deals with such controversy in his many writings, where he describes and analyses the processes by which religious symbols and institutions are reinterpreted and modified to accommodate new and evolving social and historical realities, and describes how religious ideologies themselves shape the social order.[23] He states that the key traditions of world religions remain vital and meaningful through the actions of their carriers, who maintain and shape them over long historical periods and in diverse contexts. Thus religious traditions are linked to the changing relations of authority and domination in which they are shaped and transformed. Eickelman adds that some carriers of world religions claim that their tradition possesses a core of formative ideals and immutable religious truths, and most share common rituals. Yet these ideals, truths and rituals must be open to reformulation and reinterpretation by their carriers over successive generations and in novel contexts. To Eickelman, many earlier studies tended to concentrate on the search for an Islamic 'essence'. This coincided with the premise held by many Muslims that Islamic beliefs and practices are unaffected by historical change. A number of recent studies of Islam, however, combine textual

[23] Eickelman, Dale F., *Moroccan Islam: Tradition and Society in a Pilgrimage Centre*, Austin: University of Texas Press, 1976, pages 3–4.

analysis with analysis of the social historical contexts in which notions of Islam are developed, transmitted, and reproduced.[24]

Sharīʿa *and Reality as Halves of Worship, a View of the Sufis*

As expressed by Sufi informants in the District of Shendi, there are no essential differences among the various Sufi orders regarding their teachings and the cardinal rituals. They all stick to both the *sharīʿa* and the voluntary religious services (Arab.: *nāfila / nawāfil*), and as such follow the same one path that is believed to ultimately lead to Allāh.

These Sufis see the necessity of always sticking to the Islamic texts. However, they are of the opinion that to take these texts only into account, without them being interpreted (to find out their true concealed meanings) by an expert, may put a person or a group in the wrong. As to taking the experts' interpretations into consideration, the Sufis in the urban and rural communities of the District of Shendi depend on their understanding of *sūrat al-Furqān* (25): 59:

> It is He who created the heavens and earth and what is between them in six Days, and then established Himself on the throne—He is the Lord of Mercy; He is the Best Informed.

A lay Sufi is expected to look for the proofs and the uncovering of the *ḥaqāʾiq* (Arab.: truths) and the *ʿilla* (Arab.: pretext, *ratio legis*, purpose of the reason of religious law) from the Sheikhs who are believed to be the successors or heirs of the Scholars of the Reality (of Islamic religion). If a lay Sufi tries to interpret by her or himself, she or he may not catch the true meanings or may lose the right way. To the Sufis, the Qurʾānic texts cannot be explained only via the usages and the meanings of words, mainly because the Arabic words in the different texts may have acquired other usages and meanings than those that were understood earlier by the Prophet and his Companions. They consider both *ilhām* (Arab.: inspiration) and *taʾwīl* as useful tools. *Ilhām* is the state in which Allāh infuses truth onto one's tongue or other limbs. *Taʾwīl* is the esoteric exposition of the inner, hidden meanings of texts.

To the urban and rural Sufis in the District of Shendi *sūrat al-Raḥmān* (55): 1–2: "It is the Lord of Mercy who taught the Qurʾān" means that if a human develops spiritually and her or his soul reaches the so-called "Home

---

[24] Eickelman, Dale F., *The Middle East and Central Asia: An Anthropological Approach*, New Jersey: Prentice Hall, 1997, pages 249, 252–253.

for Divine Attributes", Allāh will teach her or him *taʾwīl*, so as to be able to correctly interpret and understand the Qurʾān. Importantly, the Sufis treat some Qurʾānic texts, mainly those which deal with the obligatory religious services and the manifest judgements about what is permissible, prohibited, etc., as postulates that human beings should not subject the texts to mental measurements. They should be taken only in their apparent meanings. The human mind here is reckoned as minor.

The Sufis in Shendi town, villages north and south of it and nomads' camps argue that to be acquainted with all branches of knowledge could not be the fruits of one's efforts. A human who makes great efforts to learn could be acquainted only with some branch of knowledge (e.g., economics, law, etc.), but could not reach the depths of all branches. However, the knowledge that is bestowed upon a human from the presence of Allāh (i.e. *taʾwīl*) is believed to be free of any deficiency or ignorance, i.e. it is comprehensive of all details in all fields. For this reason, we find in the Sufi vocabulary titles like *aʿrif billāh* (Arab.: having esoteric spiritual knowledge from Allāh). Nevertheless, the Sufis say that no human being could 'thoroughly' be acquainted with Allāh's knowledge.

The Sufis in the District of Shendi maintain that the Prophet Muḥammad was ordered (by Allāh) to communicate to people the exoteric knowledge, but was given the option whether or not to communicate the esoteric knowledge. Accordingly, the Islamic religion, for these Sufis, has two aspects: exoteric (i.e. the *sharīʿa*) and esoteric (i.e. the Reality of religion). To these Sufis, one should stick oneself to both these aspects, because they complement and affect each other and together lead one to have a perfect faith in Allāh. If one restricts oneself to the *sharīʿa* only, or to the Reality of religion only, one's worship of Allāh will be fruitless and could not be accepted. These two aspects of the Islamic religion are inseparable. Each is regarded as half of worship. To the Sufis, the Anṣār al-Sunna, for example, adhere only to the *sharīʿa*, and refuse to acknowledge the esoteric aspect (or the Reality) of the Islamic religion, and hence they have gone astray. To the Sufis, such Muslim groups seem to adopt mutilated bodies of thought. For an Islamic thought to be perfect and sound, it should take hold of the whole Islamic religion, i.e., both its exoteric and esoteric aspects.

The esoteric component, which the urban, villager and nomad Sufis in the District of Shendi define as the Reality of religion, has something to do with the *nawāfil*, which mean, as mentioned before, the voluntary religious services. To these Sufis, each of the five pillars of Islam (i.e., the recital of *shahāda*, the prayers, the legal almsgiving, the fasting during the month of Ramadan, and the pilgrimage) has a *nāfila* of its same kind. A person is expected to do as much as s/he can of these *nawāfil*. Importantly, the *dhikr* (Arab.: remembrance, incessant repetition of certain words or formulae in praise of God) is a word usually used as a synonym of the *nawāfil*. Here the Sufis in the different subcultures of the District of Shendi appeal to the *ḥadīth* text:

> Allah said, … and My slave keeps on coming closer to Me through performing Nawafil (praying or doing extra deeds besides what is obligatory) till I love him, so I become his sense of hearing with which he hears, and his sense of sight with which he sees, and his hand with which he grips, and his leg with which he walks; and if he asks Me, I will give him, and if he asks My protection (Refuge), I will protect him; (i.e. give him My Refuge). …[25]

This text is explained as meaning that the obligatory religious services may or may not keep a person continuing to come closer to Allāh, but the *nawāfil* do so without fail. To the Sufis, only one who—via the *dhikr* and the *sharīʿa*—comes closer to Allāh or one onto whose limbs Allāh infuses truth and consequently becomes *aʿrif billāh* can learn the esoteric knowledge.

The Republican Brothers and the sharīʿa *as 'Non-original' in Islam*

The Republican Brothers, who appear entirely as an urban elitist group in the District of Shendi, differ from the other Muslim groups, whom they call *al-salafiyyūn*, in their definition of the *sunna*. The other groups define the *sunna* as whatever the Prophet Muḥammad said, acted or tacitly approved. The Republican Brothers understand by the term *sunna* merely whatever the Prophet acted; whatever he said or tacitly approved are parts of the *sharīʿa*. The *sunna*, for the Republican Brothers, is the level of religion that the Prophet Muḥammad, and all other prophets and a few Muslims embodied. The Republican Brothers believe that mankind is in progress[26] and on the way to adopt such a level of religion—as the law of the group and not the law of one individual as it was in the past. In other words, they define the *sunna* as "the personal example of the Prophet Muḥammad"[27] as opposed to the *sharīʿa*, which was applied to

---

[25] Ṣaḥīḥ al-Bukhārī, volume 8, book 76, number 509, see: http://www.usc.edu/schools/college/crcc/engagement/resources/texts/muslim/hadith/bukhari/076.sbt.html.

[26] Here, the Republican thought assumes that mankind shall be at more progressive stages in the future. It states that Allah now is taking all mankind up a ladder to stages of higher perfection.

[27] Esposito, J. L., 'Sunnah', in *The Oxford Dictionary of Islam*, New York: Oxford University Press, 2003, page 305.

the nation at large. The Republican Brothers call the other Muslim groups *al-salafiyyūn* also because they do not derive their judgements purely from the 'original Qur'ān'.[28]

The Islamic religion, to the Republican Brothers, rests on a seven-stage ladder starting with three successive stages, the first Islam, the faith, and the *iḥsān* (Arab.: beneficence, performance of good deeds), then shifting to three other successive ones (knowing the truth with the certainty of mind, knowing the truth with the certainty of sight, and knowing the very truth with the assured certainty), and ending in the stage of second Islam, which is believed to be the same religion that the Prophet Muḥammad practised. This means that human knowledge is continuously increasing as it is changing from the stage of faith to that of knowing the very truth with the assured certainty (i.e., the science). In accordance with this belief, the Republican Brothers consider all mankind to be ignorant at present, but as far more developed when their ignorance is compared to that of the 7th century. If another message of religion is revealed, it will make mankind cover a long distance of progress. When the Prophet Muḥammad came with the Islamic religion, he found people in the so-called 'former Time of Ignorance' (Arab.: *jāhilīya*).[29] He then passed with them over great stages of progress. Importantly, the Republican Brothers expect the return of the Prophet Muḥammad in the sense that mankind will progress to the point at which it will live up to his personal example (i.e. the *sunna*), which is the Second Message of Islam, i.e. the end of the seven-stage ladder on which the Islamic religion rests. By then, Islam will predominate throughout the world.

The Republican Brothers believe that Allāh is leading mankind to the stage of maturity that it missed when Adam committed sin, as cited in *sūrat al-Tīn* (95): 4–5: "We create man in the finest state then reduce him to the lowest of the low". To them, mankind was degraded to the lowest stage of material incarnation, which is hydrogen. It later on developed into water, into inorganic substances, into plants, into animals, and then into its present form (i.e. mankind). So, mankind has started to recover its origin. This is to say: mankind is now in progress from a constituent form into a better creation till it reaches its origin, i.e. to become human again. Such recovery will take place with the enactment of the Second Message of Islam.

---

28 This point will be clarified in the coming paragraphs.

29 Esposito, 'Jahiliyyah', *Oxford Dictionary of Islam*, New York: Oxford University Press, 2003, page 154.

Following on from the above, the Republican Brothers believe that Islam came with two messages: a first message at one end corresponding to Judaism, and a second message at the other end corresponding to Christianity. They state that Allāh sent Moses to a society with a more recent experience of the law of the jungle, hence his message (the Old Testament or the Torah) to that society was little more than the requirement to be just and fair (a life for a life, and an eye for an eye), as that was closer, and more acceptable to their primitive nature. In that way, the laws of the Old Testament came at one extreme, more in the nature of excessive materialism. Then Jesus Christ came with a message (the New Testament or the Gospel) that went to the other extreme. Hence the New Testament came more in the form of excessive spirituality, in response to the previous revelation of excessive materialism. These were, however, lofty moral commandments that remained suspended high above the primitive reality. Thus Jesus told his disciples: "You have heard that it was said, 'An eye for an eye and a tooth for a tooth.' But I say to you, Do not resist an evildoer. But if anyone strikes you on the right cheek, turn the other also"; (Matthew 5:38–39). Such correspondences to Judaism and Christianity are thought to be cited in *sūrat al-Fatḥ* (48): 29:

> Muḥammad is the Messenger of God. Those who follow him are harsh towards the disbelievers and compassionate towards each other. You see them kneeling and prostrating, seeking God's bounty and His good pleasure: on their faces they bear the marks of their prostrations. This is how they are pictured in the Torah and the Gospel: like a seed that puts forth its shoot, becomes strong, grows thick, and rises on its stem to the delight of its sowers. So God infuriates the disbelievers through them; God promises forgiveness and a great reward to those who believe and do righteous deeds.

Both messages of Islam, according to the Republican thought, are contained in the Qur'ān as revealed to the Prophet Muḥammad. The First Message was based on the *sharīʿa*, which had to come down to the primitive realities of the 7th century. Hence, it was founded on the principles of guardianship, that of Muslims over non-Muslims, of the ruler over his subjects, and of men over women. It is to be found in those parts of the Qur'ān revealed in Medina, which adjourned,[30] at that time, those parts previously revealed in Mecca. The Second Message, on the other hand,

[30] The Republican Brothers modify the use of the term "abrogated" in reference to the difference between Meccan and Medinan Qur'ānic messages, preferring instead the word "adjourned", which means "put off until a future day". This is a point that the coming few paragraphs elaborate further.

is based on the personal example of the Prophet Muḥammad himself (i.e. the *sunna*), in contrast to the *sharīʿa* for the nation at large. It is based on the principle of freedom, and is to be found in the parts of Qurʾān revealed in Mecca, which were binding on the Prophet personally, although they were adjourned with respect to the nation as a whole. This Second Message is regarded as the original Islamic religion.

The Republican Brothers tell the story that the Prophet Muḥammad came in the Meccan era with the Second message of Islam to all people, and he preached Islam at its scientific level, but it was rejected because of the infancy of society at that time. So, he was instructed—by Allāh—to migrate to Medina, hence the Medinese era, where the Second Message was adjourned, and the First Message was implemented.[31] The Prophet became the prophet of the Second Message, as implemented by himself personally, and the messenger of the First Message, in which he preached Islam at its faith level, and it was accepted and implemented by that nation. Here, the Prophet said: "I received three types of knowledge from Allāh. Allāh ordered me to communicate the first one to the upper and lower classes of people, gave me the option to or not to communicate the second one, and restricted the third one to me alone because no other one has the power over it".[32] Even the Prophet's Companion Abū Hurayra said: "I have memorized two kinds of knowledge from Allah's Apostle. I have propagated one of them to you and if I propagated the second, then my pharynx (throat) would be cut (i.e. killed)".[33] For the Republican Brothers, such *ḥadīth* texts hint at an extra knowledge ensconced in the Qurʾān for mankind when they become qualified enough to understand it.

The phenomenon of the two messages, as reflected in the Qurʾān of Mecca and that of Medina, may be clearly observed by contrasting Qurʾānic texts of the two eras. From the Qurʾān of Medina, expressing the First Message, the Republican Brothers quote *sūrat al-Baqara* (2): 193:

> Fight them until there is no more persecution, and worship is devoted to God. If they cease hostility, there can be no [further] hostility, except towards aggressors.

---

31 Here it is stated that Allāh intended by doing so just to convince people that they could not cope with the scientific level of Islam.

32 A text which is not presented in any edition of the Hadith books.

33 Ṣaḥīḥ al-Bukhārī, volume 1, book 3, number 121, see: http://www.usc.edu/schools/college/crcc/engagement/resources/texts/muslim/hadith/bukhari/003.sbt.html.

This is contrasted, for example, with the Qurʾān of Mecca, reflecting the Second Message, *sūrat al-Naḥl* (16): 125: "[Prophet], call [people] to the way of your Lord with wisdom and good teaching. Argue with them in the most courteous way, for your Lord knows best who has strayed from His way and who is rightly guided". The Republican Brothers say that being convinced of these two messages of Islam removes the contradictions which some people see between the so-called 'abrogating' and 'abrogated' verses of the Qurʾān. To them, really there are no contradictions between the Islamic texts, but it is a matter of two messages.

The phenomenon of the two messages of Islam may also be observed in other Qurʿānic and *ḥadīth* texts, which say that the Prophet Muḥammad has two nations: one of believers (*muʾminūn*) who were illiterate, and the other of submitters (*muslimūn*) who should be educated persons. This distinction is included in *sūrat Āl ʿImrān* (3): 102: "You who believe, be mindful of God, as is His due, and make sure you devote yourselves to Him, to your dying moment". God also says in *sūrat al-Jumuʿa* (62): 2–3:

> "It is He who raised a messenger, among the people who had no Scripture, to recite His revelations to them, to make them grow spiritually and teach them the Scripture and wisdom—before that they were clearly astray—to them and others yet to join them He is the Almighty, the Wise". In consequence the Prophet said: "Longing for my brothers who have not come yet"!

Then the Companions asked him: "Are we not your brothers?" He replied: "No, you are my companions".[34] To the Republican Brothers, such texts indicate that the people whose coming is prophesied are Muslims who shall follow the prophetic (scientific) model. They are believed to come just by the coming of the Second Message of Islam.

To the Republican Brothers, the First Message of Islam was detailed in the Qurʾān and the *ḥadīth*, while the Second Message was expressed only in general terms, with no details except insofar as given in the Prophet's personal example (i.e., the *sunna*). However, a man (i.e., the final Messiah) is prophesied to come from among the Muslims to detail the Second Message of Islam and its laws. Here, they quote from *sūrat al-Naml* (27): 82: "When the verdict is given against them, We shall bring a creature out of the earth, which will tell them that people had no faith in Our revelations". Such beast is the final fulfilment of the event that is to be carried out by the final Messiah as cited in *sūrat al-Aʿrāf* (7): 53:

---

[34] Musnad Ahmad: 7652, Sunan El-Nassaee: 150.

> What are they waiting for but the fulfilment of its [final prophecy]? On the Day it is fulfilled, those who had ignored it will say, "Our Lord's messenger spoke the truth. Is there anyone to intercede for us now? Or can we be sent back to behave differently from the way we behaved before?" they will really have squandered their souls, and all [the idols] they invented will have deserted them.

The final Messiah is to bring the accurate knowledge and to inform people of the true usages and meanings of the Qur'ān. Only then shall people know the real value, and the correct ways of performing religious services.

The coming of the final Messiah is, therefore, dependent upon the revival and the implementation of those parts of the Qur'ān which were adjourned in the 7th century, the Second Message, and making them the Islamic laws for today (after they had been of special application to the Prophet Muḥammad alone), thereby abrogating those parts which were appropriate and applicable in the 7th century. Whereupon the final Messiah will preach Islam at its scientific level, in the same way the Prophet Muḥammad first preached it in the Meccan era, but this time it will be accepted and implemented throughout the world, because of the maturity of society today, with its tremendous intellectual and material capacities. The Republican Brothers see that mankind now has become ready to receive the Second Message, which the final Messiah will bring forth.

The Republican Brothers argue that there is a series of prophecies from the Prophet Muḥammad on the coming of the final Messiah, and they all clearly demonstrate that he will come with the Second Message of Islam, and its laws, and not those of the First Message. It is reported, for example, that the Prophet said: "By Him in Whose hand is my life, the son of Mary (may peace be upon him) will soon descend among you as a just judge. He will break crosses, kill swine and abolish Jizya and the wealth will pour forth to such an extent that no one will accept it".[35] because he will scientifically show its benefits and because people shall do it with deep knowledge. It is added, in another report, "If only one day of this world remained. Allah would lengthen that day (according to the version of Za'idah), till He raised up in it a man who belongs to me or to my family whose father's name is the same as my father's, who will fill the earth with equity and justice as it has been filled with oppression and tyranny (according to the version of Fitr). Sufyan's version says: The world will not pass away before the Arabs are ruled by a man of my family whose name

[35] Ṣaḥīḥ al-Muslim, book 1, number 287, see: http://www.usc.edu/schools/college/crcc/engagement/resources/texts/muslim/hadith/muslim/001.smt.html.

will be the same as mine".[36] To the Republican Brothers, there is a spirit of peace in the prophecies of the final Messiah in a way that ends all sorts of enmities and antagonism. To fill the earth with equity, to them, presupposes the achievement of social justice, namely socialism, democracy and social equality between sexes, creeds, etc. In the phrase, "the wealth will pour forth to such an extent that no one will accept it" they find reference to the fruits of socialism, where through increased production and fair distribution, the wealth of earth will be shared in a way which will accommodate everybody. The phrase, "abolish Jizya," means for them that all compulsion and discrimination on grounds of religious faith, as well as any other features of guardianship derived from the Medinan Qurʾān shall be abolished and replaced by rules of tolerance, freedom and equality derived from the Meccan Qurʾān.

By enacting those previously revealed parts of the Qurʾān, Islam would be elevated from its faith level (related to the First Message) to its scientific level (related to the Second Message), where people may be distinguished according to their intellect and moral values, and not according to their faith or sex. One may not be asked about his religion or sex, but only about his clarity of thought and perfection of deed. Thus, in the "Islamic laws of the Second Message," and in accordance with the Islamic constitution, there will be no discrimination against any citizen because of his religion or sex. The constitution itself is not described as Islamic, because it does not purport to establish a theocratic regime, but rather a humanist regime where all people share and enjoy rights and duties, regardless of race, sex, religion, etc.

As the Republican Brothers show, the Second Message of Islam provides the legislative groundwork for the construction of an Islamic state where democracy and socialism are reconciled, and where social equity, which is between man and man and between man and woman as to the advantages and the law, prevails. To them, the need for this kind of state is global. The constitution that would be adopted in the state is based on the parts of Qurʾān that were revealed to the Prophet Muḥammad in Mecca. In other words, the Islamic legislation, for the Republican Brothers, should be based on what they call "the Original Qurʾānic Texts" (i.e., those texts which were previously adjourned), and not on what they call "the Offshoot Qurʾānic Texts" (i.e., those texts which have already attained their targets).

---

[36] Sunan Abū Dawūd, book 36, number 4269, see: http://www.usc.edu/schools/college/crcc/engagement/resources/texts/muslim/hadith/abudawud/036.sat.html.

The Islamic legislation, for them, is simply the process of replacing the 'offshoots' by the 'originals'.

The fact that the Republican Brothers seek to apply the Second Message of Islam and not the *sharī'a* does not mean that they intend to drop the doctrinal punishments. They maintain that they never attempt to break the restrictive ordinance of Allāh. To them, the known doctrinal punishments, such as those for murder, committing highway robbery, etc., all remain as 'minor' well-fixed standards. This is mainly because Allāh has revealed them with the ultimate aim of bestowing honour upon the human beings or treating them with civility and deference. In other words, such punishments are not intended just for killing, cutting hands off or the like, but they are aimed at protecting people's properties, honour, etc, and as such making them feel always at ease. However, the Republican Brothers think that the doctrinal punishments should be extracted merely from the Second Message of Islam, and should be applied only after all people in a given society get well-instructed, and after justice is achieved as to the maintenance of equal opportunities for all of them, and after their basic needs are sufficiently met. This means that no one should remain in a state of ignorance, inequity or poverty.

The Anṣār al-Sunna and the 'Reality' as Heretical

The Anṣār al-Sunna in Shendi town and villages north and south of it conceive the esotericists as different groups, who commonly accept as true that things are of a dual nature: inner and outer, reality and laws, hidden and manifest, etc. The properties of inner, reality, hidden, etc., stand for the same thing in the same way as the properties of outer, laws, manifest, etc., stand for the opposite thing. As stated by these Anṣār al-Sunna, the esotericists built this dichotomy on their belief that the Prophet al-Khiḍr was concerned with 'reality,' since his knowledge had been based on the *mukashafāt* (Arab.: revelations), and the Prophets Moses and Muḥammad were concerned with laws, since their knowledge had been based on the *waḥī* (Arab.: divine inspiration). To the esotericists, as these Anṣār al-Sunna say, some people could also attain the ability of *mukashafāt*, i.e. reveal the secrets, the unknown, the psyche, etc. The Anṣār al-Sunna describe such dichotomization and beliefs as non-Islamic. They argue that both Allāh and the Prophet Muḥammad proved the falsity of divination, and revealing the screened or unknown as human faculties. For them, humans enjoy no more than the normal sight, for all the human senses are finite. They resort to *sūrat al-Naml* (27): 65: "Say: 'No one in the heavens or on earth knows the unseen except God'. They do not know when they will be raised from the dead".

Also Allāh said in *sūrat al-Aʿrāf* (7): 188: "Say [Prophet], 'I have no control over benefit or harm, [even] to myself, except as God may please: if I had knowledge of what is hidden, I would have abundant good things and no harm could touch me. I am no more than a bearer of warning, and good news to those who believe'". To these Anṣār al-Sunna, the esoteric groups trust a knowledge that is bestowed upon human beings from the presence of Allāh. They deny the existence of such esoteric knowledge.

The members of the Islamic Movement in the urban and village communities of the District of Shendi have the notion that esotericism is a philosophical doctrine alien to Islam. Esotericism maintains that, as these members of the Islamic Movement argue, every Qur'ānic or *ḥadīth* text has inner and outer meanings. It shows the truth of this belief through the *ḥadīth* text, which states that when the Prophet Muḥammad had ascended to Allāh, he was acquainted with three types of knowledge. Allāh ordered him to keep one of these as a secret, gave him the freedom to communicate the second or not, and ordered him to communicate the third. The Prophet Muḥammad was ordered to communicate the *sharīʿa*. To the members of the Islamic Movement, such interpretation is refuted on the grounds that the Prophet's wife ʿĀ'isha once said: "He who says that the Prophet kept as secret some of what Allāh had revealed to him commits a great sin".[37] They argue that the Prophet did not conceal something that Allāh had revealed to him. Following on this, the members of the Islamic Movement always issue censure against those who take up the esoteric thought.

Hence, both the Anṣār al-Sunna and the members of the Islamic Movement criticise the Sufis' argument that the *sharīʿa* and the Reality are inseparable aspects of the Islamic religion, as each is half of worship. They consider this aspect of 'Reality' as heresy.

Concluding Remarks

Though they all share the opinion that the *sharīʿa* is the best divinely ordained plan for even the smallest or largest element in all aspects of social life, the followers of the Muslim groups in the District of Shendi use different-coloured lenses to view its interpretation and understanding.

---

37 This hadīth is not found in the most reliable hadīth collections.

From one point of view, the Anṣār al-Mahdī and the members of the Islamic Movement feel that a law that came for older times cannot really be applied to the modern times. They maintain that the Islamic texts, teachings and laws should continuously be reinterpreted, whether esoterically or exoterically, to cope with the many developments in our ever-changing world. This requires the giving of free play to the *ijtihād* and to rational thinking. Contrarily, the Anṣār al-Sunna believe that the Islamic religion, including the *sharīʿa*, is universal and permanent, as they stick to the understanding of *al-salaf al-ṣāliḥ*, whom they take as their model in deeds and understanding. To them, nothing in Islam could be re-fashioned. To the Sufis, in a second point, *taʾwīl*, which is bestowed from the presence of Allāh, is a useful tool for correctly interpreting and understanding the Qurʾānic texts, as it helps in reaching the truths and the purpose or the reason of the Islamic laws, and hence in looking for the reality of religion. The Islamic religion, for the Sufis, has in accord with each other two inseparable aspects: the *sharīʿa* and the Reality of religion. One should stick to both these aspects, because they complement and affect each other and together lead one to have a perfect faith in Allāh. The Anṣār al-Sunna deny *taʾwīl*, which, as they strongly argue, leads to stray beliefs and practices. In a third point, the Republican Brothers define the *sunna* as whatever the Prophet acted personally. When mankind becomes human with enough scientific qualifications in the future, it shall live up to this Prophetic model on which the Second Message (the original Islamic religion) will be based. The final Messiah is to come to detail the Second Message of Islam and its laws. The Islamic laws shall be extracted purely from this Second Message of Islam. The First Message, which was based on the conventional *sharīʿa*, will then be abolished. All other groups in the District of Shendi reject this Republican perception.

Taking these arguments into account and using Michael Gilsenan's terms, which describe Islam as the anthropologist's label for a heterogeneous collection of items, each of which has been designated Islamic by informants, one has to give a more cautious awareness of what the term *sharīʿa* comes to mean in different economic, political, and social structures and relations. Gilsenan's aim is to always situate the religious, cultural, and ideological forms and practices that people regard as Islamic in the life and development of their societies.[38] This becomes more sound

[38] Gilsenan, Michael, *Recognizing Islam: An Anthropologist's Introduction*, London & Sydney: Croom Helm, 1984, pages 11–12, 19.

when we listen to Abdul Hamid el-Zein, who argues that the diversity of experience and understanding revealed in many anthropological studies challenges the premise of the unity of religious meaning. El-Zein's contention is that there are diverse forms of Islam, each equally real, each worth describing. He suggests replacing the term *Islam* by *islams*, better to emphasize the multiplicity of Islamic expression and to show that the *islams* of elite and non-elite, literate and illiterate, theologians and artisans, tribesmen and peasants are equally valid expressions of a fundamental, unconscious set of principles.[39]

The above makes the imposition of *sharīʿa* in Sudan almost impossible. Not even two of the Muslim groups interrogated agreed on a single *sharīʿa* interpretation or understanding. If the *sharīʿa* interpretation or understanding of one group is imposed, then it will not just be the non-Muslims who will be dispossessed of the fundamental right of participation in the country's legislation, but within Islam also there would be many groups who would be deprived of this right. Disagreement resulting from such different viewpoints was clear in 1983 when President al-Numayrī announced the imposition of the Islamic penal code (Arab.: *ḥudūd*).[40] Ḥasan al-Turābī, who was the Islamic Movement's secretary general and al-Numayrī attorney general at that time, played a key role in the introduction of that Islamic penal code. Ṣādiq al-Mahdī, who has been head of the Umma Party and spiritual leader of the Anṣār al-Mahdī since 1970, was imprisoned for his opposition to the government's foreign and domestic policies, including his denunciation of the 1983 penal code. Al-Mahdī did not object to the *sharīʿa* being the laws of the land, but rather to the 'un-Islamic' manner al-Numayrī used to implement the *sharīʿa* through the 1983 Laws. The leader of the Democratic Unionist Party and the spiritual guide of the *khatmiyya* Sufi order since 1968, Muḥammad ʿUthmān al-Mirghānī, tried to keep in check the tensions stemming from the differing perspectives of secular-minded professionals in the party and the traditional religious values of the *khatmiyya* supporters by avoiding firm stances on controversial political issues. In particular, he refrained from public criticism of al-Numayrī's Islamic Laws, so as not to alienate the *khatmiyya* followers who approved of implementing the Islamic *sharīʿa*. Rather he supported the idea that al-Numayrī's Islamic Laws could be

---

[39] El-Zein, Abdul Hamid, 'Beyond Ideology and Theology: The Search for the Anthropology of Islam', *Annual Review of Anthropology*, vol. 6, 1977, page 227.

[40] Mahmoud, Mohamed , 'When *Shariʿa* Governs: The Impasse of Religious Relations in Sudan', *Islam and Christian-Muslim Relations*, Vol. 18, No. 2, 2007, page 275.

revised to expunge the 'un-Islamic' content.[41] Even the founder of the Republican Brothers, Maḥmūd Muḥammad Ṭaha, was arrested and subsequently executed for heresy in January 1985 when he opposed the implementation of the 'Islamic Laws' of 1983 as being contrary to the essence of Islam.

41 http://www.sudan.net/government/parties.html (accessed: 24.03.2003).

CHAPTER THREE

CONTRADICTING STATE IDEOLOGY IN SUDAN: CHRISTIAN-MUSLIM RELATIONS AMONG THE INTERNALLY DISPLACED PERSONS IN KHARTOUM—THE CASE OF MANDELA AND WAD AL-BASHĪR CAMPS

Salma Mohamed Abdalla

Argument

This chapter intends to highlight the contradiction between trends in inter-faith practice in the camp communities and the post-1989 state-ideology that has promoted Islam as a state religion and, to a significant extent, stigmatized and marginalized other faiths, especially Christianity. Little academic attention has been paid to perceptions of Christian-Muslim relations in the camps. I would argue that, in Mandela and Wad al-Bashīr camps, contrary to the state ideology, ordinary people of different faiths including Islam and Christianity seem to be sharing common concerns, common problems and common mentalities towards the state. Though one would have expected the stereotype of a Christian-Muslim divide to be playing out in the Camps, findings demonstrate that the divide is not detectable. A caveat to this argument is that this is not an illustration of what happens all over Khartoum, but is specific to the Internally Displaced Camps and is not necessarily replicated in the rest of the community of Khartoum State. An analysis of the impact of the state ideology on the ordinary life of greater Khartoum is outside the scope of this chapter.

Introduction

Since achieving political independence in 1956, the Sudan has experienced a low level of stability, having witnessed two periods of civil war (1955–1972 and 1983–2005) that have brought great suffering to the population.[1] There is a tendency to define the Sudanese conflict along religious lines,

---

[1] Özden, Melik, *Internally Displaced Persons: An overview of the rights of internally displaced persons of the Guiding Principles adopted by the United Nations*, Part of a Series of the Human Rights Programme Of the Europe—Third World Centre (CETIM), 2007, page 7.

as Muslims versus Christians, both within the macro politics of Sudan and by the international community.

The civil war brought from the South to Khartoum displaced persons with different faiths who settled around the capital. This chapter examines the relationship among displaced communities of different faiths and how they consider the issues that unite or divide them. The chapter illustrates the nature and processes of Christian-Muslim relations among the displaced persons in their daily lives and disproves the assumption that religion is a dividing factor inside the camps of the displaced. The chapter discusses the state's attempts to impose a particular kind of behaviour that is problematic to social interactions in displaced communities. The relationships inside the Internally Displaced Persons (IDPs) community and its connections with the host community (ordinary people, groups and government bodies) are also addressed.

The chapter's goal is to illustrate the behaviours and attitudes of members of the IDP communities regarding inter-faith dialogue in their daily life. It also describes the political structure and the role of the current government in Christian-Muslim relations in the IDP Camps and compares individuals' responses with those of the government.

The findings of this chapter are mainly based on a survey conducted in the IDP camps around Khartoum. The survey was conducted in two of the largest displaced persons' camps in Greater Khartoum, namely Mandela in Khartoum and Wad al-Bashīr in Omdurman. The primary data were collected using the methods of observation, individual interviews, group discussions and focus group discussion. To augment the primary data, relevant secondary data are utilized in this chapter.

Internally Displaced Persons

According to the United Nation's definition, Internally Displaced Persons are persons, or groups of people, who have been forced to flee or to leave their homes or places of habitual residence as a result of, or in order to avoid, in particular, the effects of armed conflict, situations of generalized violence, violations of human rights or natural or human-made disasters and who have not crossed an internationally recognized state border.[2]

---

[2] Özden, 2007, page 19.

Like all armed conflicts elsewhere in the world, the civil wars in the Sudan produced a drift of population into the large urban centres in the North and the South. The majority of the displaced from the South moved into Northern Sudan. They concentrated on the periphery of these towns, in the poorest areas generally known as spontaneous slum and squatter settlements.[3]

The Sudan has the largest number of IDPs worldwide,[4] with about 11.9% of the population considered to be displaced, mainly as a result of the wars.[5] More than one half of the population of Southern Sudan is now either living in Northern Sudan or has fled to neighbouring countries. In reality, three-quarters of the Southern population can be considered displaced.[6] Twenty-five per cent of the population in the country live in Khartoum and 40% of Khartoum inhabitants are IDPs.[7] Of the internally displaced persons, the greatest number is located in Greater Khartoum (over 44%).[8] This situation paints a poignant picture of Sudanese society, now made up of largely uprooted persons.

Most of the displaced population comes from a background of subsistence economy, where farming, pastoral or small-scale animal husbandry is the dominant mode of life. During the early stages of the war in Southern Sudan, the majority of the displaced Southern Sudanese came from amongst the Dinka ethnic group, of North Bahr al-Ghazal. Most of them moved northward, first to Southern Darfur and Kordufan provinces, where they settled and became agricultural labourers. From there, the displaced moved to urban centres further North. Paul Wani Gore says "the Shuluk and the Nuer started to move northward, they moved to Kosti and Khartoum and also the Equatorial have found the way to Khartoum".[9] In almost all cases, these ethnic groups had lost all their cattle either before they moved, or during the process of flight.

---

[3] Wani Gore, Paul, 'The Socio-economic and demographic consequences of population displacement in Sudan', *Current Studies on the Sudan*, ed. by: Medani Mohamed M. Ahmed, Khartoum: Omdurman Ahlia University, 1998, page 172.

[4] Assal, Munzoul A. M., 'Displaced Persons in Khartoum: Current realities and post-war scenarios. A Report', Cairo: The Population Council, 2004, page 1.

[5] Wani Gore, 1998, page 182.

[6] Wani Gore, 1998, page 184.

[7] Assal, 2004, page 16.

[8] Assal, 2004, page 15.

[9] Wani Gore, 1998, page 188.

The Government and IDPs in Khartoum

Generally and historically, displaced populations in Sudan were not treated well because the central government has for a very long time denied the existence of the phenomenon of displacement caused by civil war. The attitude of the government towards the displaced population has been marked by denial, indifference, and outright hostility. Long procedures and unstructured and uninformed interventions characterize the government's decision-making style and policy implementation strategy. The displaced have been viewed as a threat to political stability because IDPs are seen as foremost a security problem, and a source of social and cultural tension. This attitude is evident from the location of IDP camps on the fringe of cities where the populations have no access to social services. The government abdicated its responsibilities toward IDPs, leaving the responsibility for their welfare to Non-Governmental Organizations (NGOs). One result of this policy is the dependency among IDPs on relief food.[10] Government officials say that the IDPs, in the beginning, during the 1980s, were scattered in groups in forty-six different locations inside the capital. It was difficult for the NGOs to work on relief projects because of the lack of security and the deterioration of the environment when the IDPs were living inside Khartoum city.

In 1988 the Displaced Commission was established by the President of the Council of Ministries. It started working at the national level and was responsible for the IDPs both inside and outside Khartoum State. Later, after the transformation to the federal system of governance, the Commission of Khartoum became responsible for the IDPs in Khartoum State only. Government policy was divided into short term, midterm and long term policies.

(1) In the short term, between 1989 and 1991, the commission work concentrated on shelter and housing. The strategy to carry out the task was through collecting together the IDPs and assimilating them in many Camps. The government justification of this policy was to offer them food, clothing and water but "the policy was criticized on the grounds that it did not solicit the cooperation of the displaced population and did not involve it in the timing and selection of relocation sites; in addition, the relocation sites were not properly equipped with shelters and other essential

[10] Assal, 2004, page 1.

services".[11] The government's abdication of its responsibility for the welfare of the IDPs has resulted in dependency among IDPs on relief food.

(2) In the midterm, between 1991 and 1994, the government established four major official Camps in Khartoum State. The camps were used for relocation of random habitation inside the city. In 1992 the government called upon the International and the national NGOs to work in the IDP camps. The NGOs which started the work inside the camps in that period are: the Sudan Council of Churches (*majlis al-kanāʾis al-sūdānī*), Islamic Daʿwa Organization (*munaẓẓamat al-daʿwa al-islāmiyya*), CARE International, Red Cross, Save the Children UK, Oxfam, ACCORD and others.

(3) In 1995/1996, the commission started the long-term policy which aimed to integrate the IDPs into the urban structure. The commission started this process by counting the IDPs in Khartoum State. The task was done in collaboration with the Population National Council and United Nation's Development Programme (UNDP) with the assistance of the NGOs. The purpose was to deliver land plots to IDPs.

Although the government claims it is making an adequate effort, research demonstrates that IDPs in Khartoum live on the margins of urban life; job opportunities are virtually non-existent. Significantly, however, the IDPs are exposed to a cultural milieu that is alien to them, which leads to socio-cultural displacement, irrespective of the attitudes of their host communities. Social services are non-existent in these areas. Services such as water, electricity, sanitation and health facilities, as well as educational opportunities, are lacking. Being unskilled and lacking the ability to speak Arabic, the displaced population cannot find employment. The majority of them tend to earn their living through casual labour and other low-paid jobs.[12]

Case Studies

Mandela

Mandela camp, or Mayo Al-Mazari as it is called in the official documents, is 18 kilometres south of Khartoum centre. It was established on 30 June 1991, when the displaced were transferred from Al-Shoak Area

[11] Eltigani, Eltigani E., *War and Drought in Sudan, Essays on Population Displacement*, University Press of Florida, 1995, page 7.

[12] Wani Gore, 1998, page 189.

inside Khartoum Town. In 1990 the displaced were moved to the present Mandela area which is in the periphery of Jabal Awliyya locality. The total camp area is approximately 5 square kilometres surrounded by other low-cost districts and slums; it has a population of approximately 10,000 families.

The displaced resided in the area without the agreement of the government authorities. Both the locality (county) and the Khartoum State officials were not content. The government officials say the problems in Mandela are because people moved in and extended their slums and entered the farms' area. The owners of these farms took their cases to the court and demanded their lands back, and this problem is still to be resolved. But the citizens insisted on inhabiting the area against the formal wishes of the government and named their residence Mandela after the great South African black leader. They looked on themselves as freedom fighters and defended their cause against the apartheid government's wishes.

The government policy towards the area is based on the fact that Mandela camp is a temporary area and the residents are supposed to move to Sundus II (governmental camp). Mandela residents refuse to move because they have cleaned up the place and resided there for a long time, and they have the feeling that the government sold the place to Saudi Arabian investors.

The study area is composed of seven settlement squares: Central Square, the Eastern, the Western, Kordufan, Wau squares, Ghabbush and Wadi squares. It is to be noted that each settlement square embodies a specific dominant ethnic group along with other minor ethnic groups. The major ethnic groups are: Dinka Bahr al-Ghazal, Dinka Farno, Shiluk, Nuer, Nuba Mountains' ethnic groups, a mixture of Faratit and Equatorians, Furs and other Western Sudan groups.

The camp is an undefined, casual, and unplanned settlement. The area is an annexe of Mayo district which was an older slum; groups of immigrants came from the area of Dar al-Salaam and settled here. The reasons for displacement vary from one group to another, but the majority moved in because of war. Most of the people stay in the camp waiting for the town planning to give them plots of land for housing. They either engage in petty trade or are completely idle and entirely dependent on relief support and donations from NGOs.

Most of the residents I interviewed indicated that prior to coming to the camps they were subsistence farmers and pastoralists. Thus, given their economic livelihood prior to coming to Khartoum, most of the IDPs were less skilled for entering the urban job market.

I argue here that having fewer skills was a leading factor in the IDPs' dependency on relief support. When the flow of relief shrank at the end of 2005 and early 2006, conditions were aggravated and the area faced a serious crisis. Public services are completely absent and unemployment amounts to nearly 90% of the population. The working group is mainly composed of women who either make liquor and other local wines, or go to work in domestic service outside the camp. Unemployment generates a sense of estrangement and grief on the part of the residents towards the government. There is also a general feeling of frustration towards the Comprehensive Peace Agreement (CPA). There is a grand sultan (chief) court in Mandela market place, besides other smaller native courts based on ethnicity. Chiefs settle disputes but their courts are less important at the present and less cared for and respected.[13]

Wad al-Bashīr

Wad al-Bashīr camp is 17 kilometres distant from Khartoum centre and was established in 1991. Administratively it is part of al-Bugaa locality (West Omdurman). It is bordered by Block 43 to the North, Block 42 to the East and Block 46, named al-Couther, to the West. To the South it is bordered by John Madet area, which is divided into squares 51 and 52. The camp was included in the residential plan which was designed to remedy the casual housing problem. Planning projects took place to a certain extent and about 5000 land plots of 216 square meters per piece were handed out to families. The vast majority of families remain outside the plan, waiting to receive plots. The population originates from different ethnic groups; the largest group is Northern Bahr al-Ghazal Dinkas (Aweil). The Nubas of Southern Kordofan Mountains come second in number and then the Nuer, Shiluk and tribes of Equatoria, mainly Azandi and Latuka. From Darfur came the Fur, Zaghawa, Bargo, Masaleet; and from Northern Kordofan the Kababish Arabs. The cause of immigration of the majority of the population is war. Ethnic groups from North and central Sudan are also present, who work as retail merchants in the settlements.

---

[13] Field work observation coupled with a series of interviews conducted in Mandela.

The people in the camp share similar standards of living and there are no variations that warrant being mentioned. Poverty is the typical state of affairs and unemployment is widespread. As mentioned earlier, as a result of lack of skills, coupled with scarcity of jobs and discrimination by state institutions in the North, IDPs hold no permanent jobs. The few that are employed are mainly engaged in unskilled labour such as building and construction, domestic chores and odd jobs. As one of the social mechanisms in reaction to unemployment, generation and gender-base social groupings have emerged. The youth pass their time in the youth clubs playing games such as cards and dominoes. The women gather in the houses and old men meet in the Sultan's compounds or in the market places, drinking local liquor and chatting away their days.

It is important to note that, unlike in Mandela, in Wad al-Bashīr camp there is a noticeable number of young people who have achieved some level of education, including Sudan School Certificate (General Secondary Education completion), and a few are university graduates. This category is more fluent in English and Arabic languages. Yet, in spite of their linguistic skills and academic attainment, life has not been any better for them as unemployment is widespread, along with unspeakable levels of poverty.

Despite all the hardships in the camps, there seems to be peaceful coexistence among different ethnic groups and among different religious groups especially between Christians and Muslims, as I will be highlighting later on.

Christian-Muslim Relations in Sudan—Overview and Background

This chapter would not be complete without re-visiting Sudan's history since independence in 1956 and the state's different approaches, policies and strategies in Christian-Muslim relations' management. This analysis is important because there is the belief that the present phenomenon has its root causes in the past and the problem has developed along with the nation-building process. The historical background is divided into two phases: (1) from independence in 1956 until the coalition government in 1989. (2) *Al-injāz* Government from 1989 until 2007, after the signing of the Comprehensive Peace Agreement.

For some scholars, the undertaking of the programmes of Islamization and Arabization of the country by the central governments, while ignoring its great cultural diversity, contributes negatively to Christian-Muslim relations. It is a problem that started immediately after independence and, as Kebbede explicitly put it, “since independence all governments in Khartoum have totally neglected the economic, political, and cultural interests of the non-Muslim and non-Arab natives of southern Sudan”.[14]

Others see that religion has been misused, thereby contributing to conflict in Sudan’s civil wars. Many factors allowed religion to be abused in the Sudan to serve political ends. However this misuse stretches back to the colonial period which designed and implemented policies that created isolation and unequal development between people of the North and South to serve the avarice of the colonial power, and occasioned little genuine dialogue between people of the North and South.

The Period from 1956–1989

At Sudan’s Independence in 1956, the principles of Islam were articulated by the head of the *sharīʿa* courts, Grand *qāḍī* Ḥasan Muddathir in a pamphlet entitled “A Memorandum for the Enactment of a Sudan Constitution Derived from the Principles of Islam”. He said, “in an Islamic country like the Sudan the social organization of which has been built upon Arab customs and Islamic ways and of which the majority are Muslims, it is essential that the general principles of the constitution of such a country should be derived from the principles of Islam, and, consequently, the laws governing its people should be enacted from the principles of an Islamic constitution and in according with Islamic ideals out of which such community has been shaped”.[15]

Also at that time, the Umma Party (UP, *ḥizb al-umma*) and the Democratic Unionist Party (DUP, *al-ḥizb al-ittiḥādī al-dīmūqrāṭī*) called for *sharīʿa* to be the main source of legislation, while the Communist Party (CP, *ḥizb al-shuyuʿī al-waṭānī*) objected to the idea. The Southerners challenged the proposal because they expected it to result in their being treated as second class citizens, deprived of holding public office such as that of the head of the state and the chief of the judiciary. Finally they decided to

---

14 Kebbede, Girma (ed.), ‘Introduction’, in *Sudan’s Predicament, Civil war, displacement and ecological degradation*, Aldershot: Ashgate, 1999, page 7.

15 Tier, Akolda M., ‘Mixed Civil, Sharia and Customary Jurisdictions and laws in an ethnic conflict setting: the case of Sudan’, in *Religion and Conflict in Sudan*, Yusuf Fadl Hasan & Richard Gray (eds.), Paulines Publications Africa, Nairobi, 2002, page 79.

boycott the deliberation of the National Committee for the Constitution if Christianity was not recognized as a state religion like Islam.

Under ʿAbbūd's military regime, which started in 1957, the processes of Islamization and Arabization continued, firstly through encouraging the spread of Islamic education, secondly through the promotion of Arabic language and thirdly by hindering the activities of missionaries.

Later, in 1966, the Premier al-Ṣādiq al-Mahdī (Umma Party President) saw the identity of Sudan as an Islamic and Arabic one. The DUP and the Islamic Charter Front (ICF, *jabhat al-mithāq al-islāmī*) demanded an Islamic constitution, while the CP and the Southern political parties called for complete separation between state and religion.

In 1969, al-Numayrī took power in a military coup. Peace with the South was achieved by ending the Civil War through the Addis Ababa agreement of 1972, which guaranteed freedom of religion. Then, for non-religious reasons, al-Numayrī declared the implementation of *sharīʿa* law as the state law in September 1983. Khalil's observed that immediately

> Numayri appointed a committee to revise the laws with a view to ensuring their conformity with the Shariʿa.... several bills were drafted and promulgated by presidential decree..... Of these, two are of particular relevance.... The first prohibited the manufacture, possession and consumption of alcoholic beverages.... The other bill was enacted as the Sources of Judicial Decisions Act which...provided that where there is no legislation governing an issue before the court, judgment shall be based on the Shariʿa.... A new penal code provided for the severe Qur'anic punishments of *hudud*: hand amputation for theft, cross amputation for armed robbery, death for adultery, sedition and apostasy, crucifixion for armed rebellion and flogging for manufacture, possession or consumption of alcohol.[16]

As the above quotation illustrates, at state level Christian-Muslim relations were further strained, and southern politicians, the Church and the Sudan People's Liberation Movement/Army (SPLM/A) were distressed.

It is important to mention that the Islamic laws were declared three months after the Anya-Nya II mutiny; this was the consequence of the deterioration in North-South relations, as a result of breaching the Addis Ababa Accord. Southerners found that the September Laws violated their rights and freedom and some observers found the September laws intensified the second civil war. Many who initiated the peace talks that took

---

[16] Khalil, Mohamed Ibrahim, 'Human Rights and Islamization of the Sudan Legal System', in: *Religion and Conflict in Sudan*, Yusuf Fadl Hasan & Richard Gray (eds.), Paulines Publications Africa, Nairobi, 2002, page 60.

place between the Sudan Government and the SPLM/SPLA realized that the Civil War would not stop by force of arms.[17]

In the coalition government, al-Ṣādiq al-Mahdī, the leader of the then ruling party, found *sharīʿa* laws to have been imposed and he rejected the *ḥudūd*. Al-Mahdī aimed at introducing a new Islamic law that would safeguard the interests of non-Muslims. The DUP, the second party after Umma, did not demand the invalidation of the September Laws, while the National Islamic Front (NIF, *al-jabha al-islāmiyya al-qaumiyya*), the third party, affirmed that Muslims are a majority in the Sudan so *sharīʿa* would be the general source of law.

The Period from 1989–2007

In this period religion became graver, a source of conflict when it became a symbol of identity of power sharing, even of the management control of our resources. It was a factor when the Government of the National Salvation Revolution (NSR, *thaurat al-inqādh al-waṭanī*), which took power in 30 June 1989, used religion to serve its own political aims: "Some argue that the government's attempt at defining Islam narrowly and forcing it on the country's non-Muslim populations is at the core of conflict".[18] Therefore it can be demonstrated that the way that the state implemented Islamic *sharīʿa* Laws contributed to the less-than-harmonious relations between Christians and Muslims. There were no efforts at nation building to bring the population together in a national community. The policies were far from accepting diversity.

As defenders of the Islamic ideal, the National Islamic Front's programme constituted an important development in the religious dimension of the Southern question and in North-South relations. The government of NSR remained heavily committed to the *sharīʿa* as a religious mission.

Public Order Laws

In 1991 the government declared a penal code aimed at filling in 'Islamic' gaps in the September laws. The government declared Public Order laws which state that "a person who, in a public place, commits an act, or

[17] See for example: Kebbede 1999, Tier 2002 and Khalil 2002 among others.

[18] Sanneh, Lamin, 'Preface. Religion and Conflict in Sudan', in *Religion and Conflict in Sudan*, Yusuf Fadl Hasan & Richard Gray (eds.), Paulines Publications Africa, Nairobi, 2002, page 11.

conducts himself in a manner, contrary to public morality or wears an 'immodest' dress commits an offence punishable by flogging". As far as Khartoum State is concerned, this provision was elaborated by a 1996 Public Order Decree that penalized and provides for flogging for a wide range of hitherto common practices, such as . . . a women being in the company of a male other than a *maḥram* (a near relative with whom marriage amounts to incest).[19]

Section 5 (3) of the Penal Code of 1991 makes the punishments of *ḥudūd* and *qiṣāṣ* (Arab.: settlement, applied after killing or wounding under Islamic law) inapplicable in the Southern States and exempts their inhabitants from the provisions relating to apostasy, adultery, manufacture, use and possession of alcohol and wearing 'immodest' dress. In view of the massive displacement caused by the war, the exemption is poor consolation to Southerners now living in Northern towns.

It should be noted that many Christians identify disruption of socio-religious functions as a critical factor in Christian-Muslim relationships in the Sudan. This is attributed to the police action against IDPs' camps. This is always a volatile encounter that results in confrontations with the public, and is perceived by many, ironically both Christians and Muslims, in the IDP camps to be 'very discriminatory' in terms of implementing a dress code for the public but with Christian targets in focus. This is an illustration that vindicates my inference that there is a contradiction between the state ideology that plays the Islamic ideology card against non-Islamic views whereas the ordinary folk do not act, behave and think according to the state Muslim/non-Muslim borders.

The Public Order Law is a law which was instituted on Islamic principles, and the commitment to the (Islamic) public appearance is one of *al-injāz* government's 'achievements'. The public order law's approach is to prevent the practices which are contradictory to *sharīʿa* and the 'benign customs'; the implementation of the public order and the society's appearance is its main goal. The 'virtuous' external appearance is to protect woman through:

(1) Islamic dress.
(2) Public streets' discipline in terms of mixing of males and females.
(3) Combating negative phenomena.
(4) Increasing religiousness (Islam) in the society.
(5) Control of public transports, public parks and clubs.

---

[19] Khalil, 2002, page 61.

(6) Media.
(7) The educational and the cultural side.

In 1996 the authorities activated the laws and performed many acts accompanied by activities such as, firstly, intensifying the control attacks in the streets and public places. Secondly, they obliged female (state) employees and students to wear *ḥijāb* (Islamic dress) and thirdly, re-creation of the *muḥtasib*'s (inspector of the behaviour) role.[20]

Yom, a young IDP Christian girl of 23 years old, narrates her experience with the public order police in this respect.

> At one time there were street riots in Khartoum. I was wandering the street wearing a short sleeved blouse, a policeman came across to me and asked why I was dressed in that way. "Is this your home town that you should dress like that [as if you were] in Juba [capital town of the South]?" I gave no reply. Someone explained I might be Christian. The policeman said "Christian or not this is not her home town. She should respect the view of the rest as they are all Muslims". So I could give no answer. "This may as well be her own way of dressing but she should not wear this way here, let her do that in Juba or anywhere else", the policeman concluded.[21]

The Public Order Act declared in Khartoum State was accompanied by special courts called Public Order Courts which implemented the public order laws. These courts' procedures are faster than the regular courts where there is indictment, lawsuit, defence, and witnesses. Usually, regular cases take time, unlike in the Public Order Courts. In the CPA it says that leniency and granting the accused the benefit of doubt are legal principles of universal application, especially in the circumstances of a poor society like the Sudan, which is just emerging from war, characterized by prevalent poverty and subject to massive displacement of people. In contradiction to that principle, in the Public Order Courts the judges take a decision in a moment. According to one advocate interviewed, 60 to 100 cases can be adjudicated in one day because of the fast procedures. In those cases it is often the case that there is no opportunity for defence because the complainants are always either policemen, security officials or even public order police hence the accused has no chance to mount a defence.

---

[20] Bashīr, Bashīr M., *al-taḥawwulāt al-kubra fi'l-Sūdān 1989–2000* (The Major Transformations in Sudan between 1989 and 2000), Khartoum: Future Studies Centre, 2002, (Published in Arabic).

[21] Interview, Khartoum, March 2007.

Jihād *and Christian-Muslim Relations*

As defenders of Islamic ideals, the programme of the National Islamic Front constituted an important development in the religious dimension of the Southern question and in North-South relations. The NSR government remained committed to the *sharīʿa* both as a religious motto and as a guide to policy making. In the course of its rule it implemented many changes in plans, laws, programmes and policy execution. *Jihād* is one of the acts and policies with a direct effect on our field of interest, in particular on Muslim-Christian relations in general and especially among the IDPs.

The religious dimension of the Sudan conflict became more pronounced when the government of the National Salvation Revolution proclaimed that the war in the South is a *jihād* war with its strong religious connotations. The government advocated that *jihād* is being waged essentially in defence of the land and the Islamic faith, and that a *sharīʿa* state can only be constructed through *jihād*, which is the duty of every Muslim. The *jihād*[22] programme was launched over the whole of the South. As the government declared, the *jihād* was against the infidels.

An IDP, commenting on *jihād* said:

> Although, an infidel according to the interpretation of the Qurʾān is someone with no religion, but I am a Christian. In addition to that *jihād* is across homeland borders, but here they initiate *jihād* against the Sudanese Southerners.[23]

In 1992, the year that was officially announced as the year of *jihād,* General ʿUmar al-Bashīr was proclaimed *imām al-jihād.* On 27 April 1992, six pro-government religious leaders issued a *fatwā* (Arab.: legal opinion) legalizing *jihād* against the SPLA rebels in the Nuba Mountains, in South Kordofan, to liberate it from the infidel rebels.

> ... this kind of *fatwa,* a sheer product of religious manipulation has actually led to atrocities and indiscriminate killing that true Islam undoubtedly pre-

[22] According to the entry "Djihād" in The Encyclopaedia of Islam II the etymological meaning of this term is "effort towards a determined objective. [...] In law [...] *djihād* consists of military action with the object of the expansion of Islam and, if need be, of its defence". Thus, the concept of *jihād* describes at least three different types of struggles: a Muslim's internal struggle to live out his faith as well as possible; to build a good Muslim society, and finally holy war to defend Islam, with force if necessary.

[23] Interview, Khartoum, March 2007.

> vents. This may beg an important question whether Islam orders killing of Christians and other non-believers except in self-defence?[24]

The Popular Defence Forces (PDFs, *qawāt al-difāʿ al-shaʿbī*) and, under their auspices, the *mujāhidūn* (those who fight in *jihād*), were established, and "an additional tax called "financing the *jihād*" was levied upon the citizens in Kordofan".[25] Islamist Voluntary organizations such as *nidāʾ al-jihād* (call for *jihād*) and *munaẓẓamat al-shahīd* (martyr's organization) were established to advocate the cause of *jihād*, and *salām al-ʿizza* (peace with pride) to provide material support to *mujāhidūn* families and *zād al-mujāhid* (food for the holy warrior).

Gradually, fighting the war against the rebels in the South and other areas of Sudan became the ultimate form of the *jihād*. By 1993–1994 *jihād* had become the central theme in the government's projection of its war efforts.

To encourage and reinforce Muslim perception of Christians as infidels, the government had a policy towards the martyr's families. The government trains the sons of these so-called martyrs to replace their father. According to Kafino (Dinka Christian man, living in Mandela), the government's policy in this respect is carried out in the following way:

> When we were very little, the real meanings of things were unknown to us. We used to go to the martyr's organization. There they mix politics with religion. They should not have called the donation which government officials gather for the cause of the *jihād* against Christians 'martyr benefits'. They should call it war endowment... It is done to tempt our Christian kinsfolk.[26]

In fact, the martyr's organization is not merely a military foundation; it is a religious institution too. They exploit the economic situation of a killed soldier's heirs, and bestow foodstuffs on them at the end of the month and ask that the elder son of the deceased soldier convert to Islam. Such rations are given only in Ramaḍḥān (Muslim fasting month). That is in addition to a sheep given as a gift on the occasion of the sacrifice of *ʿīd al-aḍḥā* (Muslim yearly festival). Nothing of the sort is given at Christmas

[24] Kadouf, Hunud Abia, 'Religion and conflict in the Nuba Mountains', in *Religion and Conflict in Sudan*, Yusuf Fadl Hasan & Richard Gray (eds.), Paulines Publications Africa, Nairobi, 2002, page 109.

[25] Sidahmed, Abdel Salam, 'The Unholy War: Jihad and the Conflict in Sudan', in *Religion and Conflict in Sudan*, Yusuf Fadl Hasan & Richard Gray (eds.), Paulines Publications Africa, Nairobi, 2002, page 88.

[26] Interview, Mandela, March 2007.

or any other Christian feasts to Christians who suffer the similar fate of the loss of a bread-winner in the cause of the conflict. As far as my Christian respondents are concerned, the government utilizes such material benefits as enticements to proselytize Christians and subtly coerce them to convert to Islam in order to be able to receive such benefits.[27]

This material enticement is an aspect of the assimilation policy of the government, which aims to turn Christians into Muslims. Some Christians converted and the rest of them refused to convert. Christian IDPs feel that, partly because of their plight, they are direct targets of government assimilation strategies. They are directly made to suffer untold and humiliating experiences which will predispose them to switch to Islam in order to save themselves from physical annihilation. A respondent narrates his experience in this respect thus:

> In 2004, something happened here in Mandela. There were certain elements that approached a group of 27 people [all Christians] and tempted them to switch to Islam on the grounds of their living conditions and told them that as they were ideal, so they wanted them to become Muslims, and in return jobs will be availed to them. A number of those elements were Latokas[28] who work for the government. They targeted the youth in their 20s and recruited them to Soba permanent camp and were subjected to orientation courses. All of them were Latoka. They were taught the *wuḍū'* [Muslim ablutions before prayer] and *ṣalāt* [Muslim prayers]. Ultimately, they received no jobs.

Ironically, the state has not fulfilled its side of the bargain even to those who have converted to Islam within the framework of the Islamization project.

The Comprehensive Peace Agreement CPA (2005)

The question of *sharīʿa* and the separation of religion and state continued to provoke a lot of discussion and was the main challenge in the peace talks between the government and the SPLM/A, despite the efforts of several mediators in the years between the 1990s and 2003. Indeed, this issue is still causing much confusion and is yet to be settled, especially in relation to Khartoum, 'the National Capital'.

---

27 This opinion was expressed by interviewees.

28 The south part of Sudan is inhabited by two major ethnic groups who are divided into hundreds of tribes and clans—the Nilotics and the Equatorians. The Latoka group is among the largest Equatorian groups.

Prior to the CPA the government introduced an Islamic system of government. The constitutional Decree No.13 commands magistrates to be guided by the *sharīʿa*. Custom is subordinate to *sharīʿa* as a source of legislation although the Constitution stated that *sharīʿa* and customs should be the source of legislation. Religion has contributed to the civil war between the Government of Sudan and the rebel movements in the South, a war which continued, on and off, until a cease-fire was reached in October 2002.

However, religion was used during the last decade by both parties for the purposes of public mobilisation, seeking political and material support. During the last rounds of negotiations between the Government of Sudan and SPLM, defining the role of religion in public life was one of the thorny issues. The SPLM asked for a secular constitution which separates religion from state while the government defended the right of Muslims to implement Islamic laws. Eventually the two parties reached an agreed formula, which is embodied in the Comprehensive Peace Agreement (CPA) that was signed in January 2005. It included the protection of Southern Sudan from Islamic laws (3-2-2): "Nationally enacted legislation having effect only in respect of the states outside Southern Sudan shall have as its source of legislation *sharīʿa* and the consensus of the people".[29] In the CPA, respect for the practising of religious rites and the establishment of places for worship, the issuing and disseminating of religious material, and observing holidays on days of religious ceremonies appears in 6-5. 6-6 guaranteed that this principle is reflected in the Constitution. The laws and beliefs of those concerned shall govern all family matters. Citizenship shall not be subject to discrimination on grounds of religion or other beliefs.

The CPA includes a 'vague' charter about the National Capital in Chapter 2–4, where Khartoum shall be the capital of the Republic of the Sudan. The National Capital shall be a symbol of national unity that reflects the diversity of Sudan.

The CPA says the Administration of the National Capital shall be representative and, during the Interim period, the two Parties shall be adequately represented in the administration of the National Capital. The term 'National Capital' is vague in the CPA, because there is confusion as to whether the CPA talks about the Capital, which has no determined territory, or about Khartoum State.

---

[29] From the Comprehensive Peace Agreement (CPA), between the National Congress Party NCP and the Sudan People's Liberation Movement/Army SPLM/A, 2005, Kenya.

In the CPA, human rights and fundamental freedoms as specified in the Machakos Protocol, and in the Agreement, including respect for all religions, beliefs and customs, shall be guaranteed and enforced in the National Capital, as well as throughout the whole of Sudan and shall be enshrined in the National Interim Constitution. Law enforcement agencies of the Capital shall be representative of the population of Sudan and shall be adequately trained and made sensitive to the cultural, religious and social diversity of all Sudanese. The criticism at this point is that the training for the authority agencies is not enough without the existence of Law to protect these rights.

The CPA says, judges and law enforcement agents shall, in dispensing justice and enforcing current laws in the National Capital, follow certain guidelines:

1. Tolerance.
2. Behaviours based on cultural practices and traditions, as long as not in flagrant disregard of the law or disturbing public order shall be deemed in the eyes of the law as an exercise of personal freedoms. (It is three years now since the signing of the CPA and still Public Order Police attack Southerners during their cultural festivals regardless of the respect due to cultural practices).[30]
3. The judicial discretion of courts to impose penalties on non-Muslims shall observe the long-established legal (*sharīʿa*) principle that non-Muslims are not subject to prescribed penalties, and therefore remitted penalties shall apply. (In practice this principal is not yet implemented in the courts because every day many cases come to the courts and non-Muslims are judged according to *sharīʿa* law.)
4. A special commission shall be appointed by the Presidency to insure that the rights of non-Muslims are protected in accordance with the aforementioned guidelines and not adversely affected by the application of *sharīʿa* law in the Capital. The said commission shall make its observations and recommendations to the Presidency. Additionally, a system of mechanisms of guarantees shall be established to enable the operation of the above points, such as the establishment of specialized Attorney General Circuits to conduct investigations and pre-trial proceedings related to offences involving these principles. (This is not yet done.)

30 View expressed by one interviewee.

Presidential Decree No. (24) of the year 2006, establishing the Special Commission for the Rights of Non-Muslims (in view of the application of Islamic *sharīʿa*) in the National Capital, was decreed for the following objectives and functions:[31]

a) To ensure that the National Capital is a symbol of National unity that reflects and enriches the religious, cultural and social diversity of the Country.
b) To guarantee the Rights of Non-Muslims in the National Capital in view of the application of Islamic *sharīʿa*.
c) To further consolidate the spirit of tolerance and peaceful co-existence among the residents of the National Capital.
d) To ensure that the Rights of Non-Muslims (in view of the application of *sharīʿa* in the National Capital) are protected.
e) To ensure that all religions, beliefs and traditions are respected and that the spirit of tolerance and co-existence among the different creeds and cultures in the National Capital is consolidated.
f) To submit any observations and recommendations it deems fit to the Presidency.

The procedure of the work of the commission is to lay out policies and plans to initiate projects and programmes aiming at consolidating the true values of tolerance and co-existence in collaboration with the citizens, community leaders and concerned government entities. Its procedure requires it to take the initiative to contact any government or non-government entity to ensure that the rights of non-Muslims are well observed in view of the application of Islamic *sharīʿa* in the National Capital. And its task requires it to review complaints from citizen or entities with the view of studying and verifying such complaints through direct contact with the concerned bodies in Khartoum state.

However, the commission work cannot be implemented on the ground, because there is no law supporting its work to sustain the rights of non-Muslims in Khartoum. The training and awareness initiatives put in the CPA for the policemen and security officials to show special treatment to non-Muslims are not enough and cannot grant the protection of these rights. The word 'non-Muslim' is not identified well because in its composition the membership represents Christians and Muslims and there is no mention of nonbelievers, Jews and followers of traditional religions.

[31] From the Constitution of the Special Commission for the Rights of Non-Muslims in the National Capital, Ministry of Presidency Affairs, Republic of Sudan, 2006.

On the ground the establishment of the commission took a long time. Since its official start, no significant work has been done so far due to the slow, long and complicated procedures. Illiteracy, ignorance and mistrust can be obstacles for the non-Muslim IDPs to access such an institution to look for their rights in such forums unless the commission moves to those places. The commission has no office or agencies inside the camps and its work lacks the means of investigation and research in the IDP camps.

Christian-Muslim Relations in the IDP Camps

This section analyses Christian-Muslim relations from the point of view of the IDPs. The survey revealed important findings concerning perceptions and relationships demonstrating how displaced Muslims and Christians express their interfaith perspectives. Specifically, people's experience inside the camps is that there is no difference between Christians and Muslims. For instance, Christians find out that Islam as a religion has a great deal of positive things. In their daily living experience these people who have been lumped together by fate and not by choice, do not consider the issue of religion to be a dividing factor and live side by side with each other, regardless of their religious belief. Different religious beliefs and practices have not resulted in contests, tensions and social strife. The populations, as diverse as they are, live in mutual respect as neighbours; they exchange greetings and goodwill on days of religious festivals.

There is a strong inference from my respondents that religious festivals provide more opportunities for interfaith solidarity among friends of different religious traditions. It is a common practice in both Muslim and Christian communities to pay visits to neighbours during religious festivals and holidays. As Fardos Hamza, a 30 year old Muslim woman who lives in Wad al-Bashīr stated:

> We are neighbours, we exchange visits especially on *ʿīds* [religious festivals]. This is particularly so with our neighbour named al-Toma (Christian). When they dance [collectively] we go there to witness and participate. And so when they have funeral ceremonies, we as well played [danced] with them [that is, participated in mourning dance].[32]

The opinion expressed above is a clear indication that what is at the state level is diametrically different from people's everyday life.

[32] Interview, Wad al-Bashīr, February 2007.

Most exchanges among the residents of the IDP camps revolve around the positive things that colleagues wish for others in the immediate future. A substantial number of respondents considered markets, homes and public transport as other forums of interfaith exchanges. As a Dinka Christian man, Kafino Saterlino expressed:

> In Khartoum in all my activities we participate with Muslims and we have discussions in most cases. Yet most important and to make life easy we would have to respect others and apply the text of love to each other and so . . . Here in Mandela, I have not faced any questions about my conforming to a sect, or to a [particular] religion.[33]

In the planned areas, the lot system (Arab.: *qurʿa*) in the distribution of land plots, gives the opportunity to experience the intermixture of different tribes and different communities together in the same place. According to the officials of the camps, the *qurʿa* system doesn't differentiate among people. The recent shift in circumstances forces the IDPs to change their old system of traditions and behaviour. It makes people separate from their relatives and relocate to live with others pursuant to the lot. That is the reason why you find Christians and Muslims living together in one place in a peaceful neighbourhood, paying less attention to tribal and religious differences.

There is another level of collaboration between Christians and Muslims in the camps, which is in economy and trade. Many NGOs and Community Based Organizations, CBOs, such as, for instance, Peace and Development Association (PDA) in Wad al-Bashīr, work in the camps to implement projects that depend on investments and income generating projects such as a grocery business, boutiques, charcoal retail, and small stores etc., and chicken-raising projects in Mandela are implemented by women's groups. This system functions through grouping; it divides the IDPs into groups, each group consisting of between 15 to 20 persons. In such projects you find Christians and Muslims working together; the two communities are members in the collective projects and have their joint accounts and common markets.

An excellent example is 'Sawā Sawā' (Arab.: together, together) Association which is another example from Wad al-Bashīr. The Christian and Muslim members of the association concur on the same objectives, and share the same questions. To a great extent the projects are jointly designed and jointly implemented. So far Sawā Sawā has implemented a

33 Interview, Mandela, March 2007.

water distribution project, adult education and many other activities. In partnership with other NGOs, like UNIMIS, Save the Children and CARE, Sawā Sawā implemented child protection projects and other important projects. In these projects you find Christians and Muslims are working together in harmony.

Catholic Relief Service (CRS) is an NGO implementing banking and saving projects among the women. The researcher attended one of the graduation ceremonies when I found Christian women and Muslim women together sharing the same objective of economizing. ACCORD is implementing projects on Domestic Gardening, Crockery Handicraft and other projects. These projects depend on teamwork to guarantee the seriousness of the IDPs, which encourages them to get funding. The teams usually have Christians and Muslims working together.

In political behaviour, it is recognized that before and after the Comprehensive Peace Agreement, some of the Christian Southerners were and are supporting the NCP, the leading Islamic party which is controlling the resources. It is known in the political game that the NCP used to present material appeal and services to mobilize people. That is why it is not strange to find Southern Christians among the NCP because for some of the IDPs it is the party which will guarantee residence in Khartoum and services. But after the CPA, most of the Southerners realised that they have rights which can be achieved through other partners, such as the opposition party, the Sudan People's Liberation Movement (SPLM). Also among the latter party you find Muslims/Christians and Northerners/Southerners are working together in the vision of the 'new Sudan' regardless of religion and ethnicity.

The two parties SPLM and NCP are the most-represented parties in the IDP camps and in one house you can find two brothers belonging to the two parties with different ideologies and living together and 'eating from the same plate' regardless of the ideological differences. The point here is that religion does not constitute a barrier to the political behaviour of the IDPs in the Camps around Khartoum.

Issues Affecting Christian-Muslim Relations

Though the research has revealed that religion is not a barrier at the grassroots level, it does demonstrate that issues of conflict do exist at national and government levels. This situation is apparent when the interviewees identified elements of instrumentalization of religion in the cause of political objectives amongst the actors in the process and in the discernible patterns of religious manipulation. The majority of respondents of both religions agree that religion is used as an instrument of political interests.

Leadership

According to Priscilla, a Christian respondent, "there is a problem if you want to be a leader; it is difficult. You are marginalized and prevented to rule and climb the ladder, which is not open to anyone... discrimination because of religion is obvious".[34]

Priscilla's argument can be interpreted with the aid of a retrospective analysis of the political history of Sudan. The declaration of the Sudan as an Islamic Republic raises the question of whether a non-Muslim can be president. Al-Ṣādiq al-Mahdī, leader of Umma Party, answers the question negatively but hastens to say that this need not cause worry to Southern politicians as the Muslim majority would not vote for a non-Muslim as head of the state. By failing to make a distinction between constitutional rights, on the one hand, and the political chance of implementation of them on the other, al-Ṣādiq al-Mahdī misses the relevance of an important political controversy. Ḥasan al-Turābī, the NIF's (former) ideologue, however, concedes a non-Muslim's right to be nominated for that position. He defends his political stance by arguing that as no Southerner can ever secure the necessary majority of votes, the country would always end up with a Muslim as a head of state. Accordingly, he maintains, to concede a non-Muslim's eligibility for nomination would not, in effect, constitute infringement of the *sharīʿa.*

Education

The educational system also influences the relations between Christians and Muslims. One of the policies that complicated the situation was the Islamization of the educational system.

The current Education Curriculum and the educational system are Islamized. There is therefore a need to review the general curriculum so that it accommodates different religions in the Sudan. Criticism advanced against the educational system in Sudan revolves around the issue of the school curriculum, especially at the level of basic education. Yom Deng could not have framed the problem involved in this area in better terms:

34 Interview, Omdurman, May 2007.

> In the curricula of education, I came across nothing that reflects Christianity, not a single time. Most of the poetry illustrations are of Islamic Poems, Qur'ānic verses or *ṣaḥāba* [Prophet Muhammad's companions] speeches. Inversely and at no time, not a single instance, did I come across an illustration quoting the Bible or Christian Saints' speeches in school text books. In school curricula the Islamic content might not change altogether, but there at least should be a teacher for Christian education [in public schools]. It is improper for a small number of pupils to return to sit for Christian education lessons in the afternoon three days a week. This way a pupil cannot assimilate what is learnt. Once school fees are paid in full, knowledge should be taught in full including Christian religion. Now Christian pupils have to pay extra fees for their religious lessons.[35]

In looking at the role of religion in conflict and peace, the opinions of members of both Islam and Christianity point to a deliberately skewed emphasis on the curriculum toward inculcating Islamic knowledge and not Christian knowledge. As should be expected, such factors and practice of religious discrimination in schools and in shaping of attitudes affect inter-faith coexistence in the educational system. It contributes towards religious discrimination and intolerance through structures of public learning and the attitude of teachers. A sizeable number of Christians find that attitudes of teachers are partly responsible for the discrimination in schools. The attitudes of teachers could also influence trends of intolerance among students, as Solomon Oliha from Mandela reported:

> I was once studying in an Institute in the town. One day I was trying to leave the class when the Islamic education instructor was getting in. He stopped me at the door of the classroom and insisted that I attend. I refused and we argued. I reported to the director and it was solved there. That moved me a lot.[36]

The content of the curriculum affects relationships in private and in public schools. Christians are more concerned about the infusion of Islamic references and illustrations in different subjects in the curriculum for basic schools and the complete absence of Christian references and quotations. As a prescription from the state ideology the curriculum is simultaneously structured in such a way that it shields Muslim pupils and students from Christian influences on one hand while exposing Christian pupils and students to an overdose of Islamic ideas and materials on the other hand.

[35] Interview, Khartoum, March 2007.
[36] Interview, Khartoum, March 2007.

Policies were introduced where the entire syllabus was changed and the Islamic Qurʾānic understanding and Qurʾānic verses were in every aspect of the curriculum from mathematics to sciences. And that became difficult because the children were now being indoctrinated. Islamic verses are forced on all children; they have to learn them, otherwise they fail the exams. This was very difficult and meant people having to choose between the children going to school or having to struggle with the content of the curriculum. And when they go to school they have to inform the school that they are Christian and that Islam is a different religion from theirs.

Christian Education is not taught in government schools. There is a demand that Christian Education be taught in government schools, and Christian Education teachers be employed by the government and trained on the job. The public schools are open to all children although their rights are not wholly met. Public schools do not provide teachers for the subject of Christian education. It costs parents additional money to pay for the religious education of their children in private centres that offer such teaching services.

Civil Service

Areas of concern for Christians regarding the civil service include:

1. The rights of non-Muslims/Christians are not recognized by the government in national festivals and official holidays. There is a demand for recognition of Christian rights in religious festivals and official holidays under the CPA and in the Interim Constitution.
2. Freedom of worship is not given to all Christians and civil servants on Sunday by some public and private sectors. There is a demand for freedom of worship to be granted to all as stipulated in the CPA and the interim national constitution and interim constitution of Khartoum State.
3. Closing all eating places during the Ramadan is an infringement on the rights of non-Muslims in Khartoum State and therefore should not be continued.
4. Equal rights are not given to all civil servants according to their qualifications. There is the demand that all civil servants be treated equally and according to qualifications or merit. As has been pointed out earlier, the absence of job opportunities is one of the crucial challenges facing the displaced persons in Khartoum. Unemployment is a national problem in Sudan and most of the people suffer from it but the migrant

people in Khartoum, many of whom are Christians, feel this problem more acutely. Because in the words of Paul Jandlo:

> ...there are people who are discriminated [against] in the employment because when you go for employment you have to be asked Qurʾānic verses, if you do not recite them you are out of the interview.[37]

Similarly, there are cases like "some young people who have had problems and were not able to work in *al-ḍarāʾib* [Tax department] because they refused to employ him because taxation includes the *zakāt* and a non-Muslim cannot work there".[38]

There is a strongly held perception of "double" discrimination among the university graduates in the camps. For the graduates, they recognize the general unemployment problem in Sudan but they stressed that their situation is more complex since they are non-Muslims. In accordance with this argument many of the university graduates in the camps attested that their unemployability is attributed to the fact that they are non-Muslims. One actually expanded on this view by claiming that: "This is so because discrimination is already there in Sudan. When I presented my certificate to an interview board, it was sorted into whether Christian or Muslim and they take the latter".[39]

Similar to the state departments, some companies give priority to employing Muslims and no Christian can win a job in such institutions. As a Dinka Christian man, Kafino Saterlino stated, even if one is recruited for the job there is always the insistence for him to become Muslim first, and then be given the employment only afterwards: "My father tried to work for al-Hijra Roads and Construction Company (reputed to belong to Osama bin Laden's group of companies) but the condition to get the job was to be a Muslim".[40]

Lands

Churches are denied acquisition of land by the government in the North, because of the old missionary act of 1962, which has up to now not been removed from the statute books. The Christians demand to have the law repealed, so that the churches can apply for lands in Khartoum State and all other Northern States through the official channels in the land depart-

---

37 Interview, Khartoum, March 2007.
38 Interview, Omdurman, May 2007.
39 Interview, Wad al-Bashīr, February 2007.
40 Interview, Khartoum, March 2007.

ments. Once the law that prohibits the acquisition of land is repealed, churches can also apply for lands for Christian activities in residential areas according to the plans of the Ministry of Housing.

Both Christians and Muslims overwhelmingly agree on the occurrence of conflicts between Christians and State institutions. The reality is that the Church and the State are frequently at odds with each other over policy development, confiscation of Church properties and demolition of churches by the authorities of Khartoum State under the guise of town planning. The State has relentlessly targeted the church in demolishing its worship places, confiscating other property in the guise of development projects. Churches do not accept the explanation that their centres are demolished because of the imperative of the government to develop the country. It is frequently seen that Muslim praying centres are spared while those belonging to Christians are demolished.

There are other important issues which came out of the series of interviews during this study. One significant fact that emerged is that there is a strong potential for inter-communal violence when a religious property is under the threat of destruction or confiscation. Important parish centres had been destroyed according to Persila:

> The famous case of the church, which is now part of the [Republican] Palace, if you go next to the Mosque you will find another church property which is now a museum. It was a church, we went to pray there... now we can no longer pray there; and the government took it over and took off the tower and got the cross off. It is now like any other building.[41]

The IDPs have problems because the churches in the IDP camps were destroyed; after a long time they were allow to build one church on the condition that it cannot have a marked cross and cannot have a tower. There are other things which are prohibited and against the law for churches to do, including the use of microphones. A number of important churches in the informal residential districts were demolished for municipal planning. Such behaviour has given the government a negative profile within the IDP communities.

In addition to the government's official dealings with the Church, which many non-Muslims and some straight-forward Muslims point to as excessively repressive, some of the interviewees point out overt religious discrimination in the government practices in respect of land allocation. There is no law against building churches, but the long procedures can

41 Interview, Omdurman, May 2007.

be an obstacle that the government is using to delay the issuing of new licences for the construction of Christian worship places. Christians deal with the situation in innovative ways: a license is acquired for an alternative purpose and then converted to a church. This is not an issue for the construction of a new mosque; a licence is not required for the construction of a mosque and no mosque suffers the fate of demolition or expropriation such as that experienced for church properties. Solomon Oliha from Mandela cites another example of government action against Christians which was capable of raising social tension and souring the relationship between Christians and Muslims:

> By the military college, there was an area called *kharābāt* [ruins] near the soldiers' residential area. It is an hour's drive from Khartoum. The *kharābāt* was inhabited by the displaced in 1995. They decided to build a church. The construction reached a good point, then it was destroyed by orders of the State. People living in those marginal areas receive the status of animals, not human beings, in the way the government treats and relates with them. The church was destroyed before the *ʿīd* prayers. That was according to the instructions from the commander [who is a Muslim functionary of the State].[42]

Religious Activities

IDPs express lack of freedom for open air preaching by non-Muslims in Khartoum State and other northern states. The Christians demand freedom for open air preaching. Despite the availability of many potential opportunities for positive interfaith encounters, certain incidents continue to spark crises and occasional inter-communal violence. This happens between Christians and Muslims by proxy in different situations. This story was told by Stephen Wani:

> Once in Khartoum North, two or three years ago some colleagues of mine tried to preach the Bible in an open space. Suddenly a number of people appeared carrying swords; they looked like *anṣār* [Muslim Fanatics]. Most programmes of the Christians in Khartoum do not take place in open air or in market place like what happens in the South. There we conduct programmes in gathering places like *sūq al-ʿarabī* [in Khartoum]. Here organization [of activities] must take place in Halls or Stadiums. Official security arrangements are necessary. The problems are the fundamentalists and they are there even among us, we the Christians. They are people with dogmatic mentality henceforth we have to restrain a little our activity so we can con-

42 Interview, Mandela, March 2007.

> tinue ahead on the line and to avoid clashes. We did not try again since that incident in Khartoum.[43]

Ministry of Guidance and Endowment

Many Christians demand that in the ministry of Guidance and Endowment, the Department of Christian Affairs must be headed by a Christian. The Ministry must support churches in the same way as it supports the mosques. The Ministry of Guidance and Endowment should be called the Ministry of Religious Affairs, as it used to be, and have a state minister who is a Christian.

Judiciary

The judiciary should maintain its independence according to the CPA and the interim national constitution. And it recommended the speeding up of the formation of Special Courts for non-Muslims in Khartoum State according to article 158 of the Interim National Constitution 2005: "A system shall be established to guarantee the implementation of Article 156 of Dispensing Justice in the national Capital". There is also a demand for freedom of conversion from Islam to Christianity and vice-versa with equal treatment of converts (Christians/Muslims).

Media: Radio, News Papers & T.V.

Christian programmes and activities are not allowed on the National Radio and National T.V. and on Khartoum State Radio and T.V. Christians are not allowed to issue a Christian newspaper.

Conclusion

This chapter demonstrates that religious faith constitutes no barrier to mutual interaction and that in real life neither Islam nor Christianity necessarily results in ideological cleavages among the IDP camps of Mandela and Wad al-Bashīr. The displaced people feel no differences among themselves along religious lines in their daily life. To the people of the camps the Christian-Muslim divide is an issue largely external to them and confined

---

[43] Interview, Khartoum, March 2007.

to the national level and perhaps to other communities away from the camps. The majority of respondents, regardless of their faith, hold a perception that religion is manipulated as an instrument of political interest.

However these religions are treated very differently in formal and state circles and in structures such as political organization (SPLM, NCP), education curriculum and school structures, in the public Media (Radio, TV and state newspapers), in the distribution of job opportunities and access to land and in the implementation of public order law, to list but a few. Frequently, political actors instrumentalize religion for their own interests.

The chapter showed that many Christians view the Public Order Laws as critical factors in Christian/Muslim relations in the camps. Both Christians and Muslims agree on the occurrence of conflicts between Christians and State institutions. The reality is that the Christian organizations and the State are frequently at odds over development policy, confiscation of church properties and demolition of church buildings by the authorities under the guise of town planning. It is also noted that there is a potential for inter-communal violence when a religious property is under the threat of destruction and/or confiscation. This was the situation when the authorities of Khartoum State confiscated church premises and when many important parish centres were destroyed inside and outside the IDP camps.

The chapter reveals that political attitude and behaviour run contrary to the popular trends in inter-faith practice in the camp communities. The analysis of the perceptions of Christian-Muslim relations at this level shows that they should be valued, promoted and introduced into the state institutions by political actors, namely the governments and political parties.

PART TWO

NIGERIA: “RE-IMPLEMENTATION OF *SHARĪ‘A*”

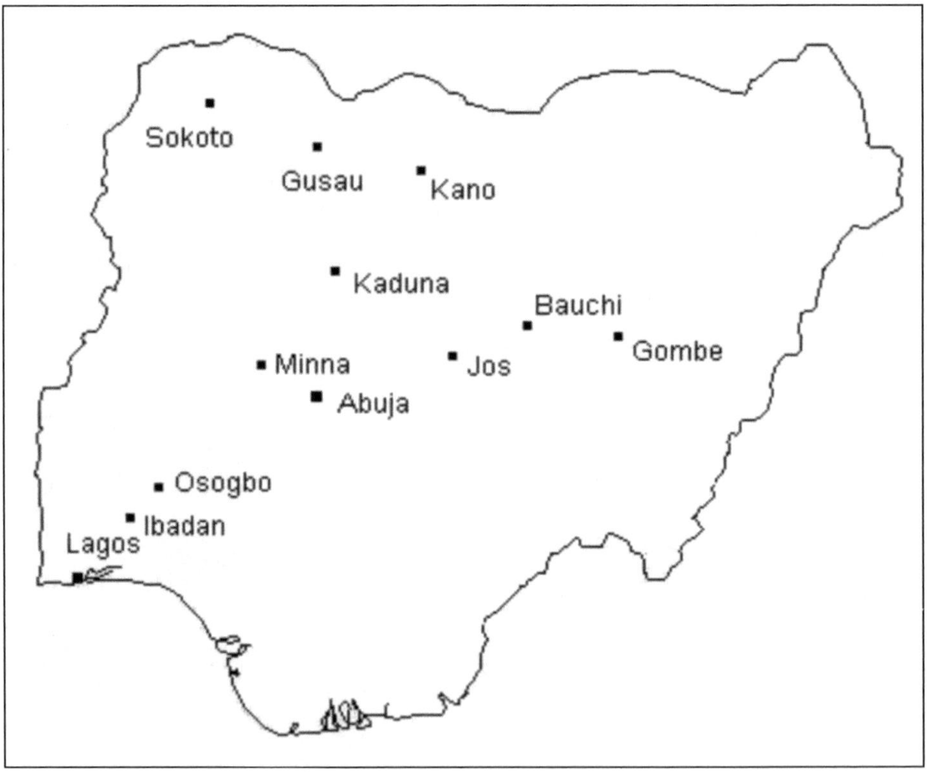

Map 3 Map of Nigeria: Showing principal places referred to in Part Two

CHAPTER FOUR

THE EVOLUTION OF THE INDEPENDENT *SHARĪʿA* PANEL IN OSUN STATE, SOUTH-WEST NIGERIA

Abdul-Fatah Kola Makinde

Introduction

Osun State is located in the tropical rain forest in the South-West of Nigeria and covers an estimated area of 8,602 square kilometres.[1] It was created on 27th August, 1991, along with eight others, by the regime of President Ibrahim Babangida. It was carved out of the former Oyo State and is bounded to the east partly by Ondo State and partly by Ekiti State, to the west by Oyo State, to the north by Kwara State and to the south by Ogun State.

It is largely inhabited by the Osun, Ijesa, Ife and Igbomina communities, who are Yoruba speaking and who form part of the larger Yoruba nation concentrated in the south-western part of Nigeria and who are also found in the diaspora.[2]

The State is densely populated and highly urbanized. According to the 1991 national population census, Osun State has a population of 2.2 million inhabitants.[3] However, based on the provisional results of the 2006 census, Osun State now has a population of 3.4 million.[4] Due to the demographic problems of Nigeria, it is difficult to give the actual percentage of Muslims in this State. It could, however, be said that Muslims are assumed to constitute more than 50 per cent of the population. The State, when it was created, had twenty-two Local Government Areas (LGAs). However,

---

[1] Adenaike, F. A. (ed.), *The Pioneers*, Ibadan: Syndicated Limited, 1991, page 6.

[2] Adenaike, 1991, page 6.

[3] Udo, R. K. and Mommon, A. B. (eds.), *Nigeria: Giant in the tropics*, Lagos: Gabumo Publishing Comp. Ltd., 1993, page 380.

[4] *The Guardian*, Wednesday 10th January 2007, front page; *Nigerian Tribune*, Wednesday 10th January 2007, pages 1 and 4 and the *Nation*, Wednesday 10th January 2007, front page.

Map 4 Map of Nigeria showing the states

with the creation of additional Local Government Areas in 1991[5] and 1997,[6] the State now has thirty Local Government Areas.

Like any other area in Yorubaland, the date when Islam was introduced to Osun State is very difficult to ascertain. As Gbadamosi observes, "it was unannounced and unplanned; and, for the most part, the first Yoruba Muslims had to worship privately and secretly".[7] According to him, what is fairly certain is that in the 17th century, mention was made of Muslims in Yorubaland. While Johnson suggests the date of the arrival of Islam in Yorubaland as 18th century,[8] Doi observes that Al-Ilori suggests an earlier date. Al-Ilori opines that it was during the period of Mansa Musa (d. 1337)

[5] Osun State Government, *Osun State so far*, Osogbo: Ministry of Information, 1992, page 14.

[6] Ministry of Information, *Information month 2000—democracy day*, Osogbo: Osun State Government Press, 2000, page 30.

[7] Gbadamosi, T. G. O., *The growth of Islam among the Yoruba, 1841–1908*, London: Longman Group Limited, 1978, page 4.

[8] Johnson, S., *The history of the Yorubas*, Lagos: CSS Bookshops, 1976, pages 38–39.

that Islam spread to most parts of Nigeria, including Yorubaland.[9] Thus, by the 18th century, Islam had spread to places like: Osogbo, Ede, Ikirun, Iwo, Ikire, Ejigbo, Ila, Inisa, Orile-Owu and many other places in the area now called Osun State.[10] Islam received a further boost in the 19th century following the *jihad* of Usman dan Fodio, which spread to Yorubaland, Oyo and Ilorin in particular.

Some parts of the South-West of Nigeria applied *sharīʿa* as a legal system before the arrival of the British colonialists in 1861 when Lagos was annexed as a British colony. There were some principal Yoruba towns where *sharīʿa* was established and applied in the domains of their *obas* (Yoruba: monarchs) during the pre-colonial era. Such towns included Ede, Ikirun and Iwo in the area now called Osun State.[11] Sanni supports this view when he writes:

> But once we had Muslim rulers in parts of the Yoruba Country from the mid-nineteenth century, for example Abibu Lagunju (1847–1900) at Ede, Lamuye (1847–1906) at Iwo, the scope and prominence of the *sharīʿa* became enhanced so much that aspects of its penal code, the public execution of robbers, was administered.[12]

The *sharīʿa* legal system had a set-back with the introduction of the colonial court system. This was because, as the indigenous legal system based on tradition still held sway, the emergence of the British legal system neither removed the native system nor promoted the establishment of a state-sponsored Islamic legal structure. The Native Council Ordinance of 1901 gave legal support to native courts which were required to administer justice according to native law and customs. The Customary law, of course, includes Muslim law as modified by the custom of each locality. Therefore, before this Ordinance came into force, the colonialists' delimitation had already eroded whatever sphere of operation was available to *sharīʿa* and its operators.[13]

However, the Muslims found something missing in the colonial courts, as they did not find justice in matters concerning their religious precepts on issues affecting their socio-personal status such as marriage, divorce

---

9 Doi A. R. I., *Islam in Nigeria*, Zaria: Gaskiya Corporation Ltd, 1984, pages 109–110.

10 Gbadamosi, 1978, page 4.

11 Noibi, D. O. S., *Islamic perspective*, Ijebu-ode: Shebiotimo Publishers, 1998, page 52.

12 Sanni, A., 'The *sharīʿa* Conundrum in Nigeria and the Zamfara Model: The Role of Nigerian Muslim Youth in the Historical Context', *Journal of Muslim Minority Affairs*, Vol. 27, No. 1, 2007, page 119.

13 Sanni, 2007, page 119.

and inheritance. Hence, in 1894 and 1923, they petitioned the colonial authority to institute for them a court whose adjudication on matters concerning their personal status would be based on *sharīʿa*.[14] Their request did not extend to penal law because the British had enacted a Penal Code which restricted the jurisdiction of the *sharīʿa* to personal status in Northern Nigeria where *sharīʿa* was in operation. In 1948, the Muslim Congress of Nigeria, with its headquarters at Ijebu-Ode, wrote to the Secretary of the colonial administration, complaining about the application of laws repugnant to the faith of Southern Nigerian Muslims. Of particular concern to the Muslims was that the judge followed whatever procedure he wished in the administration of inheritance, without regard to clear Islamic provisions in this matter.[15] This complaint, however, did not receive the required attention from the colonial administrators.

In view of the above, the Muslims in the South-West of Nigeria continued to make requests to successive governments to establish *sharīʿa* courts for the adjudication of their personal matters. The launching of *sharīʿa* by Zamfara State in 1999 opened a new door for their request. According to Sanni, the pressure was not limited to the north, as the Zamfara example had provided a strong impetus for its implementation in the south, specifically in Yorubaland.[16] The failure of the government to yield to their request made them think of an alternative way of fulfilling their religious duties; hence, the establishment of Independent *sharīʿa* Panels in some states in the South-West. Osun State was not left out of this arrangement. This chapter focuses on this state with a view to examining the evolution of an Independent *sharīʿa* Panel in the state, its activities so far and its roles in the administration of justice to Muslims in the state.

History of *Sharīʿa* Practice in Osun State

Although Osun State was created in 1991, as noted earlier, the history of the practice of *sharīʿa* in the state dates back to the arrival of Islam in the area. This is because the introduction of Islam in any part of the world always opens a door for the introduction of *sharīʿa*. According to

---

[14] Adetona, L. A., 'The dynamics of Independent Shariah Panel in Lagos State, South-West of Nigeria', *Journal of the Nigeria Association of Teachers of Arabic and Islamic Studies*, vol. 8, 2005, page 30.

[15] Sanni, 2007, page 119.

[16] Sanni, 2007, page 126.

Gbadamosi,[17] a discussion of the practice of *sharīʿa* in any part of the Muslim world must begin with the introduction of Islam into the area as a faith and as a way of life. Ambali[18] also asserts that "wherever there are Muslims, it is implicitly understood that *sharīʿa* is already introduced". It should however be noted here that the level of its application varies from one place to another; this is because the scope of *sharīʿa* encompasses all spheres of life of a Muslim. The legal aspect of *sharīʿa* is what brings about debates and controversies in most parts of the world. Therefore, *sharīʿa* in this context implies applying it in other aspects of life while the legal aspect is excluded in most cases.

In any discussion of the application of *sharīʿa* in Yorubaland, Osun State cannot be left out. This is because the State has principal Yoruba towns where *sharīʿa* was firmly established and applied. While *sharīʿa* could be said to have been applied in some towns of other Yoruba states in some aspects of Islamic Law, there is evidence that *sharīʿa* Law was applied fully in the domains of some *obas* (monarchs) in some towns in the area now called Osun State during the pre-colonial period. Such towns are: Iwo, Ede and Ikirun. Malik confirms this by mentioning Ede and Iwo, but leaving out Ikirun.[19] However, others such as Okunola[20] and Makinde[21] confirmed Ikirun as well.

It is asserted that *sharīʿa* was applied in Iwo during the reign of *Oba* Memodu (Muhammad) Lamuye who was enthroned in 1860. The *sharīʿa* was applied in his domain and the town was administered in line with *sharīʿa* until he died in 1906.[22] The Qadi appointed by Lamuye was Muhammad-Awwal Akintayo Omojiiro.[23] *Oba* Abibu Olagunju of Ede is also claimed to have applied *sharīʿa* in his domain during the second half of the 19th century. He was reported to have established the *sharīʿa* court in an area called Agbeni. It was moved to another area called Agbongbe

---

17 Gbadamosi, 2000, page 2.

18 Ambali, M. A., *The practice of Muslim family law in Nigeria*, Zaria: Tamaza Publishing Company Ltd., 1998.

19 Malik, S. H. A., 'The Shari'ah in the life of a Muslim', in *Islamic tenets and the Shari'ah*, I. A. B. Balogun (ed.), Ibadan: Sam Bookman Publishers, 2000, page 160.

20 Okunola, M. A., 'The relevance of Shari'ah to Nigeria', in *Islam in Africa*, N. Alkali, A. Adamu, A. Yadudu, R. Motem & H. Salihi (eds.), Ibadan: Spectrum Books Ltd., 1993, pages 23–35.

21 Makinde, A. K., 'The Institution of Sharīʿah in Oyo and Osun States, Nigeria, 1890–2005', Ph.D thesis, University of Ibadan, Ibadan, 2007, pages 75–78.

22 Okunola, 1993, page 25.

23 Okunola, 1993, page 25.

in 1914. The first Qadi was Alfa Sindiku (Siddiq).[24] In Ikirun, *Oba* Oyewole was reported to have applied *sharīʿa* in his domain. He established a *sharīʿa* court, which was presided over by one Alfa Bako from Ilorin as the Qadi.

Although the presence of the British colonialists in Yorubaland led to the non-recognition of the *sharīʿa* court system in this part of the country, the Muslims there did not relinquish their religion nor the *sharīʿa*.[25] This was true of the Muslims in the towns in Osun State. They continued to practice *sharīʿa* in their various mosques, particularly in matters relating to marriage, child naming and funeral ceremonies. Some of them even applied the *sharīʿa* in matters of divorce and inheritance. They however continued to demand the establishment of *sharīʿa* courts from the Government in the State.

Agitation and Demands for the Establishment of *Sharīʿa* Courts

The official launching of *sharīʿa* in Zamfara State on 27th October, 1999 sparked off agitation and a series of demands for the introduction of *sharīʿa* in other parts of Nigeria, including Yorubaland. As earlier noted, the wave of agitation was not limited to the north, as the movement for its implementation in the south, specifically in Yorubaland, had been given a strong impetus by the Zamfara example.[26] Like their counterparts in the South-West, some Muslims in Osun State championed the demand for the establishment of *sharīʿa* Courts by the government. The demand of the agitators was not to have full-blown *sharīʿa*, as was the case with the Northern States, it was to have *sharīʿa* Courts to adjudicate on matters relating to Muslim marriage, inheritance, divorce and other civil matters. Various attempts were made by the agitators to express their desire to be officially allowed to use *sharīʿa* for the adjudication of such issues. The efforts of the League of Imams and Alfas (Muslim scholars) of Osun State, directed towards joining their colleagues in other parts of Yorubaland to publicly demand the establishment of *sharīʿa* in their states, could be described as one of the attempts made by the Muslims of the state.

Such a demand was contained in the memorandum submitted to Osun State House of Assembly in December, 1999 by the League of Imams and

24 Okunola, 1993, page 25.
25 Okunola, 1992, page 25.
26 Sanni, 2007, page 126.

Alfas in the State, and signed by their Chairman, Alhaji Shaykh Mustafa Ajisafe, the Chief Imam of Osogboland, on the review of the 1999 Constitution wherein the need for the establishment of *sharīʿa* courts was clearly stated. Reference was made to the application of *sharīʿa* during the precolonial era in Yorubaland, particularly in Ede, Iwo and Ikirun, which are part and parcel of Osun State, before it was abolished by the British Colonialists. The request was put thus:

> ... the *sharīʿa* is a Constitutional right of all Nigerian Muslims, Osun State Muslims should not therefore be exceptional. It is as a result of this we want to call on the honourable members of Osun State House of Assembly to critically consider this with a view to establishing *sharīʿa* courts in Osun State since section 275 of the 1999 Constitution allows this.[27]

Different Islamic organizations or groups in the State organized a series of lectures, symposia and rallies to publicly demand the establishment of *sharīʿa* courts in the State. For example, the Osun State Area Unit of the Muslim Students' Society of Nigeria (MSSN) on Wednesday 27th October, 1999 held a rally at Ansar-ud-deen School, Sabo, Osogbo to demand *sharīʿa* in Osun State. After the address of the Area Unit Amir, Qamaruddin Bello, members conducted a peaceful protest round the town to call for the introduction of *sharīʿa* in the State. In reporting the incident, *The Punch* reported inter alia:

> ... in Osun State, over 500 Muslim adherents trooped to the streets of Osogbo, the State capital, canvassing the introduction of *sharīʿa* Law in the State.[28]

The Punch reported further:

> ... the placard carrying protesters marched through Ayetoro, Oke-fia, Oja-Oba, Old Garage and Gbongan Road, chanting Islamic songs of solidarity.[29]

Moreover, *The Punch* observed the inscriptions on the placards and reported thus:

---

27 Okunola, 1993, page 25.

28 Excerpt from the memorandum submitted to Osun State House of Assembly on review of the 1999 Constitution by the League of Imams and Alfas of Osun State on behalf of the Muslim Community of Osun State in December, 1999.

29 *The Punch*, Thursday 28th October, 1999, page 6. *The Punch* is a national widely read daily newspaper in Nigeria. It is published in Lagos, Nigeria. It is also on the website: www.punchng.com.

> ... some placards the protesters carried had such inscriptions as 'Give us *sharīʿa*', '*sharīʿa*' a blessing to all Muslims and non-Muslims.[30]

Some other dailies that reported the incident also made their reports accordingly. In the report of the Nigerian Tribune, it stated that 'Muslim Youths numbering about 2,000 marched through the streets of Osogbo, the state capital calling for the introduction of *sharīʿa* Law in the State.' It referred to MSSN as the Muslim Youths when it reported thus:

> ... the Youths who came out under the aegis of the Muslim Students Society of Nigeria (MSSN) argued that the introduction of *sharīʿa* in all States of the country would check the vices ravaging the country.[31]

Moreover, the National Council of Muslim Youth Organizations (NACOMYO), Osun State Chapter, organized a state symposium on *sharīʿa* titled: "Constitutionality of *sharīʿa*: Problems and Prospects in Application". It was held on 30th January 2000 at the Presidential Hotel Hall, Osogbo. It was well-attended by some eminent Islamic scholars, legal luminaries and important Muslim personalities from within and outside the State.[32] Immediately after the programme, some of the notable Muslim participants held a meeting at NACOMYO Secretariat to review and appraise the programme and some decisions were arrived at.[33] These included, firstly, that the awareness raised in the State through the programme should be followed up with some other enlightenment programmes on *sharīʿa*. Secondly, that a meeting of Islamic scholars and Muslim personalities who are indigenes of the State be called to review the programme with a view to actualizing the introduction of *sharīʿa* in the State, and thirdly, that a committee needed to be set up on *sharīʿa* actualization in the State.[34]

It could be said therefore that the meeting at NACOMYO Secretariat precipitated the formation of a committee on *sharīʿa* in Osun State. Since it was unanimously agreed that day that some Islamic scholars and Muslim personalities, as well as leaders of some Islamic organizations, be invited to a meeting on the issue of *sharīʿa* in the State, a follow-up was made to

---

30 *The Punch*, 28th October, 1999.

31 *The Punch*, 28th October, 1999.

32 *Nigerian Tribune*, Thursday 28th October, 2000, page 2. This is also a daily newspaper in Nigeria. It is published in Ibadan, Nigeria. Website: www.tribune.com.ng.

33 *The Guardian*, 22nd January 2000, page 4; *Saturday Tribune*, 22nd January, 2000, page 9. *The Guardian* is a widely read daily national newspaper published in Lagos, Nigeria. Website: www.ngrguardiannews.com.

34 Interview with Alh. Mustafa Olawuyi, former state co-ordinator of NACOMYO and member of executive of Osun State Muslim Community, on 25th December, 2006.

that effect. Thenceforth, Osun State Committee on *sharīʿa* was established and has since been working assiduously to educate and mobilise Muslims of the State for an official demand for the establishment of *sharīʿa* courts in the State.[35]

Additionally, a series of lectures, symposia and rallies were held either privately or publicly demanding the establishment of *sharīʿa* courts in the State. The symposium organized by the National Council of Muslim Youth Organizations, (NACOMYO), Osun State Chapter, on *sharīʿa*, earlier mentioned, seemed more educational and challenging. Hence, many Muslim individuals became more aware of the need to demand the establishment of *sharīʿa* courts on civil matters for Muslims in the State.

However, the Muslims felt dissatisfied about the lukewarm attitude of successive governments to their request to establish *sharīʿa* Courts and *sharīʿa* Courts of Appeal in Osun State. They argued that they deserved to be given the opportunity for several reasons. Firstly, because Nigeria is a multi-religious nation where every citizen is free to practise his or her religion. Secondly, because the Nigerian Constitution gives room for legal pluralism by allowing English/Common, *sharīʿa* and Customary Laws; and because the other two laws which are allowed to operate in the state do not in any way make provision for Islamic civil matters. They argued further that the English/Common law is of Christian origin,[36] taking care of the interests of the Christians, while the Customary law takes care of traditional interests, but the *sharīʿa*, which takes care of the Muslims' interests, is not established; hence, there is injustice.[37]

It is as a result of the above that the Muslim Community of the state submitted a proposal for an amendment of the Law to incorporate the application of *sharīʿa* or Islamic Law in the proposed District Customary Court and Customary Court Law of Osun State during the consideration of the District Customary and Customary Court Law Bill 2005 by the State House of Assembly. This was acknowledged by the Honourable Speaker but Muslims claim that the proposal was never properly considered despite all the efforts made by the Muslim Community.[38]

---

[35] Alh. Mustafa Olawuyi, 25th December, 2006.

[36] Malik, 2000, page 161 where he states: "Common Law originated from Christianity because it came in existence alongside the cathedrals, abbeys and parish churches which were built in the 11th and 12th centuries and that it was formulated by judges who were often prelates of the Church".

[37] Interview with Alh. Musa Raji, secretary of the Independent *sharīʿa* Panel, on 25th November, 2006.

[38] Alh. Musa Raji, 25th November, 2006.

Opposition to *Sharīʿa*

The Zamfara State *sharīʿa* initiative, which generated serious debates in the country, did not omit Osun State. As some Muslims in the state were agitating and demanding from the government the establishment of *sharīʿa* Courts in the state, some Muslims and non-Muslims, particularly the Christians, were not favourably disposed to it.[39] Although, they agreed that *sharīʿa* is meant for Muslims, their contention was that it should not in any way be enforced on people of other faiths.[40] It was stressed that since *sharīʿa* is the way of life of Muslims, the law should not be binding on non-Muslims.[41] It was even likened to Canon Law that is basically not even for all Christians but for the Catholics.[42] Therefore, the Muslims are free to practise their faith in as much as it does not affect the religious rights of others. In the words of one of these Christian leaders:

> *sharīʿa* is a way of practising their (Muslims) faith and they are free to do so as long as it does not encroach on other religionists' right.[43]

Although the Christian leaders agreed that *sharīʿa* is meant for Muslims, they opposed the idea of the government establishing *sharīʿa* Courts. Their claim is that Nigeria is a multi-religious nation and, as a result, the government should not use the resources of all citizens to support the belief of a particular religion.[44] It is their opinion that if the government gives legal backing to *sharīʿa* Courts, then the Christians will rise up to institute their own court and the government must also give it legal backing. According to them, the only thing the government can do is to provide an atmosphere that is conducive to the free practice of religion, not saying or proclaiming by its authority that this is established by the government.[45] It is also their claim that they have something similar to a legal court in Christianity where diverse cases are taken to be resolved amicably with-

---

[39] Interviews with some Christian leaders: Rev. E. O. Adeloye of the Baptist Church and immediate past State Chairman of Christian Association of Nigeria (CAN), Osun State Chapter, on 28th February, 2007; Pastor A. O. Akinosun of the Christ Apostolic Church and current State Chairman of CAN on 9th March, 2007 and Bishop G. Leke Abegunrin of the Catholic Diocese, and one time State Chairman of CAN, on 23rd April, 2007.

[40] Interviews with Adeloye, 28th February, 2007; Akinosun, 9th March, 2007; and Abegunrin, 23rd April, 2007.

[41] Interview with Rev. E. O. Adeloye, 28th February, 2007.

[42] Interview with Bishop Leke Abegunrin, 23rd April, 2007.

[43] Interview with Rev. E. O. Adeloye, 28th February, 2007.

[44] Interviews with some Christian leaders.

[45] Interview with Rev. Adeloye, 28th February, 2007.

out the involvement of the government. This is called either a committee or a tribunal, depending on the church. Therefore the government should not be involved in the establishment of *sharīʿa* Courts.[46]

The concern of the Christians about *sharīʿa*, according to the Christian leaders interviewed, is that *sharīʿa* has generated a lot of controversy and debate resulting in crises leading to the killing of many Christians, particularly in Northern Nigeria. To them, *sharīʿa* seems to allow killing and if that is what *sharīʿa* is about, it is not a law that should be accepted by Christians.[47] One of them even sees *sharīʿa* as a violation of human rights because, according to him, in any country where it is practised, nobody is free to choose his or her religion. He opined further that Nigeria is a democratic country; therefore, no religion should impose its own faith on others and the government should not interfere with the practice of any religion; and if *sharīʿa* is established, it will violate human rights because people of other faiths may be forced to abide by the *sharīʿa* law and this goes contrary to the human rights laws of the United Nations. Instances of cases where non-Muslims in some *sharīʿa* states in the north were punished or fined for being found with alcohol were cited to support his point.[48]

It is also the contention of a Christian leader that *sharīʿa* is a controversial issue which is not needed in the south because Muslims in the south can be good Muslims without *sharīʿa*.[49] It is the opinion of another Christian leader that some laws of *sharīʿa* are no longer needed in this era of civilization because they are obsolete and not relevant to our age. He expressed this as follows:

> ... the Law of Moses which you call Torah in Islam is more or less the same thing. But with age, with civilization, with education, most of these things are changing because what was then is no longer operating now, hence, we should not be judging ourselves here now with what was operating as at that time.... I studied Islam and the *sharīʿa* especially when I read a portion of the *Qurʾān* that talks about *sharīʿa*. The thing is, if most of these things are open to scholarly debate, we see that some of them are obsolete and are no longer in existence now.[50]

46 Interview with Pastor Akinosun, 9th March, 2007.
47 Interviews with some Christian leaders.
48 Interview with Pastor Akinosun, 9th March, 2007.
49 Interview with Pastor Akinosun, 9th March, 2007.
50 Interview with Rev. Adeloye, 28th February, 2007.

The views expressed above seem to have been made from the antagonists' points of view. The protagonists of *sharīʿa* never see it that way. They do not see *sharīʿa* as having a system of law that is obsolete and no longer relevant in the contemporary period. Rather, they see it as law that is relevant at all times, particularly in the area of personal status that has to do with marriage, divorce, inheritance etc. which the Muslims engage in on a daily basis.

It should be mentioned at this juncture that opposition to *sharīʿa* was not limited to the Christians. As Sanni notes, there was no lack of audible and, at times, loud voices of rejection from some Muslims. For example, the Muslim Committee for a Progressive Nigeria (MCPN) based in Lagos, a leftist group, supported the anti-*sharīʿa* campaign and described the legal system as "the most backward Muslim religious, legal, and customary instruments in the hands of the minority feudal emirs for keeping the majority of the poor and oppressed peasants and workers down".[51]

There are also some Muslim individuals who are not in support of *sharīʿa*. The vice-Amir of the United Muslim Council in Lagos State, Alhaji Mufutau Adebayo, was reported to have warned that the implementation of *sharīʿa* legal system by some states may divide the country. He warned that care must be taken before *sharīʿa* can be implemented in the country, saying that "we cannot wake up one day and say everybody must go *sharīʿa*".[52] In a related development, the *Khalifah* of Ogun State UMC, Sheikh Salisu Adenekan, was reported to have said that the implementation of *sharīʿa* in some parts of the country was aimed at destabilizing the country.[53]

Moreover, the attitude and public comments of some Muslim personalities show lack of support for *sharīʿa*. For instance, a prominent Yoruba Muslim preacher, who lives in the north, Shaykh Muhydeen Bello, produced a record entitled '*sharīʿa*' in 2001 in which he condemned the involvement of politicians in the *sharīʿa*, saying that its introduction in the north is 'a political *sharīʿa*'.[54] Moreover, Akintola asserts that some Muslim title-holders are yet to identify with *sharīʿa*. In his words:

---

51 Sanni, 2007, page 121.
52 *The Punch*, Friday 21st April 2000, page 32.
53 *The Punch*, April 2000.
54 Makinde, 2007, page 179.

> Many Muslim title holders in the south are yet to fully identify themselves with the protagonists of *sharīʿa*. Some wealthy ones among them show little or no concern.[55]

While commenting on why the issue of *sharīʿa* generated controversy, the Speaker of Osun State House of Assembly, Hon. Adejare Bello, who, incidentally, is a Muslim, observed that it is simply because the practice differs from the orthodox law i.e. the one that was introduced by the Western world to us in Africa and that the moment people see the difference they tend not to believe, or they tend to disagree with it. He, however, claims that the most important reason is that the *sharīʿa* principles are very strict and stringent; he describes the punishment for adultery as dehumanizing. Here are his words:

> More so, you will agree with me that *sharīʿa* principles are very strict and stringent. Like take for instance, fornication. If a woman fornicates, the whole body would be buried and only the head would remain outside and to be stoned to death. You know that punishment is very strict. Just fornication, not robbery, not assassination, nothing whatsoever. So for such a dehumanized (*sic*) way of treating fornication, honestly, leaves much to be desired.[56]

The Speaker comments further on the stringent nature of *sharīʿa* as a factor that makes people run away from it, as follows:

> Honestly, this is the reason why people are running away from *sharīʿa* practice, because it is always very stringent. If you say somebody steals even fowl and his hand has to be caught off, you have reduced that person to somebody that cannot make [a] livelihood for him or herself. It is difficult because if the person is a farmer and one hand is removed, he cannot farm the way he [is] supposed to and that would encourage joblessness and at the end of the day begging. That is why it is very common in the north where *sharīʿa* is being practised. So those are the things.[57]

The views expressed above by the Speaker show the level of his understanding of the *sharīʿa* criminal law. Moreover, the idea that *sharīʿa* is strict and stringent seems to be another way of condemning *sharīʿa* from the angle of its penal law. However, to the protagonists, the criminal aspect of any law cannot be totally absolved of strictness and stringency because

---

55 Akintola, I. L., *Shariah in Nigeria: an Eschatological Desideratum*, Ijebu-Ode: Shebiotimo Publication, page 15.

56 Interview with Hon. R. A. Bello, the Speaker of Osun State House of Assembly on 5th March, 2007.

57 Interview with Bello, 5th March, 2007.

criminal laws are designed to inflict punishments on those found guilty of crimes so as to serve as a deterrent to others. Similarly, there are a lot of misconceptions and misinformation about *sharīʿa* which are held even by Muslims, based on their level of understanding of the subject matter of the *sharīʿa* penal law.

It is, however, apposite to remark at this juncture that just as *sharīʿa* received opposition from the Christians and some Muslims, there was no shortage of support from some Christians. Sanni observes that one Revd. Oloto from Ibadan could not see any reason for opposition. If the Islamic system would solve the socio-economic malaise of the country, he argued, why can't we go for it? After all, it had never affected the Christians adversely nor was there any prospect of it affecting them when fully introduced all over the country. He argued that objection smacks of antinomian trends which have found proponents among the promoters of moral and social inequities which the Zamfara model has set out to correct.[58] A vicar in Osun State also agreed that *sharīʿa* is capable of solving certain corrupt practices in society. He argued that if all religions preached integrity there would be no place for corruption and social vices in society. He opined further as follows:

> I believe wholeheartedly that *sharīʿa* has a lot of things to do to reduce if not to eradicate, and I will preach that to every religious sect, that they should preach the tenets of their religion so that corruption could be eradicated.[59]

Government Response to the *Sharīʿa* Demand

As mentioned earlier, some Muslims in Osun State made a series of attempts to demand from the government the establishment of *sharīʿa* Courts and a *sharīʿa* Court of Appeal in the state in order to officially allow them the opportunity of adjudicating on issues relating to civil matters. These attempts were made through memoranda submitted to the House of Assembly and personal contacts with government functionaries. However, the controversial nature of *sharīʿa* made the Osun State government wary in considering the request of the Muslims to have *sharīʿa* Courts established in the state. The Honourable Speaker of Osun State House of Assembly acknowledged receipt of the proposal of the Muslims

58 Sanni, 2007, page 124.
59 Interview with Rev. E. O. Adeloye, 28th February, 2007.

to the House requesting that a Bill be passed into law establishing *sharīʿa* Courts in the state.[60] He explained that the Bill could not be passed into law because the Governor was not interested in introducing anything that would cause a problem in the state. To the government, the issue of *sharīʿa* is a sensitive one and has generated a lot of controversy and misunderstanding across the country, and any attempt to consider the request of the Muslims in the state might spark religious misunderstanding or crisis in the state. The Governor was reported as saying that as long as God destined him to rule the state, he would not want something that would bring controversy between the Muslims and Christians.[61]

The question of social proportion was also brought in as a factor militating against the approval by the government of the request of the Muslims. The lack of information on the demography or population in Nigeria, meaning that it could not be categorically stated whether the most populous group of the state is the Christians or the Muslims, is a contributory factor. According to the Speaker, there is an argument as to whether the state has more Muslims than Christians or vice versa, and in a situation where you have it as 40/60 or 45/55 or 50/50 and you cannot determine which group is more populous, it will be difficult to practise *sharīʿa* there in full (including in criminal matters), unlike in some parts of the North, where more than 90% of the population are Muslims.[62]

Another factor which is militating against the passage of the Bill on the establishment of *sharīʿa* Courts and a *sharīʿa* Court of Appeal in the state, according to the Honourable Speaker, is the minority of Muslims in the House of Assembly. Out of the 26 members of the House, there were 10 Muslims.[63] He confirmed receipt of the memoranda sent to the House by the Muslims, but asserted that even if the Bill was considered by the House, it will get killed because the Muslims were just 10 out of 26 members of the House. Therefore, any attempt to introduce *sharīʿa* in the state will create a problem. What people want is peace and that has been the position of the government as well; hence it is wary about the proposal. As to the claim of some Muslims in the state that *sharīʿa* Courts were not established because the Governor is a Christian, the Speaker debunked the claim saying that the Governor had never discriminated against the Muslims. He argued further, that the Muslims of the

60 Interview with Bello, 5th March, 2007.
61 Interview with Bello, 5th March, 2007.
62 Interview with Bello, 5th March, 2007.
63 Interview with Bello, 5th March, 2007.

state never had it so good, even under Muslim governors, as they had it with him, in view of some requests they had put before him and he had granted. Examples of such requests are the employment of teachers of Islamic Studies in some primary schools in the state, and the donation of N10 million (Nigerian money) to build the secretariat of the Muslim Community.[64]

Inauguration of the Independent *Sharīʿa* Panel (ISP) in Osun State

The inability of Osun State Muslim Community to achieve success in its request to the state government to establish *sharīʿa* Courts and a *sharīʿa* Court of Appeal caused it to conceive the idea of establishing an Independent *sharīʿa* Panel, as had been done in Oyo State. This was decided on to solve the immediate needs of the Muslims of the state to have their civil matters determined according to the law of their religion, pending the time the government would accede to their request.[65]

However, the idea of establishing the Independent *sharīʿa* Panel was not immediately implemented, due to the fact that the Muslim Community wanted to have a solid plan that would make the Panel acceptable to the majority of the Muslims in the state. A committee was then set up to sensitise the Muslims in the state to this plan and to strategise as to how the Panel would be inaugurated. Islamic bodies and Muslim organizations, particularly the League of Imams and Alfas, which is the umbrella body of all Imams and Islamic scholars in the state, were duly consulted. The leadership of the latter approved the idea and gave its necessary support.[66]

The sensitisation and planning dragged on for more than three years between July 2002, when the *sharīʿa* Committee submitted its report to the Muslim Community, and April 2006, when the Independent *sharīʿa* Panel was inaugurated. This was because the Muslim Community was trying to see whether the memorandum submitted to the House of Assembly for the establishment of *sharīʿa* Courts in the state might scrape through.

64 Interview with Bello, 5th March, 2007.

65 Interview with Alh. Abdur-Rasheed Ayo Olabomi, secretary of Osun State Muslim Community, on 2nd October, 2006.

66 Interview with Olabomi, 2nd October, 2006.

About two years were spent trying to mobilise and lobby the members of the House to pass the Bill.[67]

During this period, the committee also worked on the appointment of the members of the Panel. The list of candidates submitted for appointment was screened, in order to get qualified individuals who could effectively handle *sharīʿa* matters. At the initial stage, only eight people, who were not only adjudged to possess the academic pre-requisites, but also as being of virtuous and impeccable character, were appointed. Two more were later added to make the panel number ten members. However, one of them subsequently died and was replaced with another person from his zone.[68] The composition of the members of the Panel cuts across the geographical areas of the state. Some members are degree holders in Islamic Studies or Islamic Law, some are holders of a doctorate. Some of them studied in Nigeria, whilst others studied in the Arab world and hold degrees in *sharīʿa* (LLB Islamic Law).[69] The chairman of the Panel is a retired naval officer, while the members are lecturers in Universities, teachers in secondary schools or proprietors of Arabic and Islamic Institutions. All members of the Panel are Yoruba Muslims; the litigants who have patronised the Panel, so far, are also Yoruba Muslims.

On Sunday 23rd April, 2006, Osun State Independent *sharīʿa* Panel was inaugurated at the Oja-Oba central mosque, Osogbo. The inauguration ceremony was attended by eminent Muslim personalities in the state. It was inaugurated by the Chief Imam of Osogbo and chairman of the League of Imams and Alfas in Osun State, Shaykh Mustafa Ajisafe. The occasion was presided over by Barrister Ola-Olu Ali (SAN) and all the various organs of Osun State had their representatives in attendance.[70]

---

67 Interview with Olabomi, 2nd October, 2006.

68 Interview with Olabomi, 2nd October, 2006. The members of the Panel are: Alh. Abdur-Rahman A. Olaniyan, Chairman, Alh. Musa Raji, Secretary, Alh. Abdulfatah Makinde, Alh. Muhammad Jamiu Muhibullah, Alh. Sulaiman Salahudeen, Alh. Zakariyah Sanusi, Alh. Yunus Ibrahim Balogun, Alh. Rabiu Salahudeen, Dr. Ibrahim Muhammad Baki and Alh. Abdul-Ghaniy Olagunju. Dr. Ibrahim Muhammad Baki, who died, was replaced by Dr. Siraj Asrau Bilal.

69 Interview with Olabomi, 2nd October, 2006.

70 Interview with Olabomi, 2nd October, 2006.

Views of Christian Leaders on the Osun Independent *Sharīʿa* Panel (ISP)

It is appropriate to record that, although the Christian leaders interviewed claimed not to be aware of the establishment of an Independent *sharīʿa* Panel in the state, they saw nothing wrong with it. They opined that since the Panel is independent of the government and it is to handle cases amongst the Muslims of the state, they have nothing against it. During the interviews conducted with some Christian leaders in the state, in order to gather their feelings on the establishment of the Panel, one of them had this to say about it:

> Why would I now say that I have [a] problem when Muslims want to settle problems among Muslims. What is my problem? The only problem is that, if you want to settle any dispute with me, let us sit down together and reason. Don't bring *Qurʾān* into it and don't bring *sharīʿa* into it.[71]

Another Christian leader opined as follows:

> Well, I will say we cannot say it is bad because it is [an] independent something; so far the government doesn't back it up, because if the government directly or indirectly gives it their backing, it may result to another thing. There can be no any problem, if it is independent. So, it is your own cases that you will be bringing there to judge. There is nothing bad about it.... But if it is now backed up by legislation, it has become a state matter and not [a] religious matter.[72]

One other Christian leader remarked about the Panel thus:

> Well, I have not heard of that, I am just listening to you now. But, if it goes the way you have said, there is a Panel, independent of the government, taking care of Muslims' legal affairs; I don't think there is any problem. I wouldn't say, just like our own is aged old, our own tribunal, canon law tribunal, so in the same way, and we don't disturb anybody. And since that is existing, it must be that only Muslims have been feeling it that is why we are not aware. So, if it is working good for the Muslims, I see nothing wrong in that, if it is working good for them.[73]

In view of the above, it is shown from the interaction with some Christian leaders in the state that some Christians may have nothing against the establishment of the Independent *sharīʿa* Panel by the Muslims in the

---

71 Interview with Rev. Adeloye, 28th February, 2007.
72 Interview with Pastor Akinosun, 9th March, 2007.
73 Interview with Bishop Leke Abegunrin, 23rd April, 2007.

state, since it is relevant to the affairs of the Muslims only and, also, it is not backed up by the government. They claimed that they have a similar thing in their various churches which is either called a committee or a tribunal that sees to the settlement of disputes among their members. Their contention is that the involvement of the government in *sharīʿa* matters shows that it tends towards a particular religion and it is partial.[74]

Activities of Osun State Independent *Sharīʿa* Panel

The activities of Osun State Independent *sharīʿa* Panel started immediately after its inauguration on 23rd April 2006. The Panel sits every first Thursday of the month at the Oja-Oba central mosque in Osogbo, the state capital, and adjudicates on cases voluntarily brought to it through formal written application on matters such as marriage, divorce, inheritance, contract, custody and maintenance of children, Imamship or trade disputes and other personal matters where the parties concerned are Muslims.[75]

The plaintiff obtains a form from the office of Osun State Muslim Community, completes it, stating the issues to be heard, and submits the form to the same office. The Panel's secretary, who serves as registrar/clerk, collates and presents the forms for hearing during the sitting of the Panel. The secretary acts as clerk and calls cases based on the submitted forms. He takes records of the proceedings in English.[76] Each sitting of the panel has two sessions. The first one is for public enlightenment and education of the audience about various issues on *sharīʿa.* One of the panellists would be asked to give a talk on a topic that falls within the activities of the panel and the audience would be given the opportunity to ask questions. This is done within 40–50 minutes. Then they close and arrange for the sitting proper which is the second session. They go into a room provided for the Panel and come back to occupy their seats for the hearing of cases. A minimum of three and a maximum of five members are selected to listen to a case, the chairman or presiding judge is appointed from amongst them.[77]

---

74 Interview with some Christian leaders already mentioned above.
75 Interview with Raji, 25th November, 2006.
76 Interview with Raji, 25th November, 2006.
77 Interview with Raji, 25th November, 2006.

The secretary of the panel, who also acts as the clerk, presents a case and calls on the plaintiff to state his or her case. The defendant is also invited to respond while witnesses are allowed to testify. The witnesses of the plaintiff are invited first to testify, before those of the defendant are called. The secretary and members of the panel take a record individually when testimonies are given. Since cases heard for the first time may not be dispensed with immediately, in order to allow the panellists to prepare their judgement,[78] such cases would be adjourned until all the witnesses have been heard before judgements are passed.[79]

The judgement on each case is presented by consensus, through the chairman or presiding judge of the panel, who delivers it, once all members who listened to the case are in agreement. The judgement is delivered in the hearing of the audience at the sitting, while the written text of the judgement will be presented to the litigants later. However, the judgement is never enforced on any of the litigants, since the Panellists have no power to do so. Their duty is only in an advisory capacity. They educate and advise litigants to take whatever judgement is given since it is based on the *Qurʾān* and *sunna* of the Prophet. Since Muslims, by faith, are expected to submit to the judgement of the *Qurʾān* and *sunna*, the litigants accept the judgement. The Panel does not restrict itself to a particular school of thought under Islamic law; rather, it explores the law of any particular school that will be more useful and beneficial to the matter being handled.[80]

Between April 2006 and October 2007, only five cases were brought before the panel. They were:

A case of *khulʿ*: divorce at the instance of a wife
A case of *faskh*: dissolution of marriage at the discretion of a court
Two cases of inheritance
A case of Imamship dispute

The case concerning the Imamship had earlier been scheduled to be taken to a conventional court, but the parties rescinded the decision and brought the case to the Panel.

---

[78] The word 'Judgement' is used by the Panel for the decisions reached in its sittings. This is not peculiar to Osun State. It is the same in all the states where Independent *Sharīʿa* Panels (ISP) operate.

[79] Interview with Raji, 25th November, 2006.

[80] Interview with Navy Captain Abdur-Rahman Olaniyan (rtd.), chairman of the Independent *Sharīʿa* Panel, on 6th October 2006.

Out of the five cases, the three cases concerning *khulʿ*, *faskh* and Imamship dispute were handled and disposed of by the Panel. Out of the two inheritance cases, however, one was later withdrawn by the family involved, to be settled at the family level, and the family of the other one did not initially provide the necessary document for the Panel to work on. The document was later provided and the Panel took the necessary steps to ensure the distribution of the property left by the deceased to the heirs.[81]

However, between 2006 and 2011, a total of forty-three cases were handled by the Panel. The analysis of the cases is provided in the table as follows:

Year	Cases of Divorce	Cases of Inheritance	Cases of Imamship Tussle	Cases of Care of Children	Cases of Civil Disputes	Total
2006	1	1	1			3
2007	1		1			2
2008	4	1		1		6
2009	4			1		5
2010	11	3	1	1	3	19
2011	5	1			2	8
Total	26	6	3	3	5	43

(Source: Data supplied at the office of OSISP, Osogbo)

From the above table, it is shown that the number of cases coming to the Panel per year were not all that encouraging. It was in the year 2010 that the Panel recorded the highest number of cases, which was 19. The Panel recorded 3 cases in 2006; 2 in 2007; 6 in 2008; 5 in 2009 and 8 in 2011, giving a total of 43 cases. Out of these cases, 26 were for divorce; 6 for inheritance; 3 for Imamship tussle; 3 for care of children and 5 for civil disputes. It is also shown from this analysis that divorce cases had the major share, 26 out of the 43 cases recorded. What could be responsible for the low number of cases recorded so far? This is discussed under another subheading later on in the chapter.

81 Interview with Raji, 25th November, 2006.

Judgements on the Cases

It is appropriate to briefly examine some of the cases handled by the Panel and the judgements passed on them. The cases, the reasons advanced by the plaintiffs or petitioners, and the defence put forward by the defenders, as well as the judgement passed by the Panel, will be stated.

Case I: (CASE NO/OS/ISP/06/002) Case of khulʿ

This is between Adebomi Rukayat—Plaintiff, Vs Lasisi Abdul-Waheed—Defendant, both of Ido-Osun of Egbedore Local Government of Osun State. The plaintiff first brought the case to the sitting of the Panel on 6th July, 2007. She told the Panel that she fell in love with Lasisi about five years ago and *aqdun-nikāḥ* i.e. joining of hands in marriage, was done on 13th February, 2003. The programme was conducted by the Muslim Students' Society, Ido-Osun branch, while her uncle, Adebomi Rauf, and her mother as well as the parents of her husband were in attendance. According to her, her husband gave a copy of the Glorious *Qurʾān* to her as a gift. She, however, accused her husband of having affairs with another lady whom he later impregnated. As a result of this, she could not cope with the situation; hence, preferred to seek for *khulʿ* (divorce at the instance of the wife). The panellists cross-examined her, before finally deciding to summon the husband to the next hearing.[82]

After the defendant failed to attend two sittings without showing cause, the Panel decided to invite his parents, who are the *walīy* (guardians under the *sharīʿa*) and they came to confirm the story. They went further to assert that their son was also not interested in the marriage any longer. It was on the basis of this that the Panel asked whether the plaintiff was ready to return the gift presented to her for the marriage and she answered in the affirmative. The panellists thereafter gave judgement that the Glorious *Qurʾān* given to the plaintiff by the defendant be returned to him; hence, the marriage was dissolved and the plaintiff was given the opportunity of re-marrying according to the *sharīʿa*.[83]

It needs to be noted at this juncture that it was the plaintiff that requested that they be divorced based on the claim that her husband impregnated another lady. The failure of the husband to show up did not

---

[82] Interview with Alh. Musa Raji, 25th November, 2006, and excerpt from the record of the judgement.

[83] Interview with Raji, 25th November, 2006.

give room for further probing of the allegation. Although the parents confirmed the story, they did not tell the Panel whether the other lady is a co-wife, nor did they speak on the legality or illegality of the pregnancy. Their declaration that their son was also not interested in the marriage any longer made the Panel take a decision. The divorce could have been granted on *faskh* or *talaq* if the defender had showed up personally. His failure to show up probably made the Panel to grant the divorce on *khulʿ* since there was no ambiguity about the request for divorce at the instance of the plaintiff (the wife). It was on the basis of this that she was asked to return the gift of the Qurʾān which she claimed to be the entire dowry she collected from her husband.

Case II: (CASE NO/OS/ISP/06/003) Imamship Tussle

This is a case of Imamship tussle at Ilu-Aro in Egbedore Local Government. It is between Oyedeji Subair and Alh. Kazeem Abidoye—Plaintiffs Vs Alh. Jamiu Faleye—Defendant. The first sitting on the case came up on Thursday 2nd November, 2006. The plaintiffs filed an application form claiming that the respondent be restrained from parading himself as Chief Imam of Ilu-Aro for the following reasons:

- Adultery and snatching of a member's wife
- Seizing of prayer mat of one of his followers for ritual purpose
- Misappropriation of the mosque fund
- Attempting to kidnap Qurʾānic school students

The defendant did not appear on the day and another hearing date was fixed for Thursday, 7th December, 2006. During the second sitting, both the plaintiffs and the defendant appeared before the Panel and the hearing started. The defendant defended himself and tried to exonerate himself from the allegations. The plaintiffs called on witnesses to affirm their claim while the defendant also brought in his own witnesses to defend him. The plaintiffs even requested the assistance of a lawyer, Barrister Abdul-Ganiy Aminu, to serve as their solicitor.[84]

Regarding the first allegation, the defendant was accused of harbouring the wife of a member who was not seen for some time but was alleged to be found later in his house. It was therefore assumed that he must

[84] Interview with Raji, 25th November, 2006.

have committed adultery with her. He denied the allegation claiming that he had three wives whom he married legally. He declared that the woman he was accused of snatching was the wife of his former driver and that he used to play a mediating role in their persistent quarrels before the woman eventually sought divorce and married another man. The woman was summoned by the Panel to testify and she exonerated the defendant from the allegation.

On the issue of mat seizure, the defendant was accused to having requested a praying mat with a Qiblah indicator from a member, which he did not return because he wanted to use it for ritual purpose. He confirmed the collection of the mat for the purpose of determining the direction of Qiblah and never for any ritual purpose. He said he did not return the mat to the owner because of their closeness. He showed the mat to the Panel to exonerate himself from the allegation of using it for ritual purpose. The Panel also made a critical examination of the other allegations and discovered that there was no convincing evidence to establish the allegations levelled against the defendant by the plaintiffs. The Panel, however, blamed the defendant for not handling the issue with care, as a spiritual leader, which made the case degenerate to the level of litigation.

Because of the nature of the case, which required a lot of patience and a great deal of thoroughness, the case dragged on for six months before the final judgement was given on 3rd May, 2007. While giving the judgement, the Panel analysed the allegations and gave its submission on each of the points; it finally submitted that the two disputants should take the course of reconciliation according to *sharīʿa*. It then recommended as follows:

1. The Imam should apologise to the members of the Muslim Community of Ilu-Aro.
2. The Muslim Community too should forgive, forget and reconcile, for Allāh says in *sūrat Āl-ʿImrān* of the *Qurʾān* 3 verse 134 thus: "Who restrain their anger, and pardon people—God loves those who do good".
3. The two disputants should come together as a single community through amicable settlement, quoting *sūrat Āl-ʿImrān* of the *Qurʾān* 3 verse 103, where Allāh says: "Hold fast to God's rope all together, do not split into fractions".[85]

[85] Interview with Raji, 25th November, 2006.

Case III: (CASE NO/OS/ISP/06/004) Case of faskh

This is a case of dissolution of marriage at the discretion of a court, between Hidiat Adeleke (Nee Arogundada)—Plaintiff Vs Talib A. Adeleke—Defendant. While the plaintiff is from Irepodun Local Government, the defendant is from Ejigbo Local Government of Osun State, but works as a teacher in a school in Wukari, Taraba State. The plaintiff accused her husband of abandonment and neglect for over one and a half years. She stated further that their marriage was blessed with two children, but the husband abandoned her and the children. The Panel summoned the husband to appear before it. On appearance, the husband put up the following as his defence:

- That the woman left the house he provided for her without his knowledge
- She denied him sexual intercourse leading him to marry another wife
- The initial agreement was to put her in *purdah* or seclusion but she just pulled out of it without informing him

In view of the above, and particularly because of the first reason, he would never go back to her unless she went back to where he provided for her and the children.

Having heard the two sides, the Panel examined the case critically and pronounced *faskh*, dissolution of the marriage at the discretion of a court, for the following reasons:

- The man has abandoned the woman for more than one year and under the *sharīʿa* the length of abandonment that calls for divorce is three months.
- Both the husband and the wife were not ready for reconciliation.
- The man has married another wife.[86]

The Panel based its judgement on the resolution of the Islamic jurists that when the relationship of a couple is no longer at ease, they be separated. The judgement states inter alia thus:

---

[86] Interview with Raji, 25th November, 2006.

> It is a unanimous resolution of the jurists to separate a couple if their relationship is no longer at ease. Also Imam Malik and others permit separation of a couple for fear of persistent breach or hurt between the two so that relationship might not be likened to that of cat and mouse, in line with the tradition of the Prophet (SAW) which states: "where there is injury, there is no requital".... If the object of the marriage is mutual understanding and harmonious relationship, and the investigations had proved that their civil contract does not guarantee harmony any longer, the best is to separate their union. Therefore, the Panel decided to dissolve the wedlock; hence, the plaintiff is free to pack her belongings at Ibadan and marry another man of her choice.[87]

Reasons for Low Attendance at Independent *Sharīʿa* Panel (ISP)

Based on the analysis made on the number of cases taken so far, one wonders why the Panel recorded a low number of cases, if Muslims are really interested in having *sharīʿa* Court and *sharīʿa* Court of Appeal established by the government. Since the government failed to yield to their request and, as a result of that, they established an Independent *sharīʿa* Panel, one expects that the Panel would record a considerable number of cases within the years of its existence. In an attempt to probe into the cause for this, the secretary to Osun State Muslim Community gave some reasons. He stated that the first reason for the low number of cases could be attributed to the general apathy of Yoruba about taking each other to court. He argued on this point thus:

> It is true that we don't have so many cases. It is not a new thing in this part of the world, especially Yorubaland, because there is a Yoruba proverb that says "*A ki ti kootu bo ka sore*" that is, you don't take me to court and thereafter we become friends, we should be harsh enemies. Yoruba generally distaste going to court. They have that general apathy. If you come to Nigeria, even the normal courts, the normal Common Law Courts, it is believed that we have fewer cases in Yorubaland than in any part of the country because people like settling issues within the family setting at the extended family level.[88]

It may be noted at this point that the report above of the withdrawal of one inheritance case by a family, in order to settle it at the family level, illustrates the assertion of the secretary of the Muslim Community about the general apathy of the Yoruba to go to court. A lot of such cases or

---

87 An excerpt from the judgement of the Panel.

88 Interview with Alh. Abdur-Rasheed Ayo Olabomi on 26th August 2007.

conflicts are settled at other levels of the community. For example, local Mallams or scholars are in some instances invited to handle inheritance and other personal matters or conflicts in an Islamic way without the necessity of going to the Panel. This therefore left the Panel with few cases to handle.

The second point raised by the secretary is the general attitude of human beings to change, for they naturally do not easily take to change. This has prompted the idea of sensitising Muslims of the state to the benefits of *sharīʿa*. He says:

> We are now at the level of sensitizing Muslims of the benefits of the *sharīʿa*. Don't forget that we have so many years of adjudicating via Common Law and Customary Law Courts and human beings naturally do not easily take to changes. It takes time before people adapt to changes. I want to believe seriously that, the people, I mean the Muslims' interests are going by the day, of the benefits.[89]

Another reason advanced for the low level of turn-out so far, is ignorance or misconception about *sharīʿa*. While expatiating this point, the secretary asserted that "there is erroneous belief or misconception that *sharīʿa* is synonymous with amputation, stoning to death etc. We are trying to correct that impression. To tell people that *sharīʿa* is not mainly on amputation, and in our own case we are looking at *sharīʿa* from the angle of personal law of marriage, inheritance, personal inter-relation; civil cases not criminal cases. So, we believe strongly that very soon, the sensitization would take our people to have appreciable knowledge about that aspect".[90] He explained further that the second aspect of this factor has to do with the government side. He opined that "some people have the belief that, may be, the Higher Courts, Customary Courts and the other Common Law Courts would not recognize the judgements passed by the Panel. Consequently, they believe it is more or less, a dissipation of energy going to the Panel and it is our belief that, that too would be addressed".[91]

In view of the reasons advanced, however, several questions may still agitate one's mind as to the readiness of the Muslims for the establishment of *sharīʿa* Courts by the government. One may even ask whether the Muslims of the State would make use of *sharīʿa* Courts if established or whether they prefer other courts to *sharīʿa* Courts? It seems that answers

89 Interview with Olabomi, 26th August 2007.
90 Interview with Olabomi, 26th August 2007.
91 Interview with Olabomi, 26th August 2007.

to these questions could not be easily arrived at, based on the simple fact that even though the Panel is operating privately and it does not have the power of enforcing judgements, some few people still patronise it. There is the possibility that if official recognition is given to *sharīʿa* Courts by the government, Muslims may turn to it in large numbers.

Conclusion

Although Muslims in the South-West of Nigeria, including Osun State, had been agitating for the establishment of *sharīʿa* Courts since colonial days, the launching of *sharīʿa* in Zamfara State in 1999 opened a new door for agitation by the Muslims in this part of the country. Having attempted to convince the past and present governments to establish *sharīʿa* Courts with civil jurisdiction, but having failed, the Muslim Community of the Osun State decided to do it on a private basis by establishing the Independent *sharīʿa* Panel (ISP). Also, Christian groups in the state opposed the establishment of *sharīʿa* Courts in the state as a public institution. Thus, the Independent *sharīʿa* Panel functions purely outside the influence and machinery of government. Although few cases have come before the Panel, and the reasons for this have been mentioned, the ISP is making a gradual impact in society by performing a judicial role, particularly for the people who patronise it. There have been instances when some homes that could have been broken have been amicably reconciled when cases of divorce were brought before the ISP. This is because the ISP always tries its best to reconcile a couple in dispute; it is when reconciliation becomes impossible that the ISP resorts to separation. There were also instances where Imamship tussles and other disputes were amicably settled for the litigants by the ISP.

A few examples of the cases judged show the way the ISP handles matters brought before it. Excerpts are given of the judgements delivered by the ISP on the cases mentioned with their reference numbers and the real names of the litigants involved. Since the Customary or High Court does not have provision for *sharīʿa*, and *sharīʿa* Courts have not been established by the government, it seems these few individual Muslims who patronised the ISP found it to be a place where their religious interests on such civil matters could be fulfilled. The ISP could therefore be described as an arbitration panel privately established by Muslims, to cater for the interest of Muslim individuals who are willing to voluntarily bring their civil cases before it, to be adjudicated based on *sharīʿa* law. While the

State Government has not officially recognized the ISP, it has not in any way hindered its operations. Also, inasmuch as it could be said that there is no formal relationship between the ISP and the official state courts for now, the role being played by the ISP could be said to have indirectly assisted in handling some judicial responsibilities of the official courts. Although the judgements of the ISP are yet to be recognized by the state law, they could serve as documents to be presented in a court of law as evidence of arbitration.

CHAPTER FIVE

"EDUCATION IS EDUCATION": CONTEMPORARY MUSLIM VIEWS ON MUSLIM WOMEN'S EDUCATION IN NORTHERN NIGERIA

Chikas Danfulani

Introduction

The title of this chapter reflects some of the gender differences in Northern Nigeria's approaches to female education, emanating from interviews in 2007 conducted in five states of Northern Nigeria. The starting point of these interviews was a discussion of the statistics from the Ministry of Education that indicate that the northern states of Nigeria are educationally disadvantaged compared to the southern or eastern states. According to a survey by The National Bureau for Statistics conducted in early 2006, the adult female literacy rate in north-western Nigeria is 15.4% as against 31.0% for the adult male literacy rate.[1] This is by far the lowest figure for both the adult literacy rate and the female literacy rate for the whole country. Among my interlocutors for the present study were two male scholars of Islamic Studies, responding to the questions: do you agree with the current statistical figure that presents Muslim women in northern Nigeria as the most educationally disadvantaged? They reacted: "What do you mean our women are educationally disadvantaged? What is your yardstick for measuring that?" Other responses were: "You can only talk about being disadvantaged... in relation to western education, otherwise our women are educated". These responses reveal a resistance to statistical facts and also demonstrate widely-held opinions in Nigeria and even outside the country regarding educational imbalances. They also show the diversities and complexities involved in the conceptualizations of education in a society that puts a high premium on western education as a strategy for the contest of important state and civil resources such as development, employment, and so on. Above all, education is an instrument that in complex ways mediates identity and value particularly in a

[1] Ketefe, Kayode, 'Forty-seven Percent of Nigerians are illiterates', *The Punch*, Tuesday 20th June 2006, http://www.punchng.com/main/article04 (accessed 20.06.2006).

globalizing and interlinked world. In Nigeria, education and the papers that back it up (qualifications) are an important avenue to the acquisition of social capital such as government jobs.

Implicit in the query raised by one of the professors of Islamic studies are more fundamental issues about the meaning of education, its general purpose(s) and cultural determinants. In order to explore some of these issues, the study investigates the various views of some experts in Islamic education on what they think of and understand by education in Islam. To these experts, both male and female, the following questions were raised:

How do Muslims interpret the Islamic teaching on education?
Do they agree with the general impression that women in Northern Nigeria are educationally disadvantaged?
What are some contemporary factors responsible for such disadvantages?

It is in the light of the above questions that this chapter has emerged.

Method of Data Collection

This study is based on in-depth interviews conducted in Northern Nigeria with 20 Muslim educators, professionals and policymakers in 2007. The interviewees were drawn from five states in Northern Nigeria namely: Kano, Zamfara, Katsina, Sokoto and Niger; these states are all part of what is now characterized as 'the *sharīʿa* states', meaning those states that expanded *sharīʿa*, beginning with Zamfara State in 1999.[2] There are twelve states in all which fall into this category. The choice of these five states was partly influenced by the re-implementation of *sharīʿa* and partly by the statistics which indicate that the standard education rate of literacy is lowest among women in these states. The interviewees consisted of 11 males and 9 females. All the interviews were conducted in English, and most of them were recorded and fully transcribed afterwards. The study

[2] Ostien, Philip, Jamila M. Nasir & Franz Kogelmann (eds.), *Comparative Perspectives on Shari'ah in Nigeria*, Ibadan: Spectrum Books Limited, 2005; Danfulani, Umar H. D., *The Sharia Issue and Christian-Muslim Relations in Contemporary Nigeria*, Stockholm: Almqvist & Wikdsell International, 2005; and Paden, John N., *Muslim Civil Cultures and Conflict Resolution: The Challenge of Democratic Federalism in Nigeria*, Washington D.C.: Brookings Institute Press, 2006, pages 157–182.

was originally designed to examine if the re-implementation of *sharīʿa* had made any appreciable difference to education in the '*sharīʿa* States' in general and of women in particular since this is the category whose fate is most often highlighted by current statistics on education in Northern Nigeria.

Education in Northern Nigeria

Two types of education exist in Northern Nigeria: Islamic Education and Western Education.[3] Islamic Education has been in existence since the coming of Islam to Northern Nigeria in the 11th century.[4] This system began at a very traditional level known as Qurʾānic education, developing into what is referred to today as Islamic education; the latter, in content and practice, is a modern type of Qurʾānic education. This system adopts the organizational form of Nigeria's Western Educational system with some fundamental differences in the promotion of a broad Islamic cultural orientation and is operated in what are referred to as new Islamic schools.[5] This form of education is widely accepted by all Muslims in Northern Nigeria and "[it] exhibit[s] some of the varieties of educational dualism that have been developed in some Muslim countries".[6] Western Education, on the other hand, is the formal system of education introduced by the British after the British occupation of Northern Nigeria in 1903. For a long time, however, this system was rejected and resisted by Muslims for a variety of reasons which will become clear shortly. Most importantly, western education was viewed by Muslims as synonymous with Christianity, since it was popularized by the missionaries and it was believed that if allowed, it may lead to conversion of the pupils attending such schools. When it was eventually accepted, other regions such as the southern parts of the country had already made considerable progress in terms of the establishment of institutions of learning based on the British model as

3 The term '*Western Education*', as used in this article, is a popular term used in Nigeria to refer to the type of education brought by the British Colonial Authorities in 1900. This type of education differs from Islamic education both in content and curricula. It is also viewed by some Muslims in the north as 'Christian Education'; this is because the same type of education was taught in missionary schools in Northern Nigeria, thus accounting for the resistance to western education by the north for a very long time.

4 Paden, 2006, page 38.

5 Umar, 'Profiles of New Islamic Schools in Northern Nigeria', *The Maghreb Review*, Vol. 28, 2–3, 2003, page 154.

6 Umar, 2003, page 162.

well as in producing significant numbers of a formally-educated middle class. While the north generally was affected by the relative absence of western education, girls were even more affected as they were protected by their parents from attending these schools. This was mainly due to the general belief by most Muslim parents that girls who attended western schools might be exposed to western ways, thereby becoming morally loose and eventually unmarriageable.

The two types of education have gradually come to be accepted by Muslims in Northern Nigeria. However there still remains a big majority who reject, or rather resist, western education for various reasons. Several of these reasons, they claim, are based on the teaching of Islam on education which stipulates religious education as the basic education for every Muslim. This is reflected in the different views expressed and disseminated by various experts on education in Northern Nigeria. In order to contextualise these views, it is important to summarise the basic teachings of the Islamic holy book, the Qurʾān, on education, as interpreted by some Islamic scholars.

Current Interpretations of Islamic Teaching on Education

Several interpretations have been given by scholars[7] on the importance and place of education in Islam which they agree is made explicit in the Qurʾān and the *sunna* of the Prophet. The grounding of the role of education in these sacred texts as interpreted by these scholars further indicates how the issue of education was constructed early in the history of Islam. Understood as acquiring and imparting of knowledge in a systematic and methodical fashion, through teaching and learning, they conclude that education is a central theme in Islam. The Qurʾān, they argue, teaches that Allāh is the source of all knowledge. Accordingly, 50% of our informants agree that the first revelation that came to the prophet was 'read'. They base their argument on the *sūrat al-ʿAlaq* (96): 1–5 which says:

[7] See Doi, A. R., *Woman in Shari'ah*, London: Ta Ha publishers, 1996, pages 138–144; Jawad, H. A., *The Rights of women in Islam: An Authentic approach*, London, Macmillan Press, 1998, pages 16–29; Khalil, Fatima, 'Women's Rights Under Sharia', in A. M. Yakubu, A. M. Kani & M. I. Junaid (eds.), *Understanding Shari' a in Nigeria: proceedings of National seminar on Shari'a*, Ibadan: Spectrum Books Limited, 2001, page 71.

> Read! In the name of your Lord who created: He created man from a clinging form. Read! Your Lord is the Most Bountiful One who taught by [means of] the pen, who taught man what he did not know.

One informant, while responding to the question on what Islam regards as education, observes that:

> Education is like human rights, because without it how do you read the Qur'ān, how do you know Allah, how do you know what Islam is all about.... you have to read, so the Qur'ān starts with *iqrā*... read in the name of Allah. So education is an integral part of Islam. Without it you are nobody.[8]

The word *iqrā* (read) in Arabic has been interpreted by some scholars to mean education.[9] They also agree that the word is referring to 'education/knowledge' or 'rehearse'. According to Yusuf Ali's commentary on *sūrat al-'Alaq* (96):1; "the word *iqraa* may mean 'read' or 'recite or rehearse' or 'proclaim aloud,' the object understood being Allah's message". Therefore reading, reciting the Qur'ān and seeking for knowledge is very important to every Muslim. The importance of Qur'ānic recitation is evident in the annual Qur'ānic recitation and competition conducted for Muslim pupils all over Northern Nigeria.

Mahdi observes that the Qur'ān reveals, as part of the importance placed on education, that the educated cannot be compared with the uneducated, in all the ramifications of their situation, when it pointedly asks; "Can those who know and those who do not know be deemed equalled?"[10] As is the case in every society, education creates qualitative differences: the educated and uneducated belong to different social and economic classes altogether. Thus, when the Qur'ān lays emphasis on education, it seeks that everyone in the community or society should be educated to be on—or almost on—the same level. Otherwise only the educated will be granted a "high place before Allāh" because they understand and do whatever Allāh enjoins them to do.[11] According to Fatima Khalil, the Qur'ān states in *sūrat al-Mujādala* (58): 11 "... God will raise up, by many degrees,

---

[8] Interview with Hjiya Amina I. Ahmed, Minna-Niger State, 2nd March, 2007.

[9] Khalil, 2001, page 71.

[10] Qur'ān *sūrat al-Zumar* (39):9 as quoted by Saadatu Shehu Mahdi in '*Women's Rights under Sharia*' a presentation at a political briefing organized by the John D. and Catherine MacArthur foundation in Abuja, Nigeria, February 2002.

[11] Mwinyihaji, Esha Faki, *The Contribution of Islam Towards Women's Emancipation: A Case Study of the Swahili Muslims in Mombasa District*, unpublished MPhil Thesis, Moi University Eldoret, Kenya, 2001.

those of you who believe and those who have been given knowledge".[12] She argues that knowledge occupies a place of pride in Islamic teachings, therefore the search for it is considered obligatory for both male and female. This shows that the educated and faithful have a higher status both in the society and before Allāh.[13]

To emphasise the importance that the prophet placed on education, a *ḥadīth* of the Prophet, as interpreted by Adeleye, states; "He who goes out in search of knowledge is in God's path till he returns".[14] He concludes that this statement underscores that Allāh upholds education and places great respect and value on the person who seeks to be educated. Consequently any Muslim who seeks to be educated shall be rewarded just as he who goes on a *jihād* would be rewarded. The search for education is likened to doing God's will or being on the right path.

To the Muslim, the search for knowledge and education is in line with God's commands. Here, the reward a Muslim is promised for seeking education is equated with the reward a believer receives in serving Allāh. So, to seek education is service to Allāh which shall not go unrewarded: it is likened to a path that leads to paradise.[15]

In yet another popular *ḥadīth* of the Prophet, which 90% of our informants invoked to argue the importance of education, the prophet said; "Seek ye knowledge even if it be as far as China". China, in this context, referred to the remotest part of the world which was not Islamic. One informant opines: "China was given as an analogy to mean that you can go anywhere in the world to seek for knowledge".[16] By this injunction Muslims are encouraged to seek education wherever it can be found regardless of the difficulties such an enterprise entails. An added importance of this text is that it indicates that "knowledge" refers not only to religious education but also to secular education which may not be found in the immediate environment of the Muslims. Hence the use of the phrase "as far as China" to emphasise the importance that Islam places on both religious and secular education. At the time the *ḥadīth* was uttered, any "knowledge" existing in China would not have been "Islamic" knowledge but Chinese or secular knowledge, wisdom or philosophy. To Muslims,

---

[12] Qur'ān *Al-Mujādala* (58):11 quoted by Khalil, 2001.
[13] Yakubu, Kani and Junaid, 2001.
[14] Adeleye, M. O., 'Islam and Education', *The Islamic Quarterly*, vol. XXVII, no. 1, 1983, pages 140–150.
[15] Mwinyihaji, 2001.
[16] Interview with Amina Keri, Minna, Niger State, 2nd March 2007.

therefore, all knowledge is one and springs from Allāh, the lord of the universe; distance should neither limit, nor deter the Muslims' quest for knowledge. Consequently, education is an integral part of Islam, a prerequisite to a proper relationship with Allāh, for without it a Muslim is nobody; without education she or he would not know Allāh, would not know how to pray to Him, would not know how to serve Him or how to serve his/her self and serve others adequately.[17]

Education is also obligatory upon every Muslim. The *ḥadīth* of the Prophet, as quoted by several of our informants and which agrees with the interpretation given by several other scholars, is clear that both male and female should seek education when it says; "seeking knowledge is obligatory upon every male and female Muslim".[18] It is an obligation upon every Muslim, regardless of gender, to seek and acquire education. In this understanding, knowledge is gender-blind; hence education is open to all, irrespective of sex. According to one informant:

> Islam regards education as a tool and basis for everything in life and [the] basis for development, survival in this world and the hereafter. Islam places very high importance on education, the first revelation of the prophet Muhammad is on education... so it lays the foundation for everything in life. And it is obligatory for male and female, there is no discrimination. The prophet also says you can go as far as China to seek knowledge, this means also circular knowledge.[19]

By direct implication, therefore, there should be no discrimination between the sexes by Muslims in matters relating to the pursuit of any form of education. This is because the same rewards attached to the pursuit of education apply to both sexes seeking education, which is likened to walking in the path of Allāh. It is in regard to education that gender equality in Islam is most graphically framed. Above all, equality between the sexes is most evident in terms of the obligation or the imperatives of education.

To further bolster this fact, the Prophet Muḥammad did not only teach that both men and women should be educated but exemplified it by teaching both men and women of his day. This was reflected in the lives of his followers and also of his wife, Aisha, who was said to be well-educated

[17] Interview with Amina Keri, Minna, Niger State, 2nd March 2007.

[18] da Costa, Yusuf, *The Honor of Women in Islam*, Washington: The Supreme Council of America, 2002, pages 20–26. da Costa quotes the *ḥadīth* as recorded by Al-Bayhaqi and quoted by Badawi.

[19] Interview with Mrs. Sadiya Umar Bello, Sokoto, Sokoto State, 6th March 2007.

in religious matters, such that the followers of the Prophet were asked to seek half of their knowledge from Aisha.[20]

Agreeing with the rights bestowed on women by the Qurʾān,[21] Yakubu, Kani and Junaid are of the view that women are expected to seek education just as their male counterparts, when they state:

> Knowledge occupies a place of pride in Islamic teachings. The order to read was given in the very first verse of the Qurʾān. The search for knowledge was considered an obligation as much for men as for women ... the prophet reinforced this by making it a duty when he said "the search for knowledge is a duty for every Muslim male or female" Qurʾān *sūrat al-Mujādala* (58): 1.

From the foregoing, the Qurʾān does not specify which education a women should pursue, and which she should refrain from, but stresses they must seek education just like their male counterparts would.[22] Doi notes several women in the history of Islam who excelled in education. Starting from the wives of the Prophet, Aisha and Safiyah, several other women were said to have been well-versed not only in Islamic education, but also in other aspects of knowledge including poetry, history and literature. Expanding on this point, he writes:

> This list of women of the early days of Islam shows that women were not kept illiterate and ignorant, but rather were fully encouraged to participate in the process of learning and scholarship. They also knew their rights and responsibilities very well. There were instances to show that some women even challenged great scholars of their times if they said something which was against the rights granted to women by the Qurʾān and the Sunnah.[23]

Doi is in agreement with the fact that both Islamic knowledge and other branches of knowledge are obligatory upon every Muslim both male and female. Women, much like their male counterparts, have the right to seek for any form of education as long as such education does not distort the moral values inculcated in them by religious education. Jawad also notes that education is strongly encouraged in Islam for both men and women. Giving examples of how women in the early days of Islam excelled in the field of education, she notes: "Early Islamic history is replete with examples of women who showed a remarkable ability to compete with men

---

20 Interview with Dr. (Mrs) Aisha Lemu, Minna, Niger State, 2nd March 2007.
21 Yakubu, Kani and Junaid, 2001.
22 Doi, 1996, page 144.
23 Doi, 1996, page 144.

and excelled on many occasions".[24] She goes on to list the various fields of knowledge which women have ventured into and excelled at as religious studies, literature, medicine and military services. Thus, Muslims accept that education is compulsory for every Muslim, and Islamic scholars have interpreted that to mean that both men and women have the right to be educated, that is, to acquire any form of knowledge. While there is general agreement on the imperatives, based on Qurʾānic teaching and the *ḥadīths*, laid upon every Muslim to acquire education both religious and secular, the cultural applications and implementation of these sacred injunctions vary from one place to another, as is the case in Northern Nigeria, which is the focus of the next section.

Views on Female Education in Northern Nigeria

In many contemporary Islamic cultures, the basic Islamic teaching that education is obligatory for all Muslims seems to be fading away, as women are relegated to the background as far as education is concerned. In comparing contemporary Islamic society with the practice in the early days of Islam, one wonders where most Islamic societies missed the point of enforcing equal educational opportunity for both men and women. Expressing her opinion on the reason for the decline in the general educational status of women, and their status in relation to other rights accorded them by the Qurʾān, Jawad notes that:

> Firstly, certain pre-Islamic customs reappeared, especially during the Abbasid period; secondly, various social attitudes infiltrated Islamic culture from conquered peoples, and were assimilated as norms and then identified with Islam. Hence the status of Muslim women started to deteriorate. This was accelerated by catastrophic historical events such as the Mongol and the Turkish invasions and the ensuing decline of the Islamic civilization. The ambience generated by these conditions served to undermine the position of Muslim women who became less and less part of social life in general.[25]

The deterioration in the educational status of women and in the status of women in general has relegated women to the background, and their roles now are mostly those which culture and society define or prescribe. These roles are shaped by customs and traditions, giving the

[24] Jawad, 1998, page 25.
[25] Jawad, 1998, page 25.

women a subjugated position in the society. Thus women are seen as mothers and their status in the society becomes that of wives and home-makers (or household managers). In the light of the above situation, women's education was, and still is, seen as secondary since their basic duty is to raise children and become good wives to their husbands. Biological reproduction has taken precedence over social production and reproduction of knowledge for women. In addition to this culturally defined responsibility, women who excelled in education were, and still are, seen as threats to their husbands. Again, according to Jawad:

> Female education was viewed as a threat to the traditional customs and the way of life of these societies. Indeed educated women were feared and mistrusted as they could communicate potentially destructive or innovative ideas. Educated women were considered to be obtrusive. They did not appeal to men who expected them to serve them obediently.[26]

The assumption that educated women are to be distrusted as potentially dangerous, audacious, recalcitrant and incapable of making good wives and mothers resurfaced in the interviews conducted among male informants in Northern Nigeria. While all informants agreed that education is obligatory for every Muslim, the men disagreed that western education is compulsory on the women. According to them, women have certain roles such as managing the home, looking after the children and being good wives to their husbands. By 'good wives,' these male interviewees mean obedient, submissive, unquestioning and co-operative with the husband's agenda and decisions. They argue that the basic education the women should have is religious education, which is compulsory for every Muslim and for the woman in particular because she has to play the role of first teacher to her children. The woman being the first teacher means giving the children the basic Islamic education before they leave the home to attend school. As a result of this conceptualisation, some men in Northern Nigeria encourage or prefer women with Islamic education, rather than any other form of education, as wives and companions. The idea that western education corrupts women by inculcating in them the spirit of rebelliousness, intractability and obstinacy is deeply entrenched in the Northern Nigerian Muslim male psyche. Women with university education or degrees are believed to be and perceived to be very disrespectful and impetuous toward their husbands and kinsmen. University education, for example, is believed to predispose the women to speak 'too much

[26] Jawad, 1998, page 25.

grammar'; they would challenge their husbands on the basic issues of life and living. Apart from being disrespectful and insubordinate to their husbands, women with higher degrees seem to know their rights as women and as Muslims. Such knowledge, it is assumed by men in Northern Nigeria, will make the women more assertive and more self-confident in the home, which will not augur well for the sort of male dominance which prevails in Hausa culture. According to one informant:

> Those [educated] women seem to know their rights. You can tame an illiterate girl but it is difficult to tame an educated girl, don't you think so? Yes, when you go to the village and pick an illiterate girl who doesn't know anything, whatever you say, she says "yes sir"; anything you ask her to do, she does not question you. But an educated mind is an enquiring mind; sometimes she may ask you "Is that what Islam says?" When you are going out of point an educated girl will question you "you ask me to do this, is that what Islam says we should do?" Only education will make somebody think like that and begin to ask questions.[27]

This is a succinct framing of the reasons why educated women are viewed with suspicion. Illiteracy is culturally functional in this context. Explicit from the above view is the male conception of educated women as being 'wild' and 'untameable' and therefore unmanageable. The educated woman resists, questions and challenges subjugation and domination and it is this tendency that men resent most, it seems. The fear of the possibility of female defiance has gradually been factored into social and political policy-making in respect of the education of women in Northern Nigeria. While some of our informants acknowledge that women should be educated and must attain any level of education, some, however, feel that women should seek to be educated in courses that are related to their primary responsibilities which are strongly configured to be domestic and household management. In this vein, women should be teachers, nurses, caterers and engage in such professions as depict similar roles in the home. These are essentially 'service roles' with less power, authority, visibility and remuneration than other professionals such as lawyers, medical practitioners, engineers and so on. They are also viewed as 'weak', so there is a certain educational level a woman is not expected to attain due to the weakness associated with her physiology. For example, a woman

[27] Interview with Alhaji Husseini Mohammed, Director, Inspectorate Services, Sokoto State Ministry of Education, Sokoto, 5th March 2007.

cannot be a judge in a *sharīʿa* court because her primary role, which is in the home, cannot permit her to play both roles and succeed.[28]

However, the overall argument of most Muslim men in Northern Nigeria is that 'education is education', whether it is Islamic (religious) education, or any form of education. While it is obligatory for a Muslim to have religious education, it is only optional for an individual to acquire western education. Nevertheless, it is compulsory for a Muslim *umma* (Arab.: community) to acquire any other education, not only an Islamic education. Accordingly, in a Muslim *umma* there should be lawyers, teachers, doctors, engineers etc.[29] It is a collective responsibility to acquire this category of knowledge but an individual must have religious education in order to fulfil the obligations of worshipping Allāh adequately. Religious education is the foundation of the Islamic *umma* and it is incumbent upon every Muslim to acquire this foundational knowledge: but western knowledge or education is optional and complementary, sufficient but not necessary for an individual Muslim.

In the light of the above, Muslim women in Northern Nigeria are regarded as educated, despite the overall statistics that present them as educationally disadvantaged, in comparison to women in other regions of the country. Islamic education, they argue, is a necessary foundation of all forms of education and knowledge acquisition, and since these women have acquired this sort of education, they are to be regarded as educated. Accordingly, these women do not need western education in addition to what they already have in order to creditably perform their basic duties to the society and to the Muslim *umma*. Using Nana Asma'u (1793–1864), the daughter of Sheikh Usman Dan Fodio, as a role model, Muslims in Northern Nigeria believe that a woman can attain the highest level of religious education without any secular education and still be recognized as educated. Nana Asma'u was said to be well-educated in the norms and values of Islam such that she became a renowned scholar without western education and today her achievement is still recognized worldwide. Therefore women in Northern Nigeria cannot be said to be disadvantaged educationally, because more than 80% of them have some form of Islamic education. This includes Qurʾānic education, which the average Muslim has and every Muslim in Northern Nigeria is encouraged to acquire. Aside

[28] Interview with the Director, Shari'ah Research and Development Commission, Gusau, Zamfara State, 5th March 2007.

[29] Interview with Mohammad Sani, Zamfara State, 8th March 2007.

from such an argument lacking in merit because of the difference in time between when Nana Asma'u lived and the contemporary situation, proponents still insist that what was good for the early 19th century Hausa woman should be good for the women of the 21st century.

Given the above scenario, which presents Muslim women in the north as educated, the facts still remain incontrovertible that the educational status of women in the north is the lowest as compared to women in other regions of the country. Islamic education is education indeed, however, it is important to consider the functions and requirements of contemporary society because such a brand of education falls short of meeting the needs of women in the society in which they live. Islamic education is self-limiting because it cannot meet the requirements of an informational or jet age when knowledge in technology and science almost doubles every ten years. The acquisition of knowledge in informational technology is an enviable human capital that drives the motor of social and economic development, as is evident in the fast-developing countries of Asia such as Singapore, India, Thailand and China. While many women aspire to develop themselves and participate in a broadly-conceived public sphere comprising political, social, economic, religious and popular cultural enterprises and experiences, they are however hindered by the male voices that present them as 'educated' even when they cannot access a wider horizon of expression and experience. They cannot take up positions in the management of society, in government and in the production and reproduction of social knowledge. Such rationalisation thereby blocks their chances and possibilities of exploring better opportunities through western education.

All the women involved in this study admitted that Islamic education has played a dominant role in their lives and has given them respected status as Muslim women. They were, however, of the view that western education has added more to their status as Muslim women and women in the society. To them, western education has made them better Muslims, grounded and enlightened enough to face challenges as women both at home and outside the home.[30] Women strongly recognize their potential to contribute to the welfare of society through accessing western education. This position is in direct opposition to the views of men

30 These views were shared by Aisha Lemu, Amina Ahmed and Sadiyah Umar Bello. All three women were top ranking officials in the civil service and are now educationists and a lecturer respectively.

who insist that Islamic education should be sufficient for women in carrying out their domestic and wifely duties. This indicates that the women share different views from men in terms of defining what education really means. To the men, a woman who has religious education has got it all, and western education is secondary in her life, while the women see it differently. They know the value of western education and would ordinarily desire to acquire this, in addition to Islamic education. It is western knowledge that would enable a woman to reposition her life and experience in a wider context of human development and advancement. It is this that would give her the enabling tool to access a rapidly-changing social, economic, cultural, religious and political sphere where her skills and potentials would be put to use for the service of the Muslim *umma.*

Contemporary Factors Hindering the Education of Women

Quoting Byoma, Marg Csapo captures the factors hindering the education of women in Northern Nigeria. According to her, women in Northern Nigeria are considered as secondary citizens and as such the education of girls does not receive the same priority as that of the boys.[31] Fewer girls than boys are found in conventional schools. Outlining further the factors which have hindered female education in the north, Csapo enumerates the following: traditional antagonism against western-type education, marriage customs and seclusion of women, fear of moral laxity in the schools, paucity of post-primary institutions and lukewarm attitudes of political leaders. The condition of education in Northern Nigeria in the late 1970s and early 1980s when Csapo conducted her research seem not to have changed much, as the same factors militating against the education of women still hold sway.[32]

An analysis of the responses of informants for this study, on the various factors that are still hindering the education of women in the north, reveals that while these factors are not far from those enumerated by Csapo, there are, however, several additional factors that continue to perpetuate differences in women's educational status compared to men's. As revealed

[31] Csapo, M., 'Religious, Social and Economic Factors Hindering the Education of Girls in Northern Nigeria', *Comparative Education*, vol. 17, no. 3, 1981, pages 311–319, page 311.

[32] Although current data show that more women are getting educated than was the case in the 1980s, similar problems that hampered women's education then, still exist and contribute to the wide gender disparity between males and females in the north today.

by our interview interlocutors, these include: unfavourable atmosphere, poverty, polygyny, government policy and fear of moral laxity.[33]

Dress code is a very important norm in Islam. A woman is expected to dress in accordance with the prescription of the *sharīʿa*, found in *sūrat al-Nūr* (24): 31 which states:

> And tell believing women that they should lower their glances, guard their private parts, and not display their charms beyond what [it is acceptable] to reveal; they should let their headscarves fall to cover their necklines and not reveal their charms except to their husbands... they should not stamp their feet so as to draw attention to any hidden charms. Believers, all of you, turn to God so that you may prosper.

The *sharīʿa* requires women to dress in a way that does not expose their bodily appearance or ornament. Instead, women must be modest in their appearance. The issue of dress code is taken seriously in most Islamic societies. However, many Muslims in Northern Nigeria believe that the atmosphere western education presents has itself been inimical to the total moral well-being of women. With religious education it is different, because women must dress according to the norms of Islamic dress code, as interpreted by Hausa cultural practice. However, in conventional schools, women are not given the opportunity to dress the way Islam prescribes for them. When what is perceived as normative in Islam comes in conflict with the practices of western educational institutions, western education is quickly sacrificed rather than compromise religious norms. Female dress has been a strong flash-point in the argument against western education in the north of Nigeria and this has had its impact in keeping women from western-type educational institutions.

Another point of disagreement and resentment is co-education, the practice of educating both sexes together in the same school. While Islamic education allows women to study alone, without mingling with men, western education on the other hand encourages co-education. To many Muslims, this is not advisable because it is perceived as the seedbed of cultivating immoral thoughts and actions, practices contrary to the proper observance of Islamic moral codes and conduct. Co-education is viewed among Northern Nigerian Muslims, particularly males, as one

---

33 These factors emanated from the interviews conducted in five states of northern Nigeria. They still form the factors hindering the education of women in northern Nigeria today, giving an impression that there isn't much difference between the past and the present in terms of Muslim female education.

of the systems that most strongly encourages immoral behaviour among female students.[34]

It is against this backdrop that some states in Nigeria, such as Zamfara, have decided to separate the sexes by having separate schools for boys and girls, right from the primary level, with the hope that Muslim parents will be encouraged to allow their girls to acquire education. The enforcement of the use of the *ḥijāb* on all female pupils and students from primary to tertiary institutions is also an indication that the atmosphere has been very unfavourable to Muslims in the north before now. The perceived unfavourable atmosphere presented by western education, which some Muslims see as 'un-Islamic', makes western education unappealing to most Muslims in the north.

Fear of moral laxity has always been one of the strongest reasons that has hindered the education of women in Northern Nigeria. Western education encourages co-education and the fear of many Muslims in the past has been that if girls were allowed to co-educate with boys they would become morally loose. Co-education, it is believed, is the enabling condition for breeding sexual immorality among the pupils and students. Doi also shares this view and pointedly argues against the system when he states:

> Whatever trumpets the proponents of coeducation may blow in praise of the system, the sad fact still remains that a majority of girl students in the secondary schools in Europe and America spend more time in picking up illicit sexual techniques from their class mates than in collecting useful knowledge from their teachers ... therefore we should dispense with the system of coeducation and should open primary schools, secondary schools, colleges and universities exclusively for women where the teachers as well as the students are women. The uniform for all female students should satisfy the requirements laid down by the Sharī'ah for proper dress.[35]

The Islamic injunctions on women, they believe, are stricter than what is expected of men.[36] That a woman is not expected to mingle with the opposite sex is strongly advocated. She is expected to always 'lower her gaze', and most of all appear before men in the appropriate dress that conforms to the *sharī'a* norms or injunction. However, women who attend western schools are generally absolved from conforming to these injunctions. Some Muslim men would rather have their wives educated

---

[34] Doi, 1996, page 144.
[35] Doi, 1996, pages 144–45.
[36] Interview with Mohammed Suraju.

according to the prescriptions of Islam than allow them to attend western schools. The primary reason for this is the fear of these women becoming morally loose. Western schools, it is generally feared among Muslims, produce secular human beings and this inexorably leads to secularization of personal conduct and life as well as worldview. The Muslim is at odds with such a possibility, as his view is that the Muslim *umma* is based on the injunctions of Allāh as made explicit in the Qurʾān, expanded in the *sunna* and interpreted by many Islamic scholars.

Poverty is another major factor that has denied women access to education. Marriage customs in this part of the country allow for men to marry up to four wives. In many situations the breadwinner of the home is unable to provide for the basic necessities of the home due to the large number of children as a result of polygyny. In such cases, Islamic education is preferred because it is not expensive. As an informant notes:

> ... Islamic education is imparted cheaply. If I have four wives and have twenty-five children and I send them to be taught by Mallams, it may not cost me much. But if I send them to western schools they will say bring text books, bring uniforms, etc. Islamic education takes cognizance of our traditional way of life ...[37]

There are instances of polygynists having more than 25 children, so the figure cited by the informant above is not wide of the mark or strictly hypothetical. In such a situation the most affected in the family are the female children. The girl child is seen by most parents as an expendable 'item' that should quickly be married away in order to prevent the shame of premarital pregnancy and, more importantly, create space for the development of the male children. Boys are seen as assets and the pain of investing in them is not felt by parents. The situation is different for a girl who may eventually be married off and remain in seclusion for the rest of her life. The practice of keeping females in seclusion precludes investing in them educationally because they would not be required to utilise such investments in working in the public sphere. The practice of early marriage, which ensures that girls are married off between the ages 12 and 15, precludes these girls from remaining long enough in school to acquire adequate education which would be useful in social governance or public organizations.

Another issue at variance with Northern Nigerian Muslim communities is the official educational policy of the state. Government policies on

---

[37] Interview with Mohammed Husseini, 5th March 2007.

education have been unacceptable to many Muslims in the north. The Universal Primary Education (UPE) of the 1970s was meant to bridge the gap between males and females, and the most recent Universal Basic Education (UBE) introduced by the regime of Olusegun Obasanjo (1976–1979) has the improvement of girls' education as one of its aims. However, the UPE recorded very little success.[38] The schools constructed under the UPE programme have received very poor funding by the federal and state governments. They lacked adequate classrooms to accommodate the students and the facilities in these schools were not adequate to meet the needs of the students. Lack of adequate funding and misappropriation of funds subverted official government policy on education. According to the government's National Economic Empowerment and Development Strategy (NEEDS) document, "The goals of wealth creation, employment generation, poverty reduction, and value reorientation can be effectively pursued, attained, and sustained only through an efficient, relevant and functional education system".[39] The UBE programme of the Obasanjo regime, like its predecessor, falls short of proper implementation. The mechanism and infrastructure needed to achieve the identified noble objectives have not been adequately addressed. The result has been poorly-staffed schools, poorly-equipped schools, poorly-motivated teachers and general lack of academic infrastructure resulting in poor performance by students in many of these schools. This has made parents apprehensive of allowing their girls to attend any form of education apart from religious education. Parents reasoned that since the schools are not producing good results with quality products, why waste money and time on them. To many, this is an attractive, if not inescapable conclusion.[40]

Although these factors seem convincing to many Muslims in Northern Nigeria, they are, however, not without problems. It may be the case that 'education is education', as argued by some informants, and Islamic education is an alternative to western education. It is pertinent to ask: how do women who possess Islamic education alone compete effectively with those who have a combination of western and Islamic education?

---

[38] Clarke, P. B., 'Islam, Education and the Development Process in Nigeria', *Comparative Education*, vol. 14, no. 2, 1978, page 133.

[39] Nigerian National Planning Commission, *Meeting Everyone's Needs: National Economic Empowerment and Development Strategy*, Abuja: Nigerian National Planning Commission, 2004, page 35.

[40] Interview with Dr. Aisha Lemu, 2nd March 2007.

All the women interviewed during this study, when asked which education they preferred, recognised the importance of having both Islamic and western education: the need to balance the two is all the more obvious in their open agitation to improve the educational state-of-affairs among women. Women who have had the opportunity to excel in both Islamic and western education said they would not have excelled in the public sphere without having access to western education. It is incontrovertible that these women have had the opportunity to become teachers in public schools, principals, professors in renowned universities, directors and permanent secretaries in the civil service because of the acquisition of western education. One articulates the value of western education this way:

> The problem with those who have only Islamic education is that they can't relate what they know to anything in the world around them. We have lots of teachers in the course of time in our schools that went through the Islamic studies courses in the colleges of Islamic studies and universities. But the sad thing is that they can hardly relate their knowledge to modern knowledge... So to me it is important that anybody going for Islamic studies must have also broad general knowledge...[41]

This is an evident indication that insofar as Islamic education is education and it is obligatory upon every Muslim, yet it is not sufficient education if women are to be favourably positioned and equipped to compete for social, economic and political resources with other members of the society, both male and female alike. One such Muslim woman who has excelled in both systems of education has this to say "...I am happy to be a Muslim woman, a fortunate Muslim woman who has been able to benefit from both Islamic and western education". Another said, "Praise God! I am glad to be one of those who have excelled in the education sector". Views like these, shared by women, show that women who have excelled in both systems of education are able to differentiate between the two. While they accept Islamic education as important, they accept much more the need for western education as they believe that without both they would not have been where they are today.

The improvement of women's education and the development of Muslim women-folk cannot be a top priority for educational policy-makers in Northern Nigeria if Muslims are yet to come to terms with the reality and demands of modern life. Part of the reality of life in contemporary

---

[41] Interview with Dr. Aisha Lemu, 2nd March 2007.

Northern Nigeria is the underdevelopment of women generally. In no place is this underdevelopment as clear as in the educational sector. While women recognise their need for both Islamic and western forms of education, Muslim men, who are the policy makers and implementers of such educational structure, impose their ideas and preferences on their women. Such preferences insist on the sufficiency of Islamic education for women while men have access to both forms of knowledge. While justifying and rationalising their position by co-opting religiously-informed ideas, the consequence of tenaciously-defended, culturally-defined posturing is to keep women on the lower rungs of society, 'good' only because they do not complain about, or challenge, their plight; 'good' insofar as they fulfil their reproductive and domestic responsibilities. As women are viewed as submissive and subjugated, so is western education viewed as a secondary and non-obligatory form or source of knowledge for women. So, women in Northern Nigeria are presented with the limited roles and status tradition and society define for them and accept them as duties prescribed by Islam. These roles are diverse and they include domestic roles that tend to relegate women to the background and present them as subordinates to men, not only in Northern Nigeria but also in some other Muslim societies. Women are ideologically constructed as homemakers and are expected to pursue religious education which will help them bring up their children in the Islamic way. For women in Northern Nigeria to come to terms with their educational status as prescribed by the *sharīʿa* and to compete alongside men in contemporary society, they need to be given the opportunity to explore these rights, grounded in the Qurʾān and in the Constitution of Nigeria, without intrusion by any cultural norms that present a different picture to the non-educated women in the society.

Conclusion

This chapter has argued that the historical teaching of Islam on education and women's education seems to be different from the way it is practised in Northern Nigeria. While *sharīʿa* prescribes the right to acquire any form of education, irrespective of gender, the views shared by our Muslim informants in Northern Nigeria seem to differ from the interpretations given by Muslim scholars on the teaching of Islam on education, especially as it applies to women in *sharīʿa*. Statistics on education present women in the north as the most educationally disadvantaged in the whole country, as regards western education. While various reasons have been adduced as to the causes of such a socially regressive state of affairs, an appreciable number of both policy makers and lay male Muslim informants in this study seem to disagree with the statistics; according to them, such statistics are one-sided and present western education as the sole indicator of education, which to them is not obligatory for individual Muslims.

However, for most Muslim women interviewed for this study, inasmuch as Islamic education is important, western education is much more important in the way modern Nigerian society is organized. They argue that it is this type of education that has brought several women to the limelight in the public sphere and given them respected status in the society. Women who are educated in both Islamic and western knowledge, and work in the public sphere, have achieved higher standards of living than their counterparts with only Islamic education. They are more self-actualized than other women who lack such comprehensive educational attainment. This fact makes a huge difference to the quality of life of these women. This is evident in some of their views on western and Islamic education. For them, they argue that the question of whether or not to choose between western or Islamic education does not arise.[42] The incorporation of both systems is more acceptable to these women and thus they cannot be satisfied with only religious education. This is also revealed in the form of education these educated women have prescribed for their daughters, that is, all the women informants in this study who have western education have given their daughters the opportunity to acquire both systems of education and, in some cases, they acquire only the western system. This is countervailing evidence to that of male informants who insist that Islamic education is enough for women.

For the non-educated women, inasmuch as Islamic education is important, they still want to be recognized in the wider society and the only way for them to achieve this is to acquire both forms of education as their legitimate right and desire. For this reason, women who could not continue with their education because of marriage are aspiring to go back to school, get educated and become like their female counterparts who are experts in various fields of endeavour.

Even male informants, who insist that Islamic education is enough for Muslim women, do not deny the importance of western education,

[42] This view was unanimously shared by all our female informants in five states of Northern Nigeria.

because women, with a combination of Islamic and western education work in the public sphere and they live a better standard of life. Many who do not have that opportunity envy those who have had it and crave a balanced education which is useful and relevant in present-day society. It is the plea and hope of women who do not have both Islamic and western education that their spouses, as well as society, will give them the opportunity to acquire this, for only then will they be able to become better wives and mothers to their husbands and children. Some insist that this is, perhaps, the only way open to them to produce a better society for the future.

CHAPTER SIX

'WE INTRODUCED *SHARĪʿA*'—THE IZALA MOVEMENT IN NIGERIA AS INITIATOR OF *SHARĪʿA*-REIMPLEMENTATION IN THE NORTH OF THE COUNTRY: SOME REFLECTIONS

Ramzi Ben Amara

Introduction[1]

During the Fourth Nigerian Republic (since 1999), no other topic has been discussed as all-pervasively as the case of the so-called re-implementation of *sharīʿa*. This topic has appeared in the media, in public discussions, and in academia[2] everywhere in the federation. Even in western countries, the *sharīʿa* re-implementation in Nigeria which was initiated by the governor of Zamfara State, Ahmad Sani Yeriman Bakura, is well-known. Many western reports have described the *sharīʿa* as inhuman and against human rights and in many cases it is confused with the Islamic criminal law. Many questions have been raised relating to *sharīʿa*, especially concerning its constitutionality, its effect on the relationship between Muslims and Christians,[3] on freedom of religion and on the democratic process in the West African country.

After the 'success' of the *sharīʿa*-reimplementation, many Muslims, both as individuals and as organizations or institutions (including Sufis

[1] This chapter is based on the preliminary findings of my research in Nigeria (December 2006–February 2007 and February–April 2008). I am grateful to the junior and senior scholars of the VW-*sharīʿa*-Project, to Prof. Danfulani, Prof. Gaiya and the staff of the Department of Religious Studies of the University of Jos, Prof. Fwatshak, to Dr. Ostien, to Mallam Dawood, Mallam Sani, Dr. Umar Adam, and to all my informants for their kind assistance in all directions. Many thanks to Maren Milligan for her comments and corrections of the first draft of this chapter.

[2] Two examples of such discussions in academia are the following conferences: 'The *sharīʿa* Debate and the Shaping of Muslim and Christian Identities in Northern Nigeria since 1999', 11th–12th July 2003, University of Bayreuth, Germany; and 'Comparative perspectives on Shari'ah in Nigeria', 15th–17th January, 2004, University of Jos, Nigeria. Scholars from different countries and disciplines presented their findings and discussed the *sharīʿa* from various perspectives. Of course, there are many other platforms in and outside Nigeria where *sharīʿa* was debated.

[3] On the *sharīʿa*-discussion between Muslims and Christians see Danfulani, Umar H. D., *The sharīʿa issue and Christian-Muslim relations in contemporary Africa*, Stockholm: Almqvist & Wiskel International, 2005.

and non-Sufis), identified themselves with the new *sharīʿa*-project.[4] One aspect of this identification is the question "who is the real initiator of *sharīʿa*' behind Ahmad Sani Yeriman Bakura?" The present chapter attempts to answer this question from the perspective of *The Jamaʾatu Izalatil Bidʿa Wa Ikamatis Sunnah* (JIBWIS) (Society for the Removal of Innovation and Reinstatement of Tradition)[5] known as Izala.

The Izala movement—also known under its Hausa acronym ʾYan Izala—was established as an anti-Sufi association appealing to Muslims to follow the 'right' path of Islam based on the Qurʾān, *sunna* (Arab.: traditions of the Prophet), and *as-salaf as-ṣāliḥ* (Arab.: pious predecessors). Its recent development shows a reorientation with a new agenda of 'no direct confrontation'. As there has been an absence (or decrease) in both verbal and physical violence between adherents of the Izala association and of the Sufi brotherhoods,[6] the conflict with the Sufis is not as strong as it was in the 1970s and mid-1980s. Instead, we presume that Izala abandoned one of its main doctrines, which was to fight the Sufis, and switched to peaceful co-existence.

After an overview of Izala's establishment, its main figures, goals and institutions, we will examine its relationship with the Sufis in the past and present. Finally, we will consider its involvement in the re-implementation of *sharīʿa* in Nigeria and the consequences for Izala.

Historical Context of the Establishment of Izala

The launching of the Izala association took place in Jos in 1978. This time is known as a period of turbulence and political instability in the West African country. Nigeria's transition[7] from a military regime to the Second

---

[4] With the exception of the *Ikhwān Brothers* headed by Ibrahim al-Zakzaky who refused the *sharīʿa*-project, all other groups accepted it. There are other Muslims or Muslim organizations that may have opposed the re-implementation, but they did not declare it openly.

[5] See Kane, Ousmane, *Muslim modernity in Postcolonial Nigeria. A Study of the Society for the Removal of Innovation and Reinstatement of Tradition*, Leiden: Brill, 2003; the Society is known in Nigeria by its abbreviated names *Yan Izala* or *Izala*; the abbreviation JIBWIS is also common.

[6] To use Kane's words (2003) a kind of 'domestication of the Izala' took place after a long period of struggle against Sufis and Sufism, pp. 207–26.

[7] For an overview of the political and social changes during the period from the independence of Nigeria in 1960, through the First Republic (1960–66), and the Military Government from 1970 to 1979, especially concerning the establishment of the different Islamic associations and the development of the *sharīʿa* question, see Marjomaa, Risto, 'The

Republic (1979–1983) was facilitated by the new constitution of 1979 which had been debated throughout the end of the 1970s. One of the issues debated at that time was the question of a Federal Sharīʿa Court of Appeal (FSCA).[8] When the Chairman of the Constituent Assembly declared the '*sharīʿa*-debate' as finished and there was even a suggestion to delete *Section 180 (1) C*—the so called *sharīʿa* paragraph—from the constitution, Muslim deputies left the Assembly on the 10th April 1978. General Olusegun Obasanjo, the then head of state, requested those who left the Constituent Assembly to come back and continue with the negotiations. After two weeks of boycott the Assembly proceeded with its work on April 24th 1978.[9] The new constitution was presented on 29th August 1978 to the president without the FSCA-section and was enacted on 1st October 1979. However, the new version § 240 (1) allows 'any state [of the federation] that requires it' to establish a *State Sharia Court of Appeal*.[10]

Such was the political climate into which Izala was born. At that time, the Muslim community saw the growing influence of Sheikh Abubakar Mahmud Gumi (1922–1992),[11] who repudiated the Sufi brotherhoods. Not only in his published articles in Hausa, but also in his *tafsīr*-sessions (Arab.: exegesis of the Qurʾān) on Radio Kaduna between 1970 and 1974, Gumi 'raised many emotions and [much] unrest in Northern Nigeria'.[12] His anti-*ṭarīqa* book *al-ʿaqīda aṣ-ṣaḥīḥa bi muwafaqāt ash-sharīʿa* (Arab.: The Right Belief in Accordance with *sharīʿa*) in 1972 initiated a 'war' against all *bidʿa* (Arab.; un Islamic innovation) and, as such, against many Tijāniyya and Qādiriyya practices. Sheikh Nasiru Kabara (1925–1996), the leading figure

Long struggle for the Shari'a in Northern Nigeria', *Studia Orientalia (Helsinki)* 103, 2006, pages 39–66.

[8] Latin, David, 'The Sharia Debate and the origins of Nigeria's Second Republic', *The Journal of Modern African Studies*, Vol. 20, No. 3, 1982, pages 411–430, page 411; Ostien, Phil, 'An opportunity missed by Nigerian Christians', in *Muslim Christian Encounters in Africa*, Soares, Benjamin, (ed.), Leiden: Brill, 2006, pages 234–243.

[9] Hock, Klaus, *Der Islam Komplex. Zur Christlichen Wahrnehmung des Islams und der christlich-islamischen Beziehungen in Nordnigeria während der Militärherrschaft Babangidas*, Hamburg: Lit Verlag, 1996, page 194; also Abun-Nasr, Jamil, 'Islamisches Recht im nigerianischen Rechtssystem', in *Muslime in Nigeria: Religion und Gesellschaft im politischen Wandel seit den 1950er Jahren*, Abun-Nasr, Jamil (ed.), Münster-Hamburg: Lit-Verlag, 1993, page 221.

[10] Ostien, 2006, p. 240.

[11] For a detailed account of Sheikh Gumi's life, education and political influence see Loimeier, Roman, *Islamic Reform and Political Change in Northern Nigeria*, Evanston-Illinois: Northwestern University Press, 1997, pages 148–171; also his autobiography: Sheikh Abubakar Gumi with Ismaila A. Tsiga, *Where I stand*, Ibadan: Spectrum Books Limited, 1992.

[12] Loimeier, 1997, page 163.

of the Qādiriyya in Nigeria—later he became the leader of the Qādiriyya for the whole of Africa[13]—answered with his publication *kitāb al-nāṣiḥa al-ṣaḥīḥa fi'l–radd 'alā al-'aqīda al-ṣaḥīḥa* (Arab.: The Frank Advice in Reply to '*al-Aqida as-Sahiha*') the same year. Among the Tijāniyya[14] came Sani Kafanga's (d. 1989) response '*al-Minaḥ al-ḥamīda fil-radd 'alā fāsid al-'aqīda*' (Arab.: The Praiseworthy Gifts in the Reply to the One Who is Corrupted in His Faith).[15]

Sheikh Gumi conceded that his book "had not been written for general reading"[16] and preferred at first not to make it available in Hausa-language because "it was premature to translate it at that time".[17] When his student Mallam Ismaila Idris (1937–2000), then a school teacher, preached in Kaduna's Sultan Bello Mosque quoting openly from Gumi's book and attacking Sufi-brotherhoods, a debate started in many parts of Nigeria on Islamic practices.[18] Going public with Gumi's ideas has had a heavy influence on the subsequent life of Ismaila Idris.

One important difference between Sheikh Abubakar Gumi and Sheikh Ismaila Idris was that the former, although fierce in his criticism, offered it indirectly and without naming individuals or groups, while the latter was quite outspoken:

> With the coming of Sheikh Ismaila Idris things changed. Sheikh Idris was a student of Sheikh Abubakar Gumi, but he [I. Idris] was more open to say: 'this is *ḥaram* (forbidden) and this is against the *sunna*, the one who do[es] that is a *kāfir* (unbeliever)'. This is the way how Sheikh Ismaila Idris came out, not like Sheikh Abubakar Gumi who was indirect.[19]

---

[13] Loimeier, Roman, 'The Writings of Nasiru Kabara (Muḥammad al-Nāṣir al-Kabarī)', *Sudanic Africa*, vol. 2, 1991, pages 165–174.

[14] For the history of the Tijāniyya see Abun-Nasr, Jamil M., *The Tijaniyya—a Sufi Order in the Modern World*, London: Oxford University Press, 1965.

[15] I took Loimeier's (1997) translations of the Arabic titles of the three books; Loimeier gives an analysis of Gumi's critique towards Sufism and the counter-arguments of Nasiru Kabara and Sani Kafanga, see pages 197–206; concerning the theology and the doctrinal background of Abubakar Gumi and Nasiru Kabara, see the comparative study of Brigaglia, Andrea, 'Two Published Hausa Translations of the Qur'ān and Their Doctrinal Background', *Journal of Religion in Africa*, 35 (4), 2005, pages 424–449.

[16] Gumi and Tsiga, 1992, page 145.

[17] Gumi and Tsiga, 1992, page 145.

[18] Gumi and Tsiga, 1992, pages 145–146; Gumi narrated that he was in Saudi Arabia during the controversy and when he came back to Kaduna, the controversy was still going on and Mallam Idris was forced to resign his job as a teacher, but continued to preach *al-'aqīda al-ṣaḥīḥa*.

[19] Interview in Arabic language with Sheikh Abdurrahman Lawal Adam, JNI *murshid* (adviser) and Ex-Izala member in his Office, Jos Central Mosque, 27th December 2006;

Sheikh Ismaila Idris: Founder and Architect of the JIBWIS[20]

Sheikh Ismaila Idris Ibn Zakariyya is the founding father of the Izala-Society in Jos. He was born in 1937 in a village called Goskorom in Plateau State. Ismaila Idris was taught by his father until the age of fifteen and then he moved to Bauchi where he received his education in Islamic Religion and Arabic Studies from a number of Mallams, among whom were Sheikh Magaji, Sheikh Kansurawa and the Imam of the Central mosque in Bauchi, Sheikh Mahmud Bello. (This kind of education is known as *Karatun Zaure.*) After teaching there himself, Ismaila Idris moved to Kano for a degree in Arabic Studies and came later to Bauchi where he worked in a primary school. Starting in 1969, Sheikh Ismaila Idris spent five years in Kaduna where he worked as *murshid* (Arab.: adviser, instructor) for the *Jamāʿat Naṣr al-Islām* (Arab.: Society for the Victory of Islam; JNI)[21] and preached against Sufi practices.[22] The provocative style of his speeches led to the withdrawal of his position and he moved to preaching in Kakurdi Prison Yard in Kaduna. Later on, he applied to the Nigerian Army, where he was appointed as an Imam after leaving the JNI in 1974.[23] While in the army, he continued to agitate. His preaching resulted in *wahala* (Hausa: problem) and he was transferred to Ibadan in 1974, where he only stayed three months and, after a problem with the Divisional Imam/Lt. Colonel on the issue of *zakāt* (Arab.: almsgiving), the Mallam was transferred to Kontagora.[24] In Kontagora, many people started moving to the Army Mosque to pray on Friday since the Imam of the Central Mosque was a Sufi. After yet another controversy about the preaching of Sheikh Ismaila Idris, he was again transferred to his last Army station: Jos. Sheikh Ismaila Idris was appointed as an Imam of the Division and continued with his harsh criticism of Sufi practices. Many people were attracted by the Sheikh and

---

see also Sani Umar, 'Sufism and Anti-Sufism in Nigeria', MA-thesis (unpublished), 1988, page 204.

20 The term 'architect' was adapted from M. Sani Umar's unpublished BA Thesis 'Islamic Revivalism Today: the case of Jama'atu Izalat Al-Bidah Wa-Iqamat Al-Sunna', Islamic Studies, University of Jos, 1983, page 48.

21 Founded in the early 1960s as an umbrella organization for all Muslims in Nigeria; it was an idea of Abubakar Gumi, realised by the Sardauna Ahmadu Bello (1910–1966) with sponsorship from Kuwait and Saudi Arabia. For more details see Loimeier, 1997, pages 135–148.

22 Alhassan, Idris Abdullahi, 'The role of the School of High Islamic Studies Sarkin Mangu Jos in advancing the spread of Islamic culture and Arabic language for the years 1989 to 2001', BA Thesis, Arabic Studies, University of Jos, 2003, pages 61–67, in Arabic.

23 Sani Umar, 1983, page 49.

24 Alhassan, 2003, page 50.

they attended his lectures and invited him to preach in the town. The Sufi Brotherhoods, on the other hand, complained about Sheikh Idris to the Ministry of Defence. Although he was supported by one Major Alhassan, Sheikh Idris was requested to stop his preaching. Because of his refusal, he was arrested several times and finally discharged from the Army in 1978.[25]

Sheikh Idris succeeded in attracting many people in Jos, especially from among the Tijāniyya followers,[26] and this success was the basis for establishing an organization. On 8th February 1978, the launch of *Jama'atu Izalatil Bid'a Wa Ikamatis Sunnah* (JIBWIS) took place in Jos, and numerous scholars from all over Nigeria were invited. Sheikh Gumi was invited, but as he could not attend personally, he sent a delegation in the person of Sheikh Lawal Abubakar who succeeded Gumi after his death.[27] The Society was formally set up on 25th May 1978 and on that occasion the first mass rally was held in the Stadium of Jos.[28] Most of the followers at this first stage were young people. Many of Gumi's students founded local branches in different parts of Northern Nigeria. The society also gave politicians the opportunity to 'engage themselves in religious organizations'.[29]

Sheikh Muhammad Sanusi Gumbi, Kaduna, saw the establishment of Izala as being the result of the long struggle between Abubakar Gumi and Sufi brotherhoods that had started during the 1960s and continued to the end of the 1970s. The absence of an institution or organization that protected Gumi was the reason for the establishment of Izala.[30] This point of view was confirmed by M. Sani Umar who identifies Muhammad Sanusi Gumbi as well as Sheik Ismaila Idris who:

> ... soon after the ill-fated debate, the close disciples of Gumi began to realise the imperative need for a new mode of operation in the campaign against Sufism.[31]

---

[25] Alhassan, 2003, pages 51–54.

[26] According to Loimeier 1997, in Plateau State the *Tijāniyya* was stronger than the *Qādiriyya*, see page 213.

[27] Sheikh Muhammad Lawal Abubakar and Sheikh Ibrahim Arab represented Abubakar Gumi who added *Wa Ikamatis Sunnah* to the name of the Society; interview in Arabic with Ustadh Nasir Abdulmuhyi, director of the Diploma Section at the School of Islamic Studies, Sarkin Mangu, Jos, 5th December 2006 in his office.

[28] Loimeier, 1997, page 214. Many Izala followers mentioned during my fieldwork (February 2008) that the launching day of the Society in Jos took place on Sunday, 12th March 1978.

[29] Loimeier, 1997, page 214.

[30] Personal Interview with Sheikh Sanusi Gumbi, Kaduna, 17th January 2007.

[31] Umar, 1988, page 198.

The Doctrine of Izala

Loimeier observes that through the establishment of Izala, Gumi's plan to establish a mass-movement was put into practice. He had failed as an individual, according to Loimeier, to realise his program of *tajdīd* (Arab.: revival, reformation) in the JNI which is dominated by Sufis, although he was financially supported by Saudi-Arabia. Since the death of the Sardauna of Sokoto Ahmadu Bello in 1966, Gumi had lost political support and his prestige as Grand Qadi (1962–1975) of Nigeria had been affected. Gumi's strategy was to change from a 'struggle between the *malamai* [leaders, intellectuals] to a struggle at grassroots level'.[32]

Sheikh Gumi himself presented eight points summarising the main objectives of Izala. Essentially the society promotes Islam on the basis of the Qur'ān and the *sunna*, it reminds Muslims about their duties to Allāh, denies any revelation after the death of the Prophet and rejects any opinion claiming that the Prophet left something secret that will be revealed after centuries. The teaching of the society insists that the Prophetic mission has been accomplished in the Qur'ān, refuses any idea that someone can communicate with the Prophet or that the Prophet visited him physically, it contradicts any addition to the five basic pillars of Islam, promotes a better relationship and understanding among Muslims and insists that it is 'determined to guard these principles at all costs without any options for compromise'.[33]

Sheikh Sani Yahaya Jingre, the current leader of the Izala in Jos and disciple of Sheikh Ismaila Idris, recapitulates the programme of the founder of the JIBWIS as follows:

> He addressed his preaching first to soldiers and after that he invited common people to the oneness of Allah (Arab.: *tawhīd*) following the path of pious predecessors (Arab.: *al-salaf al-ṣāliḥ*).[34]

The dissemination of Idris' doctrine was facilitated by the distribution of tape recordings of his preaching all over the country. In addition to that, the mobility of the Society in organizing preaching sessions everywhere led to its expansion. The Izala introduced the so-called *wazin kasa* (Hausa: Preaching across the whole State). Sani Umar counted about seven hundred preaching-sessions held in the country at national level between the

32 Loimeier, 1997, page 208.

33 Gumi and Tsiga, 1992, pages 156–157.

34 Personal interview in Arabic with Sheikh Sani Yahaya Jingre, his office at the Izala Headquarters, Jos, 28th February 2007.

launching of the Society, in 1978, and 1988. Concerning the local context, he was not able to give an exact number.[35] This powerful combination led to the Izala's expansion. This strategy is the same today and Izala preachers travel to the furthest places in Nigeria and outside the country.

The main aim of the Izala is a 'purification' of Islam from any additional constituents that are not mentioned in the Qur'ān or sanctioned by the Prophet or by one of his successors. The *bid'a* (Arab.: innovation)-repudiated practices include: *mawlid*, celebrating of the Prophet's birthday; *ṣalāt al-fātiḥ* Tijāniyya, a special prayer that according to the Tijāniyya sufi-brotherhood is supposedly 6000 times better than reciting the Qur'ān; *dhikr*, congregational remembering, a Sufi custom; and many more:

> Ismaila Idris as well criticised the *ṣadaqa* (Arab.: voluntary alms) practised by Sufis after someone's death. He rejected the so called *ṣadaqat al yawm al-thālith* (Arab.: alms of the third day). Furthermore, Mallam Idris criticised the Sufi-habit that when someone dies, they come and supplicate Allāh for him in congregation and do the same thing after seven, then forty days from the death. Moreover, having the so called *lāzim* (Arab.: binding, obligatory custom) practised especially by the Tijāniyya and which means that someone obliges himself to do it every day [a] hundred or thousand times (praising the Prophet for [example]). Also visiting tombs of a known saint and ask for assistance was also refused by Sheikh Idris. Seeking the *baraka* (Arab.: benediction, blessing) by a Sheikh and practising *khalwa* (Arab.: isolation; being alone with God) for a particular time were also confronted.[36]

Furthermore, the Izala confirms that only Allāh knows the *ghaib* (Arab.: the hidden), nobody except the Prophet himself can perform miracles, all Muslims are equal, Sufism is a form of *shirk* (Arab.: polytheism), seeing Allāh in dreams or visions is impossible.[37]

The argument of Izala is that any addition to the religion of Islam is not allowed. Certainly, the doors of *'ilm* (Arab.: knowledge) and *ijtihād* (Arab.: effort of interpretation of existing rules) are open but should rely on proof. Apart from the Qur'ān and the tradition of the Prophet, which both constitute the basic source of Izala doctrine, there are other important sources used by Izala. Ousmane Kane points out that Izala used *kitāb al-tawḥīd* (Arab.: Treatise of the Oneness of God) by Muḥammad b. 'Abd al-Wahhāb (1703–1792) as an important source of its theology but also

---

35 Umar, 1988, page 202.
36 Interview with Abdurrahman Lawal Adam, Jos, 27th December 2006.
37 Loimeier, 1997, pages 230–231.

several other commentaries of that same work.[38] 'Abd al-Wahhāb is the founding father of the state doctrine of modern Saudi Arabia. It is based on a historical alliance between his religious authority and the political power represented by Ibn Sa'ūd (d. 1765). Theologically the oneness of God is emphasized and the condemnation of Sufism with its veneration of saints and visitation of shrines and tombs excludes mediators between the believer and God. Kane sees this theology as a source of justification of the Izala:

> The two concepts—associationism (*shirk*) and proclaiming others as unbelievers (*takfīr*)—provided the Izala religious entrepreneurs and their sympathizers a religious justification of the traditional order by which they felt oppressed.[39]

The writings of Ibn 'Abd al-Wahhāb are not the only source of the Izala doctrine. The Society also relies on other books such as those of Ibn al-Qayyim, Ibn Kathīr, Ibn Taymiyya, Ibn Abī Zayd al-Qayrawānī and many other writings of the scholars of *sunna*. The Izala follows the path of the mālikī school of law—as explained by Alhaji Adamu Girbo Muhammad, an Izala leader in Gombe. He added that "Izala is not *wahhābiyya* because the Society doesn't call for revolution in Islam, but to *shūra'* (Arab.: council)—unlike the *wahhābiyya* that revolted against the Saudi State. Some *wahhābis* rely on the ḥanbalī school of law and deny the others. The Izala follows the mālikī school of law".[40]

In order to realise its objectives and goals the Izala established a structure that would facilitate its work. In the following, an idea about this structure and the bodies of the Society will be given. Here of special significance are any changes that have happened since the establishment until today.

---

[38] Kane, 2003, pages 123–124.

[39] Kane, 2003, page 125.

[40] Interview with Alhaji Adamu Girbo Muhammad, Gombe, 20th February 2008; the connotation "Wahhabiyya" was given to the sympathizers of Ibn 'Abd al-Wahhāb's teachings. The movement is puritan and the oneness of God (*tawhīd*) belongs to its central doctrines. In the mid-18th century and the Wahhabi State in Saudi Arabia, the Wahhabiyya proclaimed *jihād* against all opponents of its understanding of *tawhīd*. For more details on that movement see Algar, Hamid, *Wahhabism: A critical Essay*. Oneonta, New York: Islamic Publications International, 2002.

The Structure and Institutions of Izala-society

The Izala's formal institution did not take place until 1978. Until its registration on 11th December 1985, the Society remained under the umbrella of the JNI. The reason for this delay was that the Ministry of Internal Affairs did not immediately approve the Izala. According to the law, any Society that needs this approval should be advertised in national newspapers and this was done by the Izala. After that, time is allowed by the Ministry for any objection. Thousands of letters were written opposing the registration of the Izala. It became official seven years after its launch through an Izala member, Saidu Badawa, who was formal Permanent Secretary at the Ministry of International Affairs in the administration of President Babangida (1985–1993).[41]

Before the official registration of the JIBWIS, no clear structure can be identified. There were two bodies/committees dealing with administrative and religious affairs respectively. Alhaji Musa Muhammad Mai Gandu led the *Council of Administration*, also called 'political leaders of the movement'. We find here an office of chairman, a secretary, and treasurer. His most important duties were to provide for permissions to preach and to organize the preachers' tours (transport, etc.). Sheikh Ismaila Idris himself chaired the *Council of Ulama* or 'Preacher's Committee' which was essentially a *majlis* (Arab.: council, committee) of religious scholars.

Eventually, a third body came into being: the so-called *Aid Groups*. The Society recognised the necessity of having people to prepare the preaching sessions (microphones, place of preaching etc.). Voluntary youths could undertake the task that had been done by JNI aid groups before. The problem was that among the JNI there were anti-Izala people and also Sufis. The idea was considered and finally the Society decided to institute its own groups.[42] The first principal of the aid group was the late Alhaji Shehu.[43]

---

[41] Interview with Mallam Sani Mudibbo, who took several positions in the Izala administration until 1987, his office in Jos, 28th February 2007; my interviewee confesses that not only Sufis opposed the registration, but also other individuals and even non-Muslims.

[42] Interview with Mallam Sani Mudibbo, Jos, 28th February 2007.

[43] Interview with Abdurrahman Lawal Adam, Jos, 27th December 2006; according to Alhaji Isa Waziri who is now the National Director of First Aid Groups (Izala Jos) since 1984, his predecessor was Muhammad Rabiu Bukur; interview with him on 20th February 2008 in Gombe.

As confirmed by several Izala leaders, the structure of the Izala today remains the same. In a booklet written in Arabic, Hausa and English, published by the headquarters of the JIBWIS in Jos,[44] the structure is described as consisting of the above mentioned three councils that, although having different duties, share the same objectives:

> The teaching and practice of Islam as strictly provided by the Qurʾān and the tradition of the Prophet Muhammad (S.A.W.) through public preaching and teachings by organizing yearly seminars, symposium, lectures, vocation, courses, write ups and the like.[45]

The later split of the Izala at the level of leadership led to a division of the institutions (schools, mosques, hospitals, etc.). The constitution and the threefold structure (local, state, national level) were kept. At each of these levels the three-council system still exists (*ʿulamāʾ*, administration and first aid groups). During my fieldwork in February 2008 I found out that the constitution had been amended in 2004 by the Jos faction. There is also a version introduced by the Kaduna faction of Izala in the mid-1990s. Both versions are not officially recognized.

Since its inception, the Izala's concern was to establish institutions that would propagate its message. An important component therefore was education. The construction of mosques is also crucial to the Izala. In order to work efficiently, a committee was created for each sector that the Izala got involved with: education, finances, health, preaching, personal and discipline, and elders' committee.[46] The JIBWIS runs schools from nursery to diploma level. There are regular primary and secondary schools, schools for Islamic Studies both for junior and senior students, schools for Qurʾānic recitation, and several other types. The duration of attendance varies between three and six years and examinations are controlled either by the Izala itself, by the Ministry of Education or by the Institute of Education ABU Zaria.[47]

---

[44] When I talk about the Society, I mean the Izala as a whole before the division in the mid-1980s and after that time I refer mainly to the Izala Jos; I am grateful to the actual head of the *Council of Ulama* and Izala-Jos leader Sheikh Sani Yahaya Jingir for providing me with a copy of this publication: JIBWIS-Headquarters-Jos-Nigeria *al-Jamāc fī Suṭūr* (the Society in a few sentences), JIBWIS-Headquarters-Jos-Nigeria, nd, (in Arabic).

[45] JIBWIS, nd, page 53.

[46] JIBWIS, nd, pages 53–56.

[47] JIBWIS, nd, pages 63–64.

To give an idea about the Izala institutions, in the year 2000 the society stated that every Local Government in Nigeria that has Izala followers should have at least two Primary Schools, one Arabic School, and one Western education school. Also every state of the federation should have at least one *taḥfīẓ* school (Arab.: memorisation school), one Secondary School and one Higher Islamic Studies School.[48] Currently, the headquarters of Izala Jos is in charge of an Advanced Diploma and Islamic Studies School in Jos, eighteen schools for Higher Islamic Studies in eight different states of the North, four Schools of Higher Islamic Studies (secondary level) in Plateau, Taraba and Gombe states, ninety-seven Saturday and Sunday Schools, fifty-two *Tahfizul Qur'ān Schools*, and four *Mu'assasa Qur'ānic Schools*.[49] In addition to that, the Izala A[50] established branches (of schools) in neighbouring countries like Ghana, Chad, Cameroon, Niger, and even in Sudan Republic. The Izala in Kaduna seems to run only a few schools, although no statistics were available at the time the research was being carried out.

One goal of the Izala strategy is the education of women and especially of married women. During my stay in Nigeria I was able to attend the School for Higher Islamic Studies, Sarkin Mangu, Jos and observed several classes teaching women. This philosophy is at the basis of the esteem in which the Izala is held all over Nigeria—as is proudly mentioned. Members of Izala are asked to ensure education of their wives. Learning material such as cassettes/books is provided by preachers of the Society in order to facilitate this undertaking and fill this gap.[51]

Mosques are as important as schools and the Izala is keen to establish new ones everywhere. The Society either constructs them by means of donations or people build mosques and then endow them to the Izala. A committee that arranges the selection of Imams, *mu'adhdhin* (Arab.: official of a mosque who summons the faithful to prayer), and appoints caretakers oversees the mosques. Mosques are not solely places for prayers, but also for preaching and educating people about their religion. Preaching is also hierarchical in the Society and starts from the District, to the local, then the State, to the national and, forth-coming, to attending the international level.[52]

48 JIBWIS, nd, page 64.
49 JIBWIS, nd, pages 65–67.
50 Izala A can be identified as a break away group from the original Izala.
51 JIBWIS, Izala Constitution, Section. 6, part. 2 §8a, nd.
52 JIBWIS, nd, page 61.

The Division of the Izala and Attempts of Reconciliation

There are a number of explanations accounting for the Izala's split into two major groups. While the Izala in Jos recognises problems of leadership, the influence of foreign ideas, the intervention of politicians and, finally, the passivity of Sheikh Ismaila, as his opponents argue, to gain support from Muslim countries, the Izala in Kaduna highlights the person of Sheikh Idris and his severe character, monetary issues and his selflessness as the reasons for the division. Although the two major Izala factions are Izala Jos and Izala Kaduna, I identified a third category: those who left the Izala and see themselves as neutral. They are not organized in any group and act individually.

To show the different perspectives on the split we will examine the explanations offered by Kaduna and Jos representatives, and by a former Izala member.

Sheikh Alhassan Said from Jos, who was initially the *ḥāfiẓ* (Arab.: reciter of the Qurʾān) of Sheikh Ismaila Idris, and who is now affiliated with the Kaduna faction of the Izala, identified the years 1985–87 as the first period of division. The year 1989 is the time in which the crisis in the Society reached its peak. In the beginning, according to Sheikh Said, the Society had been based on nothing but the Qurʾān and the *sunna*, along with the traditions of pious predecessors. After that, leaders were attached to this life and dealt with money, so that followers of the Society doubted its authority. Also, Sheikh Ismaila Idris had a harsh character and sometimes went so far as to call members of Izala *juhhāl* (Arab.: ignorant). Members started talking about him. Committees against him were organized and Sheikh Ismaila Idris was asked to reduce his duty to being a normal preacher. The other faction established their *daʿwa* (Arab.: invitation, mission) in 1992 in Kaduna. Sheikh Alhassan Said was not involved in the debate at that time and preferred to stay neutral. According to him the division happened at that time because of leadership, the personality of Sheikh Idris and his impatience.[53]

The current leader of the Izala Jos, Sheikh Sani Yahaya Jingir, sees the influence of some members of the movement by Shiite ideas as one reason for the division of the Society:

53 Interview with Sheikh Alhassan Said, Jos, 12th December 2006.

> The involvement of some preachers in political affairs caused further dispute. Furthermore the members who broke away blamed Sheikh Idris' inflexibility and passivity to look for assistance from Islamic countries. In addition to that they blame the Sheikh of embezzling the Society's money, which is not true. They held 25 meetings to show people the reasons of their division and any possibility of solving the issue was in vain.[54]

Mallam Sani Mudibbo, who held several positions in the Izala from its establishment until the mid-1980s, observes that one issue in the Society was that Sheikh Idris considered the *Council of Ulama* as being higher than any other body. To him the *ʿulamāʾ* were more important than any other executive. There was also a discussion in the Society concerning donations, as to whether they were addressed to Sheikh Idris or to the Society as a whole. Another issue was over the executive's decision that whoever committed a mistake and broke the rule of the Society should be punished. When they suggested that Sheikh Idris should also be punished, then he was able to mobilize his followers in the Society, which became divided into those who supported Sheikh Idris and those who were against him.[55]

In summary, leadership and power struggles, money, involvement with politics, and the personality of Sheikh Idris were causes for the division. My impression is that the division is still there, since the Jos faction continues to protect Sheikh Idris and his leadership, in contradistinction to those who split away and preferred either to join the Kaduna faction of Izala or to leave the Society.

There were several attempts to reconcile the factions. When Sheikh Abubakar Gumi was alive, there was an effort of reconciliation, but without success. During Babangida's rule (1985–1993), General Mamman tried to bring the Izala factions together, but failed. In 2005, Dr. Ahmad Gumi, Sheikh Abubakar Gumi's son, who lives in Saudi Arabia, came to Nigeria and invited Izala to unite, but was not successful.[56] Recently, an attempt at reconciliation was begun by the *jamāʿat ahl al-sunna fī gharb ifrīqiyya* (Society of *Ahl al-Sunna* in West Africa), a young Association from Ghana.

---

[54] Interview with Sheikh Sani Yahya Jingre, his office at the Izala headquarter, Jos, 28th February 2007.

[55] Interview with Malam Sani Muddibbo in his office, University of Jos, 28th February 2007.

[56] Interview with Sheikh Sanusi Gumbi, Kaduna, 17th January 2007.

They contacted the current leaders in 2006 to mediate between them, but they also failed.[57]

The Relationship between Izala and Sufis Past and Present

In a nutshell, the relationship between Izala and Sufis was characterised by a theological dispute on key doctrines and a struggle for hegemony in the Nigerian Muslim community. This conflict has to be seen in the light of the immense political, economic and social changes in post-Independence Nigeria.

The relationship between Izala and Sufis in Nigeria has been extensively studied by several scholars, notably Loimeier (1993 & 1997), Umar (1983 & 1988) and Kane (2003). A number of dissertations and theses have been written in the departments of Islamic, Arabic or Religious Studies in Nigeria that deal with the Izala and its relationship to the Tijāniyya and Qādiriyya brotherhoods.[58] In fact, looking back in history, we observe a long-standing conflict among the Sufis. Loimeier describes how the Tijāniyya and Qādiriyya struggled for hegemony, especially during the 1950/60s because of a religious, economic and political concurrence between the two.[59] This situation changed dramatically at the beginning of the 1970s when the Sufis joined forces to fight against Abubakar Gumi. Since 1978, the opposing parties have been Sufis vs. Izala. Without going into detail on the doctrinal differences (see above) I want to give an idea about the beginning of the conflict and then compare it to the present situation as seen by the leaders of both Sufis and Izala.

The situation between Izala and Sufis was aggravated when Abubakar Gumi, whilst preaching in the Sultan Bello Mosque, declared that every person who recited *ṣalāt al-fātiḥ* Tijāniyya (a *tijānī* prayer) was an unbeliever and could be killed. He added that any marriage to such a person was invalid until this person abandoned his affiliation with the Tijāniyya. In reaction to Gumi, seventy Sufi scholars published a manifesto in which they sharply criticised Gumi. They accused him of practising arbitrary *tafsīr* (Arab.: exegesis), endangering the peaceful coexistence between Muslims

---

[57] Interview with Sheikh Dalha Abubakar Abdallah, leader of Izala in Lagos, Agege, 18th February 2007.

[58] During my fieldwork in Nigeria, I collected several B.A. and M.A. dissertations, and PhD theses at the Department of Religious Studies of the University of Jos and Bayero University, Kano.

[59] Loimeier, 1993, pages 129–137.

and non-Muslims, monopolising the media, and falsifying *ḥadīths*. The two Sufi brotherhoods invited Gumi to a public debate and suggested a list of forty-two possible subjects for the discussion. In 1978, a common initiative of Tijāniyya and Qādiriyya met in Illorin and subsequently published a document explaining their position. They also pointed at Gumi's contacts with Saudi Arabia. Instead of triggering friction within the Muslim community they suggested that the Izala had better concentrate on the debate with the Christians. According to the Sufis, the Izala followers had lost their faith due to Western education.[60]

According to Loimeier, after 1978, the attacks on the Izala were limited to the more powerful Tijāniyya. Only once, in 1987, did the Izala criticise the Qādiriyya explicitly, when referring to a work by ʿAbd al-Qādir al-Jilānī (founder of the Qādiriyya, d. 1166) in which he claims to have seen God. Nasiru Kabara (1925–1996), then leader of the Qādiriyya, answered that any person who insults ʿAbd al-Qādir al-Jilānī attacked the Prophet himself. He explained that the Sufi idiom which is not easily accessible could be the cause of misunderstanding.[61]

The conflict between Izala and Sufis did not remain simply verbal but extended sometimes to an intra-Muslim conflict and, from 1978 to 1980, the physical violence escalated. Following these events, the Izala concentrated on educational activities and the conflict subsided throughout the 1980s, turning into a clash between Muslims and Christians.[62] Interestingly, more internal problems surfaced in the Izala at the same time, eventually leading to their division (see above).

Today the situation differs radically from the past decades. In conversation, Izala and Sufi leaders still speak of doctrinal differences but the conflict is reduced. Several factors explain the change. Firstly, the death of almost all the main antagonists: Sheikh Gumi and Sheikh Idris on the Izala side and Sheikh N. Kabara on *ṭarīqa* side. Secondly, the division of the Izala movement and its 'domestication'.[63] Thirdly, the emergence of a conflict between Muslims and Christians which resulted in a new union within the 'house of Islam'. When the *sharīʿa* debate started in 1999, most Muslims in Nigeria saw the need for unity against what they perceived as a common 'enemy': that is all *sharīʿa* opponents, especially Christians, who heavily opposed the *sharīʿa* project.

---

60 Loimeier, 1993, pages 152–154.
61 Loimeier, 1993, pages 156–157.
62 Loimeier, 1993, pages 216–221.
63 Kane, 2003, pages 207–297.

What is the Izala perspective on the re-implementation of *sharīʿa*? Did they contribute to the project? How do they view their role in retrospect?

The *Sharīʿa* Re-Implementation: Izala as Initiator?

The first to implement Sharia Penal Code was Zamfara State, in January 2000. Ahmad Sani Yeriman Bakura was the governor who initially passed the *sharīʿa* law that he had promised during his election campaign in 1999. Speculation about his motives are widespread. Some claimed this measure was pure propaganda and others took advantage of this unique opportunity to promote Islamic law in the North of the federation:

> What . . . at first glance looked like the clever gambit of a single governor . . . to gain popular support and to secure his own political survival developed into a chain reaction throughout the predominantly Muslim-inhabited northern states of Nigeria.[64]

Eleven other northern states followed Zamfara's model and also introduced *sharīʿa* Penal Codes.[65] The new *sharīʿa* law does not only change matters of jurisdiction but also involves certain social and moral values. Societal control increased and several programmes for purifying Muslims from social vices, such as drinking alcohol and sexual impropriety, have been introduced. There were campaigns to fight against prostitution and gambling. In public the segregation between male and female Muslims should be respected. During my stay in Nigeria, several people whom I talked to assured me of this aspect of change, although they confessed that it has been minimal. The *sharīʿa* was welcomed and seen as a solution to the problems of the country.

It appears that most Muslim groups openly welcomed the *sharīʿa* re-implementation, apart from the Shiites, under the leadership of Ibraheem al-Zakzaky.[66] Al-Zakzaky and his group—known as Muslim Brothers and called Yan Shiʿa (Shiite people) by the majority of Muslims—opposed

---

[64] Kogelmann, Franz, 'The "Sharia factor" in Nigeria's 2003 Elections', in Soares, Benjamin F. (ed.): *Muslim-Christian Encounters in Africa*, Leiden: Brill, 2006, pages 257–258.

[65] For further information on the process of reimplementation of *sharīʿa* see, Peters, Ruud, *Islamic Criminal Law in Nigeria*, Ibadan: Spectrum Books Limited, 2003; these states are Sokoto, Niger, Kebbi, Bauchi, Borno, Katsina, Kano, Gombe, Jigawa, Kaduna and Yobe.

[66] See Suleiman, G. Ibrahim, 'Mallam Ibrahim El-Zakzaky and the Question of Shiʿism', B.A. Dissertation in Islamic Studies, University of Jos, 2005.

the reimplementation. The movement of al-Zakzaky is influenced by the Iranian revolution of 1979. This influence developed to a full Shiite orientation. The movement calls itself "The Islamic Movement". The rise of Shiite doctrine originated in Nigeria's social, economic and political challenges during the colonial era and especially throughout the post-independence period.[67] Inspired by the success of the Revolution in Iran, and as a result of the turmoil of Nigeria in many directions, Sheikh Ibraheem al-Zakzaky started introducing Shiite ideas to the West African country. Sheikh al-Zakzaky was born in Zaria in 1950 and has studied at Ahmadu Bello University in the same city. He was among the active members of the Muslim Students Society (MSS) before he broke with it. He was among the students who demonstrated against the state. He visited Iran in the 1980s and came back to recruit new members of his "Islamic Movement". He regards Islam as a solution to the country's problems and propagated these ideas through lectures and public gatherings in Northern Nigeria. He opposed the nation-state with all its symbols and defined it as a *ṭāghūt* (Arab.: symbol of idolatry, evil). In many cases, demonstrations by al-Zakzaky's followers turned to violent contest with the police. al-Zakzaky himself was imprisoned several times because of his ideas and opposition to the federal state.[68]

In a lecture given at Bayero University, Kano in December 1999, al-Zakzaky tried to clarify his position towards *sharīʿa*. After defining the word '*sharīʿa*,' he classified Islamic countries applying *sharīʿa* into three major categories:

1. Traditional ones that applied the *sharīʿa* for a long time and that were hardly colonised by western colonialists.
2. Countries that applied *sharīʿa* partially: these countries have been colonised and after independence they started practising a 'post-colonial system of democracy'.
3. Finally, countries where the *sharīʿa* is total and where an Islamic revolution took place.[69]

[67] Suleiman, 2005, pages 5–8.

[68] Suleiman, 2005, pages 8–10.

[69] al-Zakzaky, Ibraheem, 'Application of Shari'ah in the contemporary world: Lessons from some Muslim countries', a Paper presented to the national Conference on the Application of Shari'ah organized by the Department of Islamic Law, Faculty of Law, Bayero University and RAMNAN Law Consult, Kano, Bayero University, 1st to 3rd December 1999, page 8.

After giving the examples of Pakistan, Sudan and finally of Iran, al-Zakzaky came to the conclusion that *sharīʿa* was successful only in Iran because it is under an Islamic state. He sees the success of a full *sharīʿa* implementation only within a system of government which is 'purely Islamic'. Concerning Nigeria, al-Zakzaky predicts two conflicts when the *sharīʿa* is applied:

> One conflict will be with the constitution which will claim superiority over the Shariʿah and will, therefore, place the Shariʿah under its control and regulations. The Other conflict will be with the Shariʿah itself which, as the Law of Almighty God, claims superiority over all laws and therefore cannot accept the supremacy of the Nigerian constitution.[70]

Al-Zakzaky concludes by saying that the application of *sharīʿa* under a government system which is not Islamic will subject it (*sharīʿa*) to 'restrictions, manipulations and possible abuse'.[71]

Unlike al-Zakzaky, the Izala movement was one of the groups that demonstrated its support of *sharīʿa* re-implementation. This is not surprising since the project conforms to the Izala doctrine of calling people back to Islam and islamisation of the society. This is obvious in its concern with Islamic education and *daʿwa*, and with the Qurʾān and *sunna*. The Izala also encourages women to wear *ḥijāb*. The Izala criticises social injustices and opposes corruption. But are they the initiators of the *sharīʿa*-Re-implementation project?

Ustadh Nasir Abdelmuhyi, director of the School of Higher Islamic Studies, Izala headquarters in Jos, claimed that:

> The Society was among the first who called for the implementation of *sharīʿa* and thank God, the Governor of Zamfara, was the first who listened to the call of Izala and practiced *sharīʿa*. This is one of the good things done by the *Jamāʿa* [Izala].[72]

Sheikh Dalha Abubakar, the Izala leader in Lagos State added that the *sharīʿa* in Nigeria was re-implemented so fast because of Izala. The sheikhs were preaching and doing *daʿwa* in Zamfara after an invitation from Ahmad Sani Yeriman Bakura, who was not yet governor but campaigning. On this occasion he gave a lecture saying:

---

[70] al-Zakzaky, 1999, page 13.
[71] al-Zakzaky, 1999, page 15.
[72] Interview with Ustadh Nasir Abdulmuhyi, Jos, 5th December 2006 in his office.

> I promise you—my Society; our Society—that if you elect me as governor, then I will implement the Islamic *sharīʿa*. I will do that because this Society taught and linked us to what is useful for us and through it we understood that the religion is Islam and *sharīʿa* is the best thing in life that a human being can reach. *sharīʿa* is the way of satisfaction of Allah. If you elect me now as Zamfara Governor, I will apply *sharīʿa*![73]

After he had been elected as governor of Zamfara State, Sheikh Ismaila Idris reminded him about his promise in a letter:

> I thank Allah for you, but I want to remind you that you promised Allah to apply his *sharīʿa* and since you have the opportunity to do it, then hurry up. It is a wealth that should not be delayed.[74]

Ismaila Idris also requested all Izala leaders to support Ahmad Sani at this crucial time: "Go to him, support his project, assist him with what you can, and tell him that you are on his side. I am also with you!"[75]

A number of Izala leaders claim to be behind Sani's *sharīʿa* project. It is impossible to prove such a statement, as many Muslims in Nigeria saw the *sharīʿa* project as being supported by the majority of Muslims in the country and not only the Izala. The leader of *Jamāʿat Tajdīd al-Islām* 'Society of Revival of Islam' (JTI), Sheikh Abubakar Mujahid, pointed out that the re-implementation of *sharīʿa* in Nigeria was achieved through the contribution of many groups: Izala, Sufis, JTI and others:

> ... the tariqa and Izala played the role of sensitizing people. People of the Umma did the legal aspect, and JTI tried to find answers to the issues like corruption; the Zakat of course it was in our (task) and look how to collect Zakat.[76]

Sani Mudibbo, former Izala National secretary, confirms that implementing *sharīʿa* or transforming Nigeria into an Islamic state was not the initial agenda of the Izala. Instead, the movement was determined to fight *bidʿa* and Sufism more than any other thing.

This point of view is backed up by O'Brien in her article on *sharīʿa* in Nigeria. She writes that the Izala was neither the first group that called people to apply Islamic Law nor the one that monopolised its application:

73 Interview with Dalha Abubakar Abdallah, Lagos, 18th February 2007.
74 Interview with Dalha Abubakar Abdallah, Lagos, 18th February 2007.
75 Interview with Dalha Abubakar Abdallah, Lagos, 18th February 2007.
76 Interview with Sheikh Abubakar Mujahid, Zaria, 5th January 2007.

> Les réformistes d'inspiration wahhabite connu sous le nom d'Izala et leurs nombreuses branches, dont certaines reçoivent des financements Saoudiens, n'ont pas été les premiers a réclamer la charia, pas plus qu'ils n'ont monopolisé son application, au profit des principales confréries soufis, la Qadiriyya et la Tijaniyya.[77]

Sharīʿa is not simply the result of an anti-Sufi reform. Rather the Izala adapted several times to the political conditions. Therefore O'Brien sees Izala as 'reformist' but not as 'islamist revolutionist'.[78]

Conclusion

The objective of this chapter was to situate the Izala within the project of re-implementing *sharīʿa* in Northern Nigeria and to examine whether or not the movement initiated the project. The re-implementation of *sharīʿa*, although initiated as part of a political campaign, was seen as a solution to the problems of Nigerian Muslims. The whole project offered Izala a unique opportunity to confirm its own doctrine of establishing the *sunna* and Islamising society. *Sharīʿa* and Izala can go side by side and the movement that concentrated for decades on education and fighting *bidʿa* became an active member of the project of the *umma*. In fact, opposing *sharīʿa* means opposing Islam and that can be related to social isolation. *Sharīʿa* was an identity marker of Muslims in northern Nigeria. It was seen as a chance to undo years of repression of Islamic law. *Sharīʿa* was related to change and the reform of society. *Sharīʿa* became a unifying issue despite the heterogeneity of the Nigerian society and existence of other religious groups in the *sharīʿa* states.

Izala understood the rules of the game. Since the conflict with the Sufis had ceased and the Izala was divided and 'domesticated', the movement was threatened with passing into oblivion. The hypothesis is that Izala changed its strategy and supported the re-implementation of *sharīʿa*. One set of Izala leaders insist that the movement initiated Islamic law; on the other hand many voices disagree with this statement, so the supposition is difficult to prove. What can be said is that the resurgence of the Izala in the public sphere conspicuously occurred at the same time as the re-implementation of *sharīʿa* in Nigeria.

---

[77] O'Brien, Susan M. 'La Charia contestée: Démocratie, débat et diversité musulmane dans les 'état Charia' du Nigeria', *Politique Africaine* 106, 2007, page 48.

[78] O'Brien, 2007, page 52.

PART THREE

KENYA: "PLACE OF *SHARĪ'A* IN THE CONSTITUTION"

Map 5 Map of Kenya: Showing principal places referred to in Part Three

CHAPTER SEVEN

DEBATES ON KADHI'S COURTS AND CHRISTIAN-MUSLIM RELATIONS IN ISIOLO TOWN: THEMATIC ISSUES AND EMERGENT TRENDS

Halkano Abdi Wario

Introduction

Since 1992, Kenya has been characterised by demands for new constitutional dispensations. It has also seen heightened competing interests emerge in which religion and politicised ethnicity have played a pivotal role in the political game of the day. The same scenario has been replicated at a grass roots level. Elsewhere, as in the Kenyan case, the increased calls for recognition and empowerment of courts applying aspects of *sharīʿa* almost instantly elicit strong negative responses from Christian communities. One of the contentious issues in the referendum on a draft constitution was the issue of Kadhi's courts. Should they be empowered, or left to stay as in the current Constitution? The resultant debates are the concern of this chapter. The findings of the research have strong implications for Christian-Muslim relations. The chapter examines how different views evolved in Isiolo, a small Northern Kenyan town. The town has a history of strained Christian-Muslim relations. Contests over resources and ownership of the town feature highly in every new conflict. The chapter explores the role of ethno-religious ascriptions and elite mobilization in the increasing misunderstandings about Kadhi's courts. It also illustrates that, despite efforts by concerned civic educators to teach the residents, the resultant decisions were informed by insufficient knowledge about courts' functions.

The purpose of this chapter is threefold. Firstly, it problematises the two main concepts used herein, Kadhi's courts and Christian-Muslim relations, by outlining their conceptual and practical frameworks. Secondly, it analyses the seven main thematic issues arising out of debates, as perceived by Muslims and Christians of Isiolo Town in Kenya. This involves exploring the complex issues that came to be part of the debate, despite being explicitly unrelated to the operations of the Kadhi's courts, and how the debate shaped the resultant skewed understanding of the constitutional debates during the Referendum campaigns in Kenya during 2005.

Finally, the chapter concludes by examining emergent trends that arose as a result of the debates on Kadhi's courts and Christian-Muslim relations.

Isiolo Town,[1] considered to be the gateway to Northern Kenya, is a melting pot of peoples and different cultures of Northeast Africa. The town developed in the early 20th century as a colonial administrative outpost and a centre for the then Northern Frontier District (NFD), which was separately administered from the rest of the country, as well as being the staging-post for long-distance trade and hunting expeditions during its early years.[2] Following Independence in 1963, the *shifta*[3] conflicts in Northern Kenya during the mid to late 1960s and the collapse of the pastoral economy, the greater population of the destitute were drawn to the town by the demands for services, labour, farm and livestock products and petty trade. From early days, Asian and Somali traders provided the economic activities in the form of small retail shops (Swah.: *duka*), while the Turkana, Waso Borana[4] and Samburu herders served as their main customers. Since then the Igembe and Tigania Meru subgroups, who had been displaced from the Meru region due to population pressure and scarcity of farm land, have moved into the town to set up consumer business. Apart from engaging in keeping livestock, the former pastoralists are also involved in small scale subsistence farming through irrigation.

Religious communities in the town include Muslims and Christians of the following denominations: Roman Catholics, Methodists, Presbyterians and Anglicans, as well as a host of Pentecostal churches. Ethnic and religious identities more often than not overlap, providing the actors with multiple identities. Ethnically and culturally, the population divides into what is colloquially referred to as the Bantu speakers, represented by the Meru;

---

[1] According to *Isiolo District Poverty Reduction Strategy Paper: Consultative Report for the Period 2001–2004*, Ministry of Finance and Planning, page 3, the estimated population of the Isiolo Central division, of which the town is the centre, was 52,588 persons as at 1999.

[2] Hjort, Anders, *Savanna town: Rural Ties and Urban Opportunities in Northern Kenya*, Stockholm: Stockholm Studies of Social Anthropology, 1979.

[3] *Shifta* wars refer to the secessionist conflicts waged from 1963 to 1969 by the Somali and a section of, largely Muslim, Waso Borana in order to join their culturally and religious brethren in the Republic of Somalia. The term *Shifta* has its origin in an Amharic word, meaning bandit.

[4] Waso Borana refers to the Borana group which emigrated from Ethiopia due to expansionist wars of Menelik in the late 19th century. According to Mario I. Aguilar's *Being Oromo in Kenya*, Trenton: Africa World Press, 1998, these Borana groups who occupy Merti, Garba Tulla, Isiolo Town, and Sericho were separated from their kinsmen in the homelands in Ethiopia in early 20th century due to colonial rule and, as a result, religious diversification is a common feature.

the Cushitic communities of the Borana[5] and the Somali; and the Nilotic speakers of Turkana and Samburu. These, however, are not self-identifying cultural categories. Rather, the communities divide themselves into their ethnic groups, where self-identity is stronger within groups than across groups. While the Meru, a significant minority in the town, are predominantly Christian, the Borana and Somali are largely Muslim. In essence, the national perception of a Muslim minority in a predominantly Christian majority state is negated in the town's demographic balance as the majority-minority dynamics are reversed. However, it should be noted that in each religious community there exists a high ethnic consciousness, which often translates itself in the form of, for instance, the Borana, the Somali, the Meru, the Turkana and Samburu. This is also reflected in the settlement patterns of different communities, with each of the groups occupying different areas of the town. Besides this, the more pastoral groups frequently clash over scarce resources, such as grazing lands and water.[6] Conflicts in the area have a great propensity to depict the fluid and volatile identities of ethno-religious crises, as the division between the two is often blurred.

The Conceptual and Practical Contours of Kadhi's Courts

Post-1990, Africa has been characterised by the (re)introduction of political pluralism, the liberation of airwaves and enhanced adherence to human rights and freedoms. The period has also witnessed agitation to put in place constitutional dispensations that reflect the will of the citizenry, to replace the irredeemably amended independence constitution. Since the fall of the Soviet bloc, in most African countries, ideologies that had gained currency due to Cold War rivalry ran out of ammunition.

[5] Different spellings have been used by researchers to refer to Borana, a branch of Oromo found in Isiolo, Marsabit and Moyale Districts of Northern Kenya and Southern Ethiopia. They include Boran, Booran, Boorana and Borana. Booran(a) is considered by Aguilar (1998) as closer to the phonetic sound of the word. The long 'o' is a long vowel while the second vowel 'a' is accented and the terminal vowel 'a' is optional and is usually dropped in phonetically restricted environments. Legesse, Asmarom, *Oromo Democracy: An Indigenous African Political System*, Trenton and Asmara: Red Sea Press, 2006. For uniformity I use 'Borana' in the chapter, as no standard format has been accepted and all the variants are considered legitimate.

[6] See Ruto, P., M. Adan & I. Masinde, *Conflicts in Northern Kenya: A Focus on the Internally Displaced conflict victims in Northern Kenya*, Nairobi: ITGA-EA & DTP Martin Karimi Publishers, 2003, for further reading on conflicts in Northern Kenya.

Ethnicity and other forms of identities took the centre-stage as the rallying ground for political, economic, and social and cultural bargains and negotiations.[7]

In Kenya, members of different religious communities face similar socio-economic and political predicaments; however, the drive for the new rules of the game has often led to divergent, if not incompatible, views on constitutional matters regarding issues such as the status of Kadhi's courts. Although the calls for their empowerment and expansion were largely expressed to the Constitution of Kenya Review Commission (CKRC) when it collated and collected the views from Kenyans of all walks of life in the early 2000s, such calls cannot be divorced from the opening up of the democratic space in 1992 and the subsequent opportunity it offered to members and elites of the different faiths to add their input to the tools of governance in the spirit of a 'people-driven' process. In the following section, the chapter examines the constitutional development of Kadhi's courts from an historical perspective.

Kadhi's Courts: An Historical Continuum

Along the East African coast, the institution of Kadhi's courts existed much earlier than the period of establishment of British colonization. The weak Sultanate of Zanzibar ceded to the British the Coastal Strip as a protectorate, with the guarantee that certain issues be given protection. An 1895 agreement between the two powers made a resolution that the new administrators will respect and protect all mosques and religious festivals, and that Kadhis and *ʿulamāʾ* shall continue to receive all honours, among other issues. The agreement explicitly stated that "Mohammedan religion will remain the public and established creed in all Sultan's territories, and all cases and law suits between natives will continue to be decided according to Sheria".[8] The colonial administration set up a

[7] Oloo, A. G. R., 'The Contemporary Opposition in Kenya: Between Internal Traits and Manipulation', in *Kenya: The Struggle for Democracy*, G. R. Murunga & S. W. Nasong'o (eds.), Dakar: Codesria Books, 2007, pages 90–128; Omolo, Ken, 'Political Ethnicity in Democratisation Process in Kenya', *African Studies*, 61:2, 2002, pages 209–221; Ajulu, Rok, 'Politicized Ethnicity, Competitive Politics and Conflicts in Kenya: A Historical Perspective', *African Studies*, 61:2, 2002, pages 251–268; Nasong'o, S. W., *Contending Political Paradigms in Africa: Rationality and Politics of Democratization in Kenya and Zambia*, New York and London: Routledge, 2005.

[8] Mungeam, G. H., *Kenya: Select Historical Documents 1884–1961*, Nairobi: EAEP, 1978, page 68.

tri-partite legal system: Common law (Colonial) courts, Kadhi's courts and Customary courts. The last two had no jurisdiction over criminal cases and they remained subordinate courts, mandated to handle personal law for their adherents under strict supervision of the High Court. The colonial administration co-opted local *ʿulamāʾ* as civil servants to serve in the Kadhi's courts; such officials often hailed from leading coastal families.[9]

The status of the Kadhi's courts in the colony was different from that of the Protectorate. Muslims in other parts of the colony such as Mumias, and the Northern Frontier District, were not subject to the rule of the Sultanate of Zanzibar, nor were they part of the Coastal Strip. There were no legally binding agreements that endorsed establishment of such courts in the colony. On the eventual establishment of similar courts outside the Protectorate, Hassan Mwakimako observes that:

> The difference between a protectorate and a colony in terms of the applicability of Islamic laws and in particular the appointment of Muslim officials designated as Kadhi was a dilemma facing immigrant and indigenous Muslim communities who while domiciled in the colony still demanded to have special legal interactions with colonial authorities as it was the practice at the Coast. The practicability of such demands manifested in Mumias as Muslims failed to appreciate the colonial governments' preference for a geographical categorization of spheres of influences as far as the establishment of Kadhi courts and an application of Sharia laws demanding instead a universalistic religious-based establishment of legal structures and application of rules.[10]

The colonial administrators appointed a few learned individuals, deemed to possess adequate knowledge of Muslim personal law, as registrars of Muslim marriages and divorces, on a semi-official basis. Nonetheless, they were referred to as kadhis by the colony's Muslim subjects. Isiolo was the headquarters of the then 'closed' Northern Frontier District (NFD). Colonial archival sources indicate that there were no Native courts or courts with jurisdiction over Muslim personal law until the mid-1940s. Before then, among such communities as the Somali, local sheikhs and clan elders often presided over cases of civil, and sometimes criminal, nature. By the mid-1940s there was a registrar of Muslim marriages and divorces ('kadhi') based in the NFD. Sheikh Abdulla bin Ali, a Somali resident of

---

[9] Bang, A., 'Intellectuals and Civil Servants: Early 20th Century Zanzibar Ulama and the Colonial State', *Islam in East Africa: New Sources*, Biancamaria Scarcia Amoretti (ed.), Rome: Herder, 2001, page 59.

[10] Hassan Mwakimako, '*Kadhi* Court and Appointment of *Kadhi* in Kenya Colony', *Religion Compass* 2/4, 2008, page 427.

Wajir, served as the first 'kadhi'. He frequently travelled between Isiolo, Wajir and other towns to hear scheduled Muslim personal law cases. These duties were carried out in co-ordination with the District Commissioners of all the six districts in the NFD, namely: Garba Tulla, Wajir, Garissa, Mandera, Moyale and Isiolo. During this period most of the disputants were urbanized Somali and a few Borana. Outside the towns, an admixture of customary and Islamic law were popularly applied. J. N. D. Anderson aptly observes that:

> Most disputes are settled by *ad hoc* arbitration 'tribunals', which apparently apply an admixture of tribal and Islamic law as they see fit. There is only one official *Qadi* at Isiolo, the headquarters of the Province; but there are registrars of marriages (who act as unofficial *Qadis*) at Wajir, Moyale, Garissa, etc. There are also a few 'holy men'—i.e. local leaders of dervish [Sufi] orders—who sometimes act in a semi-judicial capacity.[11]

The early 1960s was a period of intense constitutional negotiation in East Africa. The 1895 Agreement between the British and the Sultanate was revisited by the soon-to-be independent African governments. The Sultan of Zanzibar gave up his sovereignty over the Coastal Strip (10-Mile Strip) in exchange for a constitutional guarantee for a number of issues pertinent to the welfare of the coastal Muslims. This included, among others, the continued existence and recognition of the institution of Kadhi's courts in Independent Kenya.

The courts were, hence, enshrined in the Constitution. Through a number of Acts, the parliament outlined the functions of the subordinate courts to determine matters of Muslim law on personal status, marriage, divorce, and inheritance, in proceedings in which all parties involved profess the Islamic faith. Kadhis, strictly speaking, are Muslim judges who preside over these courts and they are employees of the Judicial Service Commission, having proved to have adequate knowledge of Islamic law. Currently there are about 17 such courts dotted all over the country to serve Muslim clients. There is a Kadhi's chamber at Isiolo Law Courts.

The post-1992 period in Kenya was marked by increased demands for a new constitution as the Independence Constitution was seen to have been manipulated severally to create an 'imperial' presidency and to entrench bad governance. The national constitutional conferences, held at the Bomas of Kenya in the early 2000s, were the apex of such public

[11] Anderson, J. N. D., 'Kenya', in *Islamic Law in Africa*, London: Cass, 1970, page 113.

demands. The Draft Constitution of 2004 (Bomas Draft),[12] had provision for devolution of power, equitable distribution of national resources, affirmative action, the redress of historical injustice, solutions to perennial land questions and provided for the empowerment of Kadhi's courts, among other issues.

The radical recommendations of constitutional changes were strongly opposed by the government. In place of the Bomas Draft, the government presented a new draft constitution, entitled the Proposed New Constitution of Kenya and known as the 'Wako Draft',[13] for public discussion; this was taken to a vote by means of a referendum which was held on 21st November 2005. The position of Kadhi's courts was argued to have been weakened in this draft, unlike the situation in the Bomas draft. We shall return to these documents in our discussion of thematic issues.

Christian-Muslim Relations: What Is It All About?

Going by the number of publications dedicated to its study, Christian-Muslim relations remains a popular academic discourse.[14] It can be argued that the very term 'Christian-Muslim relations', devoid of determinism, may at first appear to suggest uniformity of intent and practice, although it is grounded in the assumption of variability and change.[15] The foci of this subject in Africa range from scriptural implications of the various religious texts on the relations and instances of co-operation and co-existence, to political and social challenges arising out of strained relations. The subject further considers the roles played by education and other forms of socialization on relations between religions. It also covers the effects of globalization on the relations, and the impact of increased

---

12 *The Draft Constitution of Kenya 2004*, (CKRC) adopted by the National Constitutional Conference on the 15th March 2004, known as the 'Bomas Draft'. The conference was held at a venue called Bomas of Kenya.

13 This draft constitution was popularly referred to as the Wako Draft; it was named after the Attorney General, Mr. Amos Wako, whose office was responsible for the formulation of the Draft from earlier draft bills and the current Constitution. *The Proposed New Constitution of Kenya.* Special Issue Kenya Gazette Supplement No. 63, Nairobi, 22nd August 2005, known as the 'Wako Draft'.

14 A search of the Bibliography of *Islam in Contemporary Sub-Saharan Africa*, by Paul Schrijver (ed.), Leiden: African Studies Centre, 2006, revealed almost 100 articles that included the words 'Christian-Muslim'.

15 Mwakimako, H., 'Christian-Muslim Relations in Kenya: A Catalogue of Events and Meanings', *Islam and Christian Muslim Relations*, Vol. 18, No. 2, 287–307, April 2007, page 288.

demands for observance of religious laws in post-colonial secular states in multi-ethnic and multi-religious societies, amongst others.

The popularity of the subject has also been motivated by the need to understand the growing tension between Muslims and Christians in a globalized world, faced with uncertainty over competition for scarce resources and opportunities, increased calls for application and recognition of religious laws by religious groups, and protection of their rights as minorities. The sustained campaigns of prejudice, suspicions and stereotyping through media and other public forums by members of rival religions are raising much concern, as well as interest, in academic researches. While the study of Christian-Muslim relations may signal the urge to understand the tensions and dissonance between and among religious communities, more often than not, the relations are characterized by cordial co-existence in every day interactions in the social arena. In most parts of Africa, there is a strong movement to encourage good Christian-Muslim relations through seminars, workshops, visits, and open discussions. Although such efforts are often elitist in nature, they nevertheless represent the primary basis for dialogue and interfaith approaches to solve conflicts.

Competition over socio-economic and political goods such as land, perceived marginalization of one's group by a ruling class associated with a rival religious community, and fear of the other have been identified as fuelling strained Christian-Muslim relations.[16] Hence, "when perceived imbalance in distribution of resources with identity differences exists, we have potential for conflicts".[17] It must be borne in mind that "religious beliefs create boundaries between people not only when distorted or misused; for, religion binds persons into . . . communities of those who believe in Jesus, Allah or Krishna".[18]

---

[16] Njozi, H. M., *Mwembechai Killings and the Political Future of Tanzania*, Ottawa: Globalink Communications, 2000; Hashim, Abdulkadir, 'Muslim State Relations in Kenya after the Referendum on the Constitution', in *AASR Bulletin* 24, November 2005, pages 21–27; Kubai, A., 'Christian-Muslim Relations in Kenya since Independence', *Interface between Research and Dialogue: Christian-Muslim Relations in Africa*, Klaus Hock (ed.), Münster: LIT, 2004, pages 32–65.

[17] Yusuf, H. B., 'Managing Muslim-Christian Conflicts in Northern Nigeria: A Case Study of Kaduna State', *Islam and Christian-Muslim Relations*, Vol. 18, No. 2, April 2007, page 241.

[18] Gecaga, M. G., 'Religious Movements and Democratization in Kenya: Between the Sacred and the Profane', *Kenya: The Struggle for Democracy*, G. R. Murunga & S. W. Nasong'o (eds.), Dakar: Codesria Books, 2007, page 63.

Discourse on Christian-Muslim relations can best be studied by focusing not on general issues, but rather on specific contextual situations that show how conflict, or the lack of it, is usually shaped by historical and socio-economic circumstances. The best approach is therefore 'contextualization from below', so as to appreciate the authenticity and uniqueness of people's experience.[19] In this chapter the author has reconsidered contextualization in terms of themes that formed the Muslim-Christian debates in Isiolo over the constitutional position of Kadhi's court. While the first two themes reflect the debates as articulated by Muslims and Christians in the national arena and in Isiolo, the remaining themes are mainly specific to this town.

Thematic Issues from the Debates on Kadhi's Courts in Isiolo Town

These themes are based on interviews and observations conducted between August 2006 and April 2007. The analysis of the data does not necessarily suggest homogeneity and consensus among members of one religious or ethnic group, but rather represents the dominant perspectives. The terms 'Christians' and 'Muslims', as used here, are loosely defined without denying the diversities of voices and persuasions in each group. This is because the respondents identify themselves as such. In total, 32 interviews were conducted.

Purposive sampling technique was used to identify key informants, with care being taken to ensure that the sample groups were not affected by religious, ethnic, gender and educational biases. The sample population was categorized into 6 clusters to capture different segments of the society, namely: religious leaders, civil society officials, ordinary men and women, youth groups, community leaders and former officials of the Constitution of Kenya Review Commission (CKRC). Semi-structured questions were administered during individual and group interviews. Official and unofficial social forums, in which debates about constitutional matters were discussed, were also attended. These included civic awareness programmes, sermons in places of worship such as mosques, and informal afternoon public discussions, which were common along the main streets of Isiolo. Included among the interviewees were local representatives

[19] Mwakimako, 2007, page 95.

of the Supreme Council of Kenya Muslims (SUPKEM) and the National Council of Churches of Kenya (NCCK), religious leaders from the Jamia and Rahma Mosques, Roman Catholic Church, the Methodist Church and Redeemed Gospel Churches and the Kadhi of Isiolo. Secondary materials consulted included various documents from the CKRC, the Constitution of Kenya, various draft constitutions such as Kilifi, Bomas and Ufungamano drafts, publications and press statements from national and local religious organizations and instructional materials used by various civic education providers. The textual analyses of the data were done using the grounded theory approach that entailed identifying categories, concepts and themes. Recurrent ideas were then regrouped under the seven thematic issues as set out below.

Theme One: Views about Kadhi's Courts by Muslims and Christians

There is a consensus about the historical existence of the courts in Kenya. The existence of Kadhi's courts in Kenya might, however, mean different things to different religions. For a majority of the Muslims in the area, it is an historical validation of the courts' continued existence and improvement; whereas, for the Christians, the government of Kenya entered into agreements with other regional states at the time of independence without much thought and without wider consultation. Such agreements, which resulted in the entrenchment of Kadhi's courts, therefore should be abrogated. The sentiment expressed by one informant captures the argument this way:

> Yes, my feeling is that in the first place the courts should not have been there and now that we are rewriting the constitution it should go. Because, if we go back to the origin of it all, it started along the Coast only. There was an agreement which was made in the colonial period. But now we are saying because now we want to write a good constitution, some of the things which bring problems should be done away with, or be removed. So that has been a big question all through. Why should this one recognize one religious system while others should not be recognized?[20]

For the Muslims, the court has come to symbolize the only institution in the Constitution that protects their interests as members of a minority religion in a country where Christian belief dominates. The Courts have

[20] Personal interview with Pastor Geoffrey, 11th December 2006, at Deliverance Church, Isiolo.

therefore become "a symbol of both Muslim governance and its vulnerability in the post-colonial era".[21] Because the Kadhis are weaving a role between the secular and religious legal structures, negotiating for a place for their non-secular judicial system, Muslims in general believe that they cannot envisage the rightful enjoyment of their freedoms and rights in the absence of these courts in Kenya. The respondents in Isiolo air similar concerns about the importance of the courts in their daily lives. Sheikh Harun, echoing the symbolic status of the courts for the Muslims, local and national, opines that:

> Kadhi's Courts are the only body that exists in the Constitution that Muslims can truly claim to be theirs and be proud of. If a new constitution is constructed, it must take into account the opinions and interests of the Muslim community into the new laws. This is what we are after. Interests of the Muslims must be guaranteed generally by the Constitution and not partially by it.[22]

The fact that these courts have always catered exclusively for parties professing Islam elicited negative responses from the majority of Christians, who subscribe to the idea of 'one country, one legal system'. The entrenchment of these courts into the Constitution of Kenya was interpreted as state recognition and favouritism of Islam. To the Muslims, such reactions are motivated by envy, suspicion and propaganda, because the courts only handle matters of personal law for Muslims. In the view of the Muslims, the constitutional role that the Kadhi's Courts play should not concern non-Muslims who are not affected by their decisions.

The proposed changes in the Bomas Draft that became part of the Referendum debates include the granting of appellate jurisdiction to Kadhi's courts, and reforms aimed at enhancing their functional capacities as corridors of justice. Muslim rejection of the Wako Draft arose out of the fear that such changes were removed and the status of the courts further weakened. In practice, the courts lack such jurisdiction, as appeals lie ultimately with the High Court and the Court of Appeal, where the application of secular laws takes precedence over Muslim personal law. The decisions made in such cases are subject to contest on the basis of Islamic jurisprudence. Though appeals are rare, and appellate decisions

21 Hirsch, S. F., *Pronouncing and Persevering: Gender and Discourses of Disputing in African Islamic Court*, Chicago and London: University of Chicago Press, 1998, page 136.

22 Personal interview with Sheikh Harun on 11th December 2006, at Bomen Hotel, Isiolo.

even rarer, the possibility of such a process has been noted to challenge the authority and legitimacy of these courts in post-colonial Kenya.[23] These views were largely expressed by the Muslim religious and community leaders in the town.

The call in earlier draft bills for appellate jurisdiction for the courts and their enhanced status was largely viewed by Christians as being a calculated and gradual move to introduce Islamic *sharīʿa* in a fuller form, just like in Nigeria or the Sudan. Examples from these countries were often voiced to show opposition to the courts. Such moves were also seen as costly to the economy, as two parallel systems of law will be enforced, and it was considered that conflicts between the two systems will be inevitable. Furthermore, the very existence of non-secular legal structures in a secular state was often cited as contradictory to the Constitution and Article 10 of the Wako Draft that "the state and religion shall be separate, there is no state religion and the state shall treat all religions equally". For the majority of the local Muslim respondents, these courts are not religious courts and they should be seen in the context of judiciary; Kadhis are only civil servants presiding over matters of personal laws.

Theme Two: Majority-Minority Dichotomy

Prior to the 21st November 2005 referendum, the issue of Kadhi's courts was interpreted in terms of a demographic struggle over political issues. Each religious community blamed the other for amassing their followers to sway the results to their side.

Christian-Muslim relations in Kenya have often been seen through the lens of a majority-minority spectrum. And "considering the fact that Muslims in Kenya consider themselves to be living in the shadow of [a] dominant Christian population (estimated at 75%) the social, political and economic issues of conflicts become implicitly religious".[24]

The suggestion that the courts should be established as an act of parliament, instead of being entrenched into the Constitution, was also opposed on the grounds that because the numbers of Muslim parliamentarians are relatively small, there were fears that the dominant Christian presence in parliament could easily throw out the courts' provision from the laws. Isiolo being in an area considered as underdeveloped in terms of infrastructure, poverty levels, representation in national leadership, and

---

[23] Hirsch, 1998.
[24] Kubai, 2004, page 39.

general insecurity, discourse about marginalization gained greater currency there. The blame was not just put on the government but also on the religious persuasion of the ruling elite.

There was a tendency to look at the state and the religious community from which the ruling elite hails, as being one and the same and hence in pursuit of similar objectives. Media portrayal of president and cabinet ministers' attendance at church services, national prayer meetings and fund-raising for church activities helped to reinforce the above association.

When the Wako Draft left out some crucial reforms such as appellate jurisdiction, which had been suggested by the Bomas Draft on Kadhi's courts, the local Muslims viewed the action as being carried out by a Christian regime bent on trampling on their religious freedoms for religious and ethnic reasons. The Wako Draft was also said to have been changed to remove the clauses that proposed some sort of 'Marshall Plan' to help Northern Kenya catch up with the rest of the country. Other contentious issues such as the devolution of power and equitable resource distribution consolidated the stance of each group.

The experience of the Secessionist (*shifta*) wars of the 1960s also had the effect of inculcating fear and a feeling of indifference among the dominant local Cushitic populace towards the state and its machineries.[25] This is the region that Negley Farson, an American author writing in the 1940s, captured in his narrative as "... [The] one half of Kenya about which the other half knows nothing and seems to care even less".[26] Each religious community has a perception that their demographic strength in the country is larger than it actually is, while no census data of religious affiliation exist. Christians estimate their percentage to be from 75% to 90%, while Muslims put their percentage as being from 10% to 30%. It is not uncommon for adherents to cite the higher percentages. In such an atmosphere of religious rivalry one may conclude that the Kenya experience is "that of a Muslim minority living with a Christian majority who did not lose the opportunity of turning a numerical majority into a religious advantage".[27]

---

[25] Aguilar, 1998; M'Inoti, Kathurima, 'Beyond the "Emergency" in the North Eastern Province: The Legal Regime under the N. E. Province and Contiguous Districts Regulations, 1966', in *Constitutional law and politics in Africa: A Case Study of Kenya*, K. Kibwana (ed.), Nairobi: Claripress, 1998, pages 315–338.

[26] Words of American Negley Farson in *Last Chance in Africa* (1949) quoted in K. M'Inoti, 1998, page 320.

[27] Mwakimako, 2007, page 95.

It must be noted that a number of Christians voted against the Wako Draft due to mobilization by the Orange Democratic Movement in western parts of the country. This is because this is an opposition zone, and ethnic and not religious reasons accounted for this move.[28] The communities from Mount Kenya area, which include co-ethnics of the local Meru, overwhelmingly voted for the Wako Draft. In fact Central Province was the only Province to vote in favour; all other provinces rejected the Wako Draft.[29] The overlap of religious and ethnic ascriptions reinforced the rivalry and suspicion between religions with ethnic rivalry and suspicions.

As mentioned earlier, the national majority-minority dichotomy is reversed in Isiolo town. Muslims form the majority while Christians form a significant minority. The demographic balance has implications on how things are debated in town. The majority believe that because of their numerical strength and the historical ties of the town's origin, they have the upper hand on how issues are dealt with. They are most likely to interpret divergent opinions that touch their religion and culture as a direct challenge to their 'hegemonic' control over the town. Such a picture of a majority-minority struggle was reflected in the thoughts of one informant:

> On the existence of Kadhi's Courts in the Constitution, the Christians took it up with a different perception. They considered that the government was favouring the Muslims a lot. So the Christians said that because "we are the majority, let us use this fact for us to be recognized by the state". It was just by the blessing of God that politics crept in and distorted their unity. They opposed it because of the existence of Kadhi's Court. You see Margaret Wanjiru and the likes said that if Kadhi's Courts is there, they shall reject it.[30]

Theme Three: Influence from without on the Debate

The national debates, fears, suspicions and inspirations of co-religionists and co-ethnics were localized and integrated into the body of local discourses about Kadhi's courts. Religious leaders, local politicians and civil

---

[28] Muturi puts the point this way: 'What I see is that during the Referendum, distinctly there has not been any friction along religious lines. Of course Muslims were fighting for their rights, they felt that rights have [been] violated and therefore they must have to fight against the Draft, but Christians for those who are politically inclined to the ODM, they were also fighting against the Draft. It is not an issue of religion now.' Personal interview with C. Muturi on 20th November 2006, at Isiolo Market, Isiolo.

[29] See *Daily Nation* 23rd November 2005 for results by province.

[30] Personal interview with Mama Amina on 4th December 2006, at Bomen Hotel, Isiolo.

society officials acted as the bridge between the national and local concerns for their groups. Press statements, radio and television debates and publications from religious organizations such as the National Council of Churches of Kenya (NCCK), the Supreme Council of Kenya (SUPKEM), the National Muslim Leadership Forum (NAMLEF) and the Kenya Episcopal Council (KEC) shaped the course of the debate. For instance, Nairobi Jamia Mosque's *Friday Bulletin*, a weekly Muslim news update, had an important role. These bulletins were regularly dispatched by the *ʿulamāʾ* to keep the faithful informed of the current concerns and challenges facing Islam in Kenya.

Global discourse about *sharīʿa* application in Africa and the world entered the debate. Some informants associate the current proposals to improve the working of the court with the hidden urgency to implement criminal law. Arguments about amputation of hands for theft and stoning to death for adultery epitomize these fears. A number of local Muslim respondents see the hand of the United States of America behind the concerted efforts of Pentecostal churches in their opposition to Kadhi's Courts.[31] These churches, through an umbrella body called the Kenya Church, called for the removal of Kadhi's Courts or any other religious courts from the Constitution and the draft bills. However, the presence of these churches is not very pronounced in Isiolo. The effects of their arguments on the Christians of other denominations in the area are not very clear.

The call for the removal of the courts was also interpreted by Muslims as a part of the global efforts to check the growth of 'Islamism', in the 'war against terror' campaigns, in Sub-Saharan Africa. To the local Muslim population, there is an implicit connection between the call to curb the courts' improvement and the reduction of their status in the Wako Draft. The state is perceived as being party to such moves. Fresh in the minds of the informants were the proposed Terrorism Bill and the closing down

[31] H. Ismail, who was suspicious of the vocal role of the Kenya Church, observes that: 'What many Muslims believe is that there is an external influence fighting against the Kadhi's courts. Muslims and Muslim solidarity and Islam as an institution are being fought by other factors, particularly American interests. This is what it is. They are ones who are trying to use these evangelical churches to weaken the Muslim stand, which they call actually conservativeness, or it is we who are being influenced to be like them. You know, Muslims do their things in their own way not in their Western ways. I think most of these churches were paid groups. These are the ones shouting loudest, not even the Catholics and others.' Personal interview with H. Ismail, on 14th December 2006, at Green Lodge, Isiolo.

of some Muslim Non-Governmental Organizations (NGOs)[32] for alleged connections to terrorist groups, and the rapid and indiscriminate manner in which the government then accused Muslims of complicity in the 1998 US embassy bombings. The NGOs provided social services, such as education and health in addition to *daʿwa* activities. The wider inference drawn from the closure of Muslim-oriented groups was that a Christian-led government was facilitating the hindrance of the propagation of Islam.[33]

Theme Four: Linking Past Conflicts to the Present Concerns

The debates about the courts became embroiled in discussing earlier protracted clashes over resources such as land, economic opportunities, political leadership, and conflicts over control of educational institutions and boundary disputes. Every new potential conflict was viewed as an extension of the past ones or an opportunity to settle scores with a rival religious or ethnic group. The fact that the majority of local Muslims opposed the Wako Draft and many Christians supported it, was a clear indication to each group that the others' stand is motivated by the wars of supremacy in the town. This reduced the referendum debate to some sort of 'do or die' event. One informant argued that where a rival ethnic group was supporting the Draft, they must have vested interests. He says "when the constitutional debate came to town, people observed that where these Meru are pushing strongly the way they are doing, they must have vested interests. So we said: Let us deny them!"[34] Recalling earlier boundary disputes and the resultant carry-over of old conflicts, one informant narrates that:

> There was a time when Kuti (the local Member of Parliament) came and spoke about the issues of boundaries. It happened that the boundaries have been brought even closer to Kiwanja cha Ndege (the area close to Isiolo airstrip). We were even told that soon it will come as close as Isiolo Girls' and then it is redrawn behind Lobos (a hotel in Kulamawe area of Isiolo town). So now you see the Borana community feels that these people, because they are leading in the government now, they have embarked on oppressing us

---

32 See Mohamed Salih's 'Islamic NGOs in Africa: Promise and Peril of Islamic Voluntarism' in Alex de Vaal (ed.), *Islamism and its Enemies in the Horn of Africa*, London: Hurst & Company, 2004, pages 146–181. Salih notes that five Muslim NGOs were thrown out of the country for alleged links with terrorism. Most of them had offices in Isiolo; they include Mercy International, Al Haramain Foundation, Help Africa People, IIRO and Ibrahim al Ibrahim (page 175).

33 Mwakimako, 2007, page 293.

34 Group interview with IYAP, 22nd March 2007.

> and grabbing our land. One day we even heard that Isiolo town itself is in Meru. Now, one is left wondering how Isiolo town can be in Meru. Now we cannot side with them and they cannot side with us.[35]

It should be noted that the "land question, its ownership, access and use, has come to occupy a central place in public policy and political discourse in Kenya. This is because land has been the crux of cultural, economic and socio-political change".[36] In Isiolo, almost all past conflicts relate in one way or another to the land question. It defines who is an outsider, and therefore not part of the decision making and voting process, and who is an insider, with full rights on how issues are run in town. The town is near the border of Meru and Isiolo Districts and hence it is more cosmopolitan than other divisions in the District. In Isiolo, land is legally considered as trust land and the Isiolo County Council holds it on behalf of the local communities. Being on the border with Meru District, current concerns among the Borana and other pastoral residents are the 'ever shrinking' physical boundaries of their District and the encroachment of Meru District, and the implied symbolic loss to a rival ethno-religious group. The clauses concerning land ownership as proposed in the Wako Draft did not satisfy the dominant groups in the town. Abdulla Dima, citing errors in Wako Draft, avers that:

> Now later what happened was that in the Wako's Draft... they still called [it] community land but to define it, it sort of diluted the definition that was done by the Boma [drafts] but still call it community land of some kind. But it even stated that in the implementation, the land is going to be held by a commission on behalf of the community for three to four years before the rightful owners are going to be defined. But people know who owns the land, they know who the rightful owners are, it really became an issue.[37]

The town has attracted peoples of diverse origins. Population growth and pressure on grazing lands, transformation of property rights from communal to private tenure, political instability and economic insecurity have pushed pastoral groups in the area to abandon their lands and concentrate around settlements and towns.[38] In addition, individualization of

---

[35] Group interview with IYAP, 22nd March 2007.

[36] CKRC, *The Final Report of the Constitution of Kenya Review Commission*, Nairobi: CKRC, 10th February 2005, page 271.

[37] Personal interview with Abdulla Dima, on 8th December 2006, Isiolo.

[38] Fratkin, E., 'The Problems of Pastoral Land Tenure System in Kenya: Demographic, Economic and Political Process among Maasai, Samburu, Boran and Rendille, 1950–1990', *Working Paper in African Studies*, No. 177, Boston Africa Studies Center, 1994.

lands for settlement is often unregulated. For some communities, the loss of communal lands to persons labelled as 'outsiders' is unfair. Corruption in land allocation procedures by the very Council entrusted with its care is considered as rife by the majority of residents.[39]

Ultimately the debate ignites the old wounds of struggle for supremacy over the town's political, socio-economic and religious space. Such clashes were common features before 2002; they often involved members of different ethnic groups, or pitted one religion against the other, with each group imputing religious motives to the opponents' actions. Nothing more than electoral exercises, such as voting for preferred candidates in general elections, and the highly charged Referendum option of 'Yes' or 'No', makes the rivalry emerge. The majority ethnic groups and religions contest the labelling of the town as cosmopolitan and hence free for all. Each group is observed to rush to history to validate their claims of ownership of the town and its implied benefits. The ultimate question, as one informant puts it,[40] is 'who owns Isiolo?' The answer to this question is emotively contested.

Theme Five: The Ethnic Factor in the Debate

Group solidarity, whether religious or ethnic, is very strong in Isiolo and it is 'strengthened when actors see their ethnic group as a means of gaining access to valued resources, but this relationship is contingent on the availability of these resources to the individual outside the ethnic group'.[41] The dominant Cushitic groups considered themselves as being outside the group who are in receipt of state benefits and identify the largely Christian Meru as one of the chief beneficiaries of government support in their home districts.

The support given to the Wako Draft by communities from Mount Kenya region was perceived as being motivated by the need to keep their co-ethnics in power. During the Referendum campaigns, while Central

---

[39] *Isiolo District Poverty Reduction Strategy Paper*, 2001.

[40] In a personal interview with Bonaya Bankare, 27th March 2007, who says this: "Most of the communities feel that Isiolo is theirs; if you ask the Somali right now, they will say that Isiolo is ours, as we were here since World War I. You ask the Borana, they will say it is ours, because we are the majority. You ask the Turkana, they will say it is ours, as we were among the first people. You ask the Meru, they will say we are the first merchants, we were here before others, check even the buildings are ours".

[41] Hempel, Lynn, 'What's it worth to you? The Questionable Value of Instrumentalist Approaches to Ethnic Identification', in *Ethnicity, Ethnic Conflict and Peace Process: Comparative Perspectives*, E. A. Tirykian (ed.), London: Sage, 2004, page 141.

Province and its environs backed the government, the Nyanza and Western Kenya provinces opposed the Draft and "analyses of the referendum, which dominated public and private debate, immediately acquired an 'ethnic logic', as ethnic groups were labelled 'orange', 'banana' or 'divided"'.[42] The promotion of 'Us' versus 'Them' raised the stakes in the referendum debate and eliminated the chances of compromise or even understanding of opponents' points of views.

Those in opposition wanted to show the government their dissatisfaction at being left out from being beneficiaries of the 'national cake', as "having political power opens up the opportunity to gain access to and distribute state resources... hence, the frequent reference in African politics to ethnic groups asserting that it is 'our turn to eat'".[43] Discourses on inequality and the perceived lack of concern from the state formed the rallying points for political mobilization and strengthened the resolve to oppose the draft and all its contents. Put differently, "when economic inequality in incomes, wealth and access to services or political power coincides with group differences, ethnicity may assume importance in shaping and mobilizing individuals for collective actions".[44]

Theme Six: The Christian Courts Saga

Article 195 of the Wako Draft established religious courts, which were to include Christian courts, Kadhi's courts and Hindu courts. The jurisdictions of these courts were to determine cases of personal law of their respective faith in which the parties involved profess that faith. The inclusion of the Christian and Hindu courts, previously not in the Constitution, elicited varied responses from the local Muslims and Christians. It also had implications for the debates on Kadhi's courts. Reverend Munywa of the Methodist Church of Kenya, Isiolo, points out that each church has what he calls 'Standing Orders'[45] that guide the conduct of members. Raising the issue of cases arising out of marriages, given the diversity of denominations in Kenya, consensus would be hard to reach, particularly as to

42 Lynch, Gabrielle, 'The Fruits of Perception: "Ethnic Politics" and the case of Kenya's Constitutional Referendum,' *African Studies*, 65, 2, December 2006, pages 233–268. The Electoral Commission of Kenya gave fruit symbols to the Yes and No vote in the referendum. Banana stood for the positive vote while Orange symbolized the negative vote. As a result of the campaigns, these fruits got a whole new meaning during this period.

43 Steeves, J., 'Beyond Democratic Consolidation in Kenya: Ethnicity, Leadership and "unbounded" politics', *African Identities*, Vol. 4, No. 2, pp. 195–211, 2006, page 197.

44 Hempel, 2004, page 128.

45 In some Christian denominations Standing Orders are called Canon Law.

what the Christian personal law would look like, and who should preside over its sessions. He attributes the inclusion of the Christian courts to a misconception about Kadhi's courts:

> Christians thought that Muslims want separate courts for themselves, so that if they do anything they would be taken to Kadhi's Courts and they, as Christians, would be taken to the usual courts. And that the person in charge is the Chief Kadhi. When people were discussing this issue, it emerged as if Muslims were being favoured. Then the Christians argued that now that Muslims have been given these courts, let us also be given Christian Courts. Then some Christians and some government officials went ahead and requested the religious courts without discussing how they shall operate, what it will consist of, who will be included, the hierarchy of the officials, as to who is the highest and the lowest.[46]

For the sake of some Christians, the Attorney General wanted to insert the clauses on Christian courts so as to silence them from opposing the draft, and hence ensure its success. It was also argued that it had been put in place in order to create equal ground for each religion to run its own personal law in a constitutionally-recognized manner; this is because the sole inclusion of Kadhi's courts could be interpreted as favouritism of Islam by the state. The diversity of Christian denominations was cited as an impediment to operability of these courts. Some raised the problem of a lack of consensus on how the officials will be selected. They also doubted how the various churches will agree on a common law for the handling of issues on a common personal law, and matters consequential to them, when each church has its own standing orders for the same.

The majority of local Muslims voiced similar sentiments as above, but also commented that the courts were added as a gradual step towards the total removal of all religious courts, including Kadhi's courts, once one of the courts proved unworkable. The draft was also accused of watering down the gains made under the Bomas Draft that involved contributions and negotiations of all stakeholders. The proposed changes raised at the Bomas Conference for the enhancement of Kadhi's courts were also cited as the reasons behind the inclusion of Christian courts. Evangelical churches under the auspices of the Kenya Church were nonetheless opposed to the inclusion of the Christian, Hindu and Kadhi's courts.

---

46 Personal interview with Reverend Munywa, on 9th October, 2006, at Isiolo's Methodist Church of Kenya.

The fact that the one of the principal sources of laws of Kenya is the English Common Law gained prominence in Kadhi's courts' debates. English Common Law, it is argued by Muslims, is based on Judeo-Christian traditions which imply that there was actually no basis for Christian courts as their laws form the backbone of the legal system in the country. Abdulla Dima recalls that it was only during the formulation of the Kilifi draft constitution that the clauses on the Christian and Hindu courts were added. He further points out that:

> Kenya's current judicial system, established by the British colonial administration, was almost synonymous with Christian culture. Therefore there was no need for separate courts for Christians and this was understood, and even during the process of collecting views, there is nowhere at any time when actually Christians either as individual or as a group have raised the issue of the Christian courts.[47]

Theme Seven: Civic Education for the Referendum and Choices Made

Prior to the Referendum, the CKRC selected national, provincial, district and constituency civic education providers (CEPs). CKRC *Source Book for Civic Education*[48] identifies the objective of the exercise as being to provide Kenyans with information, knowledge, and skills on the content of the Proposed New Constitution, to ensure that they make informed decisions whether to accept or reject it through a referendum. A 'win-win' approach was encouraged by the CKRC to ensure that the referendum remains a bargaining process and not a weapon to settle differences or even narrow antagonisms and prejudices. Apart from the officially approved CEPs, in Isiolo, unofficial civic educators played an instrumental role in raising civic consciousness and mobilization.

The CKRC educators approved, trained and funded for both Isiolo North and Isiolo South Constituencies included: Women's Access Programme (Isiolo District), Garba Tulla Development Organization (Garba Tulla), Lobby and Advocacy Service Team, Global Child Hope, Friends of Nomad's International (Northern Kenya), Northern Mosques and Madrassa Network (Isiolo Town, Merti, Garba Tulla, Sericho and Kinna), Ndugu Sangu Christian Community Development (Isiolo Town and

---

[47] Personal interview with Abdulla Dima, on 8th December 2006, Isiolo.

[48] CKRC, *Source Book for Civic Education: Referendum 2005*, Nairobi, CKRC, September 2005.

surrounding areas), Sericho Community Consortium (Sericho), Ngare Mara Development Consortium (Ngare Mara), and Oldo Nyiro Based Community Consortium (Oldo Nyiro).[49] Despite the geographical distribution of the chosen organizations, the civic education exercises were observed not to have reached the people well, especially those on the fringes of the town and the far-flung corners of the District. Inadequacy of time, personnel and resources were cited as the reasons behind the ineffectiveness of the programme. Unofficial civic educators included the local imams, youth leaders, priests and pastors of both Catholic and Protestant churches, and politicians. Through local initiatives, *Majlis ʿulamāʾ* and organizations such as the Council of Imams and Preachers of Kenya and representatives of SUPKEM and NCCK played an immense role in shaping the decisions of their faithful.

To "fully operationalise civic education, society must have a degree of tranquillity, enabling infrastructure to facilitate the movement of civic educators, and, a general will of the state to allow the exercise to take place".[50] However, most of the CEPs were led by personalities, who, to a great extent served as opinion leaders for their respective ethnic and religious constituencies and hence were highly-interested parties as to the kind of choices the voters made at the end of the day.[51] Sheikh Harun notes that:

> People, in some areas, turned away the educators and even insulted them. People, in such areas, said that they did not want what the educators were teaching them, saying that they are supporting Orange and so they did not want anything to do with new opinions. And that they did not want anything to do with such new ideas. Simply they had made [up] their mind about the things in the draft constitution.[52]

It has been suggested that the residents had made their choices before the official commencement of the referendum campaigns in October of 2005, based on unofficial civic educators, such as the religious institutions,

[49] CKRC List of District CEPs, CBOs as approved by Plenary on the 19th September 2005. Source www.kenyaconstitution.org (accessed 21.03.2006).

[50] Bellucci, S., Katumanga, M. & Otenyo, E., '"Political" education versus "Civic" Education in colonial and Independent Kenya', *Africa: Rivista trimestrale di studi e documentazione Dell'Instituto italiano per I'Africa e I'Oriente*, 62.1, 2007, page 2.

[51] Personal interview with Father Mathenge on 8th December 2006, at Kiwanjani Catholic Church, Isiolo.

[52] Personal interview with Sheikh Harun on 11th December 2006, at Bomen Hotel, Isiolo.

and informal talks.[53] While the CEPs were expected to educate the citizens about varieties of pertinent issues in the draft bill, the majority of the local residents were more interested in what affected them most. They frequently asked about what would happen to their land and the status of the Kadhi's courts.[54] Low literacy, poor political consciousness and rivalry between the Banana and Orange camps also affected the exercise. Poverty, unemployment, drought and famine in the first quarter of 2005 were observed to have reduced local people's bargaining powers and made them vulnerable to political manipulation. State patronage and use of incentives by those for and against the Wako Draft complicated the decision-making for the referendum. On the presence of threats and coercion of local leaders to campaign for the Wako Draft, Ahmed Hussein observes that:

> Of course threats were there. But many were not directed to the people, but to their leaders. There are cases where leaders come out and say to the people "look, this one is going to amount to my [being] sacked as an assistant minister and the government will never recognize me and give us development projects again if we are not going to take sides with the government". These were the issues that were not only coercive but also intimidating. Yes this can amount to force.[55]

It is a common practice in Isiolo for the approved CEPs to 'sublet' or 'outsource' their services at a lesser fee to organizations affiliated to them and to consume the bulk of the funding for their own use. The draft and the current constitutions presented to the CEPs are written in 'legalese' and were often not only voluminous but also incomprehensible to even the elite in the local civil society. This had the effect of reducing the whole of the constitutional debates to parochial issues related to the everyday concerns of the local Isiolo residents.

The perceptions of the youth, both Christian and Muslim, demonstrated greater coherence and accommodation of Kadhi's courts debates than those of the older respondents. However they have also expressed similar sentiments on their attitude towards members of the rival religion. Muslim women have higher levels of understanding of the need for empowerment of the courts than do ordinary men of the same religion.

---

[53] Personal interview with Sheikh Harun on 11th December 2006, at Bomen Hotel, Isiolo.

[54] Personal interview with Adan Jirma on 9th December 2006, at his Tulu Roba home, Isiolo.

[55] Personal interview with Ahmed Hussein, 20th December 2006, Safi Estate, Isiolo.

Christian women, on the other hand, demonstrate little awareness of the workings of the courts but do not have such a strong opposition as their co-religionist men. Youth of both religions express the need for the urgent redress of the social ills that afflict them most, such as unemployment, inequality and drug abuse, compared to the older respondents. It must be noted that in the events of strained relations between Muslims and Christians, it is the youth that becomes actively involved in skirmishes due to mobilization.

Emergent Trends from the Debates on Kadhi's Courts

Consultation at Kadhi's courts is relatively low; this is partly due to the existence of alternative, and to some extent complementary, mechanisms for conflict resolution for domestic matters that include marriage, divorce and inheritance. Local Muslims mix the customary and Islamic laws amicably for their daily needs. For instance among the Borana, the role of clan elders (Borana: *jarole*) is crucial in solving marital conflicts and, more often than not, matters of inheritance are decided not according to Islamic jurisprudence but through *aada sera Borana* (Borana customary law).[56] The elders function as a court with broad and flexible powers to interpret evidence, impose judgements, and manage the process of reconciliation.[57] The *jarole* or other local religious mediators use their judgement and position of moral ascendancy to find an acceptable solution. Traditionally, the parties involved in the conflict are likely to accept the decision and reconcile their differences.[58] The decisions of the elders do not involve loss of face and are backed by social pressures. For instance, the role of elders in mediation is often extended to minor criminal cases in places such as Merti and Garba Tulla. The underlying belief is that taking someone to judicial courts means handing over someone to 'foreigners' (Borana: *nyap*) whose decision may be regretted later. It is common to hear "*dubi affan borannat debissa*" meaning, let us take the mediation process back to the

[56] See Mario Aguilar's *Being Oromo In Kenya*, 1998, for understanding of *Nagaa Borana* (peace of Borana) and how the Waso Borana maintain harmony in their domestic and socio-economic and political sphere, pages 19–22. *Aada Sera Borana* means the customary traditions of the Borana.

[57] Ruto P., M. Adan & I. Masinde, *Indigenous Democracy: Traditional Conflict Resolution Mechanisms—Pokot, Turkana, Samburu and Marakwet*, Nairobi: ITDG-East Africa, 2004, page 4.

[58] Ruto et al., 2004, page 5.

local conflict resolution mechanism. Imams of local mosques conduct marriages and mediate in marital disputes and it is only for the issuance of marriage certificates and other forms of legal documents that the Kadhi is consulted. The infrequent consultation of the courts can be attributed to lack of adequate awareness about them and also the influence they have, because of their relatively short history in Isiolo Town, in comparison with the coastal region of Kenya.

Despite the above challenges, the majority of Muslims in the area showed great support for the expansion and improvement of the courts. This is largely due to the effects of elite mobilization, opposition from rival local and national ethnic and religious groups towards them, and the conviction that supporting them will have the greater benefit for the general Muslim populace in Kenya. Hirsch makes a similar observation among the Swahili, as follows: "though Muslim men have been harsh critics of kadhis who have historically been viewed as collaborators with the state, they join with kadhis to oppose the state in order to protect and promote Islamic legal practices".[59]

For the majority of the Christians in the town, the existence of Kadhi's courts in the constitution of Kenya is a recent discovery and, due to that, little if anything is known of their function and efficacy in dispensing justice in marital matters. Such specialized knowledge was observed to be available to the clergy. Misinformation and stereotyping of other faiths is common in Isiolo.

Muslim men in Isiolo town were observed to be very critical of the local kadhi. Their condemnation points to an accusation of being pro-women and being hasty in decision-making. Youthful Muslims question why a kadhi who understands Islamic, secular and local customary laws (Arab.: *ʿurf*), cannot be appointed despite the availability of such qualified persons who studied in the Sudan and the Middle East. Susan Hirsch sums up the predicament facing the kadhis in this way:

> The Kadhis are, for most part, ethnically Swahili ... Kadhis are generally assigned to courts outside their communities of origin. Frequent transfers mean that Kadhis are relatively unable to establish strong ties in their own towns of appointment and are uninterested in doing so.[60]

---

59 Hirsch, 1998, page 136.
60 Hirsch, 1998, page 122.

A number of Muslims in the area view the Kadhi as someone who should be more than just a judicial officer. He is expected to perform other duties such as preaching at mosques or other religious forums from time to time, interacting and co-operating with local *ʿulamāʾ* and sheikhs in Islamic activities, and generally adhering to Islamic codes of conduct in his everyday life. If all the above are not evident in a Kadhi, then contempt and indifference toward the institution and the person increases. This often happens in Isiolo. The complexity of this issue is heightened by the multiplicity of roles and functions that the Chief Kadhi performs at the national level.

In a sense, the debates on Kadhi's courts and the general participation of Muslims in the Referendum campaigns consolidated their votes and strengthened their bargaining power in the political future of the country. The resounding defeat that the government suffered at the hands of the Orange Democratic Movement (ODM) in the referendum was argued to have been impossible without the Muslims' minority vote. In all subsequent campaigns, there has been a concerted effort by the government and presidential candidates from the opposition parties to garner the community's support. All manners of promises have been made, commissions to address their grievances such as marginalization and harassment have recently been formed, and talks about signing of memoranda of understanding between national Muslim leadership and presidential candidates have become the norm. More than ever before, the future of Christian-Muslim relations and Muslim-State relations seem to be heading for a brighter future.

The Isiolo Interfaith Committee proved ineffective in curbing the religious divisions created by the Referendum debates. This committee had been instrumental in the past in diffusing tension between religions. Members include Muslim sheikhs and imams and Christian priests and pastors from Roman Catholic and Protestant churches. Christian-Muslim relations have been observed to be cordial after the Referendum, as life continued as normal and people put aside constitutional matters for some time. The interfaith committee mainly meets through seminars and workshops sponsored by donor agencies. Resolutions arrived at are often grandiose and far removed from the challenges that people of different religions and ethnic groups face in Isiolo.

Despite the failure of the Law of Succession Act (CAP 160) in the 1980s in formulating unified laws of succession for all the religions in Kenya, and its subsequent repeal in 1991 to exempt Muslims, there are signs of its revival, such as the Act of Parliament under the title of Marriage

Bill 2007.[61] Already its negative implications on the functions of Kadhi's courts have been mentioned as unwarranted. NAMLEF and other Muslim organizations have voiced strong criticism against it, on the basis that it contradicts the understanding of marriage, divorce, paternity, inheritance, custodianship and women's rights in Islamic jurisprudence. Should such a bill pass in Parliament, the crisis of Islamic law under Kadhi's courts will be far from over.

On 4th August 2010, another constitutional referendum was held on whether to adopt a proposed new constitution passed by the national assembly on 1st April 2010. The proposed draft was approved by 66.9% of the total votes cast. Among the issues that the 'no/red' leaders cited as anomalies that warranted its rejection were the retention of the Kadhi's courts, fears that the draft may allow for abortion on demand, and that its proposed clauses on land were discriminatory. The majority of mainstream and evangelical churches campaigned against the draft. The 'yes/green' team was led by President Mwai Kibaki and Prime Minister Raila Odinga, as well as by a host of other senior politicians, while the 'no/red' team was led by William Ruto. On 27th August 2010, the new constitution was officially promulgated, replacing the independence constitution. The new constitution proposes devolved forms of government, greater and equitable resource distribution, better gender representation and redress of pertinent issues such as corruption, abuse of human rights and historical injustices. The status of the Kadhi's courts, however, remains relatively unchanged from that within the old constitution.

Conclusion

It is imperative to note that the debate on Kadhi's courts in Isiolo is a complex one. The past history and present concerns are reinforced by the lack of consensus on the issues that surround the courts. The referendum campaigns also moved from the discussions of constitutional matters to political struggle at the national levels and the struggle for supremacy at the local level such as at Isiolo. Lack of adequate understanding of the

[61] In the month of August 2007, SUPKEM, in a paid-for press statement in the leading local dailies, expressed dissatisfaction with the government over four impending parliamentary bills for being rushed through the national assembly without wider consultation, their incompatibility with Islamic laws and the implications for the already existing statutes. The bills are: The Marriage Bill, 2007; The Matrimonial Property Bill, 2007; The Domestic Violence (Family Protection) Bill, 2007; and the Equal Opportunities Bill, 2007.

workings of the courts did not deter the actors across the religious lines from misconceiving the opinions of their rival ethno-religious grouping within the town. The regime in power has failed to do so within their time-span. It is hoped that the question of Kadhi's Courts will, in future, be discussed in an atmosphere of trust and co-operation, more so for the benefit of residents of such areas as Isiolo where Christian-Muslim relations and inter-ethnic relations have been soured.

CHAPTER EIGHT

"NECESSITY REMOVES RESTRICTIONS": SWAHILI MUSLIM WOMEN'S PERSPECTIVES ON THEIR PARTICIPATION IN THE PUBLIC SPHERE

Esha Faki Mwinyihaji

Introduction

This chapter examines factors that facilitate the increased participation of Swahili Muslim women in the public sphere, specifically in political leadership, in Mombasa, Kenya. The quest to make an entrance into leadership in the public sphere requires a thorough questioning of the 'truth' claims, by which the Swahili community functions. This chapter gives a brief background of the Swahili in general and their involvement in the politics of Mombasa. It focuses on the means that Swahili Muslim women have used in order to reclaim their opportunity of participating in the public sphere, especially in Mombasa. Like elsewhere in the world, the public sphere is not a neutral arena for social actors; it is a highly contested terrain, demanding the deployment of strategies and tactics of involvement in political competition.

The prospects of empowering Swahili Muslim women are being questioned along Islamic doctrinal and cultural grounds. Muslim women amongst the Swahili are forced by necessity to confront and contest interpretations of religious texts deemed responsible for reinforcing patriarchal structures and male-dominated religious forms of authority. Because of entrenched unequal forms of education, most Swahili Muslim women lack resources on how to debate, mobilize and lobby their way into leadership positions outside the home. Most significantly, they are few in political leadership. Recently, in a few instances, Swahili Muslim women have been visible in higher managerial ranks in large corporations and women's organizations.[1] However, to a large extent, the aspirations

[1] Examples include a former Coast Provincial Medical Director who was a Swahili Muslim woman; others include senior managers in co-operative organizations such as banks and parastatals.

and potentials of Swahili Muslim women to engage in what comprises leadership in the public sphere, notably the wielding of political power and authority, have yet to be realized.

Conceptual Theorization and Key Terms

The notion of a 'public sphere' has been a subject of debate for many scholars since the eighteenth century.[2] Implicit in the concept 'public sphere' is the separation of formal structures of religious and political authority from the space of household and kin, especially in European societies. More appropriate to the present discussion, which is centred in a Muslim society, is the approach of Eisenstadt and Schluchter.[3] According to these scholars, the 'public sphere' is conceptualized as an arena where culture is created, contested and in flux for both traditional and modern societies. Furthermore, societies and civilizations do not develop autonomously but through a continuous interaction between the cultural codes of these societies and their exposure to new internal and external challenges.

In the context of this discussion, the phrase 'public sphere' refers to an arena or social space where meanings of social issues are articulated, shared and negotiated: that which takes place in the public sphere may possibly influence political action. The public sphere, here, will serve as a general social horizon of experience in which everything that is actually or seemingly relevant for all members of society is integrated. This chapter is concerned only with political leadership as a visible marker of Swahili Muslim women's participation in the wider public sphere.

Swahili Muslims have been continuously exposed to new internal and external challenges and have developed rich cultural interpretations and practices. The participation of Swahili women has not always been confined to domestic life. Swahili Muslim women have actively participated in political leadership in their cultural milieu. However, during the last century, Swahili Muslim women's visibility in political leadership has been declining.

We hold that Swahili Muslim women are venturing into the public sphere out of necessity. The concept of 'necessity' is generated by Swahili

---

[2] Hoexter M., S. N. Eisenstadt & N. Levtzion (eds.), *The Public Sphere in Muslim Societies*, Albany: State University of New York, 2002, page 2.

[3] Eisenstadt, S. N. & W. Schluchter, 'Introduction: Paths to Modernities—A Comparative View', *Daedalus* 127:3, 1998, pages 1–18.

Muslim women's narratives during the course of this research. It is derived from Islamic legal precepts (*al-Qawāʿid al-Fiqhiyya*). According to *sharīʿa* principles, necessity dictates exceptions. Islam is not oblivious to the exigencies of life, to their magnitude, nor to human weakness and capacity to face them. It permits the Muslim, under the compulsion of necessity, to eat a prohibited food in quantities sufficient to remove the necessity and save himself from death; the context is after listing the prohibited foods in the form of dead animals, blood, and pork (*sūrat al-Baqara* (2): 173). Moreover, this is repeated four times in the Qur'ān after each mention of the prohibited foods.[4] On the basis of these and similar verses in the Qur'ān, Islamic jurists formulated an important principle, namely, that 'necessity removes restrictions' (Arab.: *al-dharūrāt tubīḥ al-maḥẓūrāt*). The title of this chapter is derived from this legal precept. This principle allows Muslims who are having trouble to engage in things that are initially forbidden.

Al-Qaradawi demonstrates that necessity allows the use of *ḥarām*, in cases wider than the food laws:

> In permitting the use of *ḥarām* under necessity, Islam is true to its spirit and general principles. This spirit, which we find permeating its laws, is to make life easy and less oppressive for human beings, and to lift the burdens and yokes imposed by earlier systems and religions.[5]

This precept is adopted as a defence mechanism for Swahili Muslim women to counter the assertions of modern clerical teachings that are geared towards enforcing seclusion and exclusion of women from political leadership. It is highly recommended that a Muslim woman's best place is the home (*sūrat al-Nūr* (24): 31).

Some Swahili consider the idea of women remaining at home to be true to Islamic spirit. In as far as Islam recommends a woman to stay at home, she may also go out for her needs, be it prayers, studies and other lawful needs, both religious and secular.[6] Hence, the Swahili Muslim women are seeking to liberate themselves from such patriarchal and religious restrictions that hinder them from active engagement in public sphere. They are seeking to unshackle themselves due to necessities incurred in the modern ways of living.

---

4 Al-Qaradawi, Y., 1960, *The Lawful and the Prohibited in Islam* (*Al-Halal Wal Haram Fil Islam*), New Dehli: Millat Book Centre, pages 36–37.

5 Al-Qaradawi, 1960, page 37.

6 Al-Qaradawi, 1960, page 167.

Mombasa: A Geographical and Historical Background

Mombasa is a cosmopolitan city, inhabited by many communities. It covers an area of 275 square kilometres.[7] Administratively, Mombasa is divided into four divisions: Changamwe, Island, Kisauni and Likoni. Kisauni division occupies the north coast, while Likoni covers the south coast. Island division mostly covers the Main Island. Changamwe occupies the Western mainland. The Swahili mainly live in Island and Changamwe divisions, among Arabs and Indians. A small portion of the Swahili are found in Kisauni and Likoni divisions.

Mombasa, like the rest of the East African Coast, has had contact with the outside world for millennia. In particular, there has been contact with the maritime states of the Indian Ocean such as the Persian Gulf, Arabia, India and China. The anonymous Greek traveller who wrote the *Periplus of the Erythrean Sea* visited the East Coast in the first century and saw trade being carried out between the merchants from Arabia and the local inhabitants.[8] When travellers like al-Masʿūdī (10th century), al-Idrīsī (12th century) and Ibn Baṭṭūṭa (14th century) visited the coast, towns like Zanzibar and Malindi were already in existence. The advent of Islam and subsequently its establishment in the coastal settlements led to an enduring influence on the cultural history of the Swahili city-states and village settlements.[9]

The identity of the Swahili is a paradox for many scholars. This is due to the Swahili community's dynamic capacity to absorb external features and influences through gradual integration of a multiplicity of outsiders into their society.[10] It is imperative to ask ourselves 'who are the Swahili?' This question has often prompted a quest for 'origins', a search for that historical moment *at* which, as well as the historical process *by* which, the Swahili can be said to have come into being.[11] Some scholars do not believe that the Swahili exist as an ethnic group; to them, the Swahili

---

[7] *Mombasa District Development Plan*, 1989–1993, page 1.

[8] Abdulaziz, M. H., *Muyaka: 19th century Swahili Popular Poetry*, Nairobi: Kenya Literature Bureau, 1979, page 7.

[9] Horton, M. and J. Middleton, *The Swahili: the social landscape of a mercantile society*, Oxford: Blackwell, 2000, pages 16, 47.

[10] Kresse, Kai, *Philosophising in Mombasa: Knowledge, Islam and Intellectual Practice on the Swahili Coast*, Edinburgh: Edinburgh University Press Ltd, 2007, pages 36–37; Loimeier, Roman and Rüdiger Seesemann (editors), *The Global Worlds of the Swahili*, Hamburg: LIT Verlag, 2006, pages 55–66.

[11] Mazrui, Alamin M. & Ibrahim Noor Shariff, *The Swahili: Idiom and Identity of an African People*, New Jersey: Africa World Press, 1994, page 17.

are a mixture of Arabic and African races.[12] On the contrary, others recognise that the Swahili are an ethnic group that is distinct from other African ethnic communities and definitely very different from the Arabs.[13] The Swahili are an urban Muslim Community that emerged on the East African coast around 800.[14] One very striking characteristic trait of the Swahili is their assimilation of newcomers.[15]

The participation of Swahili Muslims generally in the Kenyan public sphere has neither been constant nor has it progressed since colonial times. The Swahili ruled the coastal city states for many centuries prior to European colonial rule. They controlled the power and wealth in these city states. The Swahili were mainly fishermen and farmers, as well as being engaged in trade both overseas and with the hinterland of Kenya.[16] This peaceful trade was disrupted by the coming of the Portuguese in the late 15th century. At the end of the 17th century, the Omanis took over control of the East African coast, ruling the various towns as well as dominating trade. In the 19th century, Omani Arabs, ruling from a sultanate established on Zanzibar Island, attained control of political and social dominion on the coast in addition to running an active shipping trade. This period saw the emphasis on the Arabic elements of Swahili culture. Zanzibar served as a nexus for the Swahili with new fashions in clothing, religion and governance. The advent of British imperialism in the late nineteenth century disrupted the Omani influence and also brought an end to the slave trade. The slaves had been depended upon to provide labour on the farms owned by Swahili as well as Arabs.

The public sphere in Mombasa has always been a contested space and Mombasa did not belong to the Swahili alone but also to their closest allies, the Mijikenda,[17] as well as to Arabs and Indians who were

---

[12] Maxon, Robert M., *East Africa: Introductory History*, Nairobi: EAE Publishers, 1986, page 40.

[13] Kim, C. C., *Islam Among the Swahili in East Africa*, Nairobi: Acton Publishers, 2004, page 10.

[14] Horton, M. and John Middleton, 2000, pages 46ff.

[15] Askew, Kelly Michelle, 'Female Circles and Male Lines: Gender Dynamics on the Swahili Coast', *Africa Today*, Volume 46, Number 3/4, Summer/Autumn 1999, pages 67–102

[16] Cruise O'Brien, Donal, 'Coping with the Christians: The Muslim predicament in Kenya', in *Religion and Politics in East Africa*, Bernt Hansen & Michael Twaddle (eds.), Oxford: James Currey, 1995, 200–219, page 212; Middleton, John, *The World of the Swahili*, New Haven: Yale University Press, 1992.

[17] Mijikenda: nine closely related but distinct peoples who share a common linguistic and cultural heritage. The Nine are: Kauma, Giriama, Chonyi, Jibana, Kambe, Ribe, Rabai,

engaged in trade. Mombasa has maintained its cosmopolitan state with many people from the hinterland of Kenya. The Swahili no longer have the command and control of the coast in the way they did during the al-Mazrūʿī and Āl Bū Saʿīd periods.[18] They have been adversely affected from an administrative point of view as well as over the question of land ownership.

They lost control of considerable areas of land, partly due to a misunderstanding by the Kenya Land Commission to whom they put their case for land ownership in 1932. Some of the Swahili homelands were taken over by the government as Crown Land. For example, the land currently occupied by Wa-Jomvu on the Maunguja channel is still considered Crown Land and the people who have lived there for years are considered to be squatters. It was reported in an interview that currently squatters are demanding land from the government that belongs to absentee property owners, especially in Kisauni areas.[19]

Hence, there is stiff competition for political control from all the forces involved, be they up-country people who have settled in Mombasa, Arabs, Indians or the Swahili. The *Mwambao* movement failed because of disunity of the interested parties.[20] There are many rivalries between the Swahili families in the support of a male electoral candidate. This makes the entrance of women into the political public sphere even more complicated. However, this is not to say that Swahili Muslim women are not making progress in the arena.

The initiatives and the obstacles to Swahili Muslim women's entrance into the public sphere during the years since independence are now examined. Interviews and observations were carried out between May 2007 and April 2008 in order to identify the factors which are seen as necessitating Swahili Muslim women's participation. The analysis of the data does not necessarily suggest homogeneity and consensus among Swahili Muslim women, rather it represents the dominant perspectives that were found in the course of the research.

Duruma and Digo; Spear, Thomas, *The Kaya Complex*, Nairobi: Kenya Literature Bureau, 1978, page 4.

[18] Jewel, J. H. A., *Mombasa: The Friendly town*, Nairobi: East African Publishing House, 1976; Kresse, 2007, pages 52–53.

[19] Interview with Mishi Abdul, at Kisauni, on 15th May 2007.

[20] *Mwambao* was a separatist movement of the people of Coast Region following Independence. Salim, Ahmed Idha, *Swahili Speaking Peoples of Kenya's Coast, 1895–1945*, Nairobi: East Africa Publishing House, 1973.

Necessity and the Idiom of Leadership amongst Swahili Muslim Women

When traced back in history, it is possible to argue for the existence of cultural idioms and religious nuances which Swahili Muslim women have used to distinguish themselves and to seek leadership prowess in the public sphere. In the histories of the Swahili there are motivational stories of heroines like Mwanamkisi who ruled Kongowea.[21] It was harder for Swahili Muslim women to have active political participation in Mombasa in the 1960s and 1970s. The women who have been active political leaders, like Shamsa Muhashamy, have had the support of their husbands. Shamsa explains that she got a lot of support from her second husband, Ali Salim Jeneby, who was a man of politics; so, with his support she began working in the public sphere.[22] Shamsa represents the first attempt by Swahili Muslim women after independence to take an active role in the public sphere. Prior to this, many women from patrician families never made a public display of themselves. It was considered shameful and improper to go out in public.[23] For instance, Swahili Muslim women hardly ever visited butcheries and fish shops, which were considered areas where men visited and sat down to talk. One informant, in particular, insisted that although she was married for forty years, in all these years she never visited the butchery to buy meat or went to a fish shop. She contrasted this with her current status as a widow; her husband is no longer there to run the errand for her. She said that she hates going to these two places because the men there continuously stare, or often initiate gossip about women. However, circumstances have forced her to change with time.

In politics today, looking through the local government lists in the Mombasa municipality, the participation of Swahili Muslim women has been minimal. There have been only four Swahili Muslim women councillors since independence, all of whom initially were nominated members. These women are Aisha Busaidy, Bijuma Bwajuma, Somoe Abdallah Amour and Shuweikha Rashid.

Of the four women, Aisha Busaidy, now deceased, was a favourite of many women, always appearing in *Maendeleo Ya Wanawake* (Women's Development) programmes within Mombasa. She was known to many

---

21 Jewel, 1976, page 17.

22 Mirza, S. & M. Strobel (eds. and trans.), *Three Swahili Women: Life histories from Mombasa*, Bloomington: Indiana University Press, 1989, page 110.

23 Kresse, 2007, page 53.

as Ashuu. Aisha was initially a nominated member but was later elected as a councillor for Kibokoni ward.

Bijuma Bwajuma, now deceased, was nominated during the tenure of her relative, Mayor Ahmed Shahame Mwidani. She campaigned for him, so some saw this as one way the former mayor was repaying the efforts of his strong supporters. Bijuma Bwajuma had no formal education, and mostly used Swahili as the language to address people at public rallies. She was a very charismatic leader and could mobilise many Swahili women into voting for the candidate she was campaigning for.

Somoe Abdallah Amour, after her period in office as a nominated member, subsequently migrated to the United Kingdom.

Shuweikha Rashid is also a well-known woman, who, when she was interviewed, had just participated in the opening of the Mombasa Agricultural Show. She boasted of having shared the dais with the president as being something which some men are still very jealous about. Concerning her involvement in politics, she observed:

> For a woman to be involved in and gain entrance into the political arena she has to be at least twenty times better than a man. It was not for me to gain access but I fought my competitors hard and was able to succeed. People like the late Sharriff Nassir were not very happy to see me brushing shoulders with the people in government at that time.[24]

The sentiments of Shuweikha support our argument that the public sphere is a contested space that is not freely available for women to take, especially in the political field. They have to compete with the other contestants who are men, rather than with other Swahili Muslim women, and, if they are to succeed, have to use the same tools as the men to advance their campaigns. Shuweikha's sentiments also imply that Swahili Muslim women are well involved in the political arena. They are slowly breaking the boundaries of custom and religion in order to fully participate in the public sphere. The 2007 Kenyan elections saw the entry of three Swahili Muslim women into politics in Mombasa Municipality. They owe their entry to the popularity of the party ticket, namely the Orange Democratic Movement (ODM) as well as to their earlier involvement in Women's Groups.[25] They initially worked with women's groups in various projects

[24] Shuweikha Rashid, Kibokoni, Mombasa, 31st August 2007.

[25] Maimuna Salim, Shanzu, 20th March 2008; Maimuna Omar Waziri, Junda, 19th March 2008.

such as dealing with HIV/AIDS victims, youth programmes and starting funding initiatives for women.

These women's groups deserve a special mention because they are the genesis of Swahili Muslim women's breakthrough to the public sphere. All the politically active Swahili Muslim women were initially involved in women's activities in their localities. They also served as important campaigners with prominent political leaders in their constituencies. They provided potential voters to male politicians. Afye Rama, an unsuccessful Parliamentary candidate in the 2007 general elections, asserted: "If I could be able to mobilise supporters to all these previous male politicians, why can't I become a candidate myself".[26] These sentiments were also echoed by most Swahili Muslim women who contested the 2007 general election in Kenya. Swahili Muslim women's groups served as important areas for these women's participation in the public sphere. In fact, they serve as informal venues for Swahili Muslim women's entrance and participation in the public sphere. These Swahili Muslims women's groups are legitimated by the notion that they are women-only groups and there are no avenues for mixed gender activities. Politically, they serve to empower prospective contestants with a valid record of accomplishment in terms of achievements. The Swahili Muslim women contend that they may be able to make more progress in their communities if they are given a formal type of leadership.[27] It should be acknowledged that some male politicians make many pledges to garner the support of these women and then normally 'drop them' when they have achieved their objectives.

It was observed that single women, or women who are unattached, seem to be seen more in the public sphere. These are women who are widows, divorcées, or who are unmarried. In addition, women who are married as second wives, or even those who are marrying for the second time, seem to have greater involvement in activities in the public sphere. Women with supportive spouses also participate more in the public sphere.[28] This can be seen as a bid to better their family life and the community at large.

---

[26] Afye Rama, Fort Jesus, 17th March 2008.

[27] Maimuna Salim, Shanzu, 20th March 2008; Maimuna Omar Waziri, Junda, 19th March 2008.

[28] Maimuna Salim, Shanzu, 20th March 2008; Maimuna Omar Waziri, Junda, 19th March 2008.

Some Swahili Muslim men view it as despicable for a married woman to stand on a public platform and deliver a speech.[29] Swahili Muslim men with a strong religious inclination see it as provocative for a woman to sit on a dais. At times, a public appearance is associated with making a public display of a woman's beauty. Today's Swahili Muslim women parliamentary aspirants appear in public without veils. This seems to support the sentiments of religious theologians that the appearance by women in the public sphere is a source of *fitna* (Arab.: civil strife) and, because of that, women should only appear when absolutely necessary.[30] In the past, as noted by both older Swahili Muslim women and some scholars,[31] there was separation of men and women in public gatherings such as weddings and funerals. Especially at weddings, the women's quarters were shielded from the public. Today, at most weddings of the Swahili, men and women tend to mix freely, especially if there is a musician at the wedding. Where there are *Taarab* Music[32] performances in town, men and women mix and at times dance together. In these gatherings, there is no regard for seclusion or veiling; there seems to be a laxity of observation of Islamic rules such as the prohibition of music and the free mixing of men and women. This trend shows that there are factors other than *sharīʿa* that legitimise women's entrance into the public sphere. Modernity has exposed the Swahili to new kinds of lifestyles that are castigated by Islam.

However, this ideal seems to be theoretical for the majority of Swahili Muslim women. Many have ventured into the public sphere due to necessity, especially because of economic needs. The structures that were there to safeguard their comfortable life-styles in their homes have crumbled. They no longer own land and farms in order to have enough money to maintain their standard of living. The British colonial period marked the decline of Swahili economic and political structures.[33] The two pillars of economic resources along the coast, land and labour, have been diminished. The move from the old harbour in Mombasa to the modern port of Kilindini led to a further decline in their trading prowess.[34] Very few

---

29 Amina Zuberi, Fort Jesus, 25th March 2008.

30 Fatma Sufi, Munawarah, 26th March 2007.

31 Mirza & Strobel, 1976.

32 *Taarab* music, a blend of Arab and Indian styles which developed in the 19th century, is very popular in Kenya and Tanzania.

33 Janmohamed, K. K., *A history of Mombasa c. 1895–1939; some aspects of economic and social life in an East African port town during colonial rule*, unpublished PhD thesis, Northwestern University, 1978, page 161.

34 Kresse, 2007, page 48.

Swahili families were able to prevent their farms from being appropriated by the colonial government, leaving many Swahili in economic need.

Another necessity that is driving the Swahili Muslim women into the public sphere is the influx of 'up-country' people to the coast.[35] The coast belongs even less to the Swahili and they now form a minority in their own homeland. With the fall of economic and political structures, Mombasa was transformed into an urban centre dependent on up-country people for leadership. The up-country people share Mombasa with the Swahili and are very enterprising and, at times, are seen to be aggressive in economic circles.

The Swahili were initially reluctant to send their children to secular schools for fear of conversion to Christianity. This contributed to their being disadvantaged in education, allowing people from the hinterland in Kenya to take up many positions of leadership in co-operative organizations. This has forced Swahili Muslim women to develop similar strategies to effectively compete with them. Hence, they are now present in the public sphere, seeking economic sustenance. In the past, a woman from one of the patrician families (*Waungwana*) wielded power, whereby she at least owned the house which she lived in. However, her affairs outside the house were taken care of by her male relatives as she was seen to not have enough experience in matters outside the house. A Swahili Muslim woman acted as a silent owner while male relatives managed her affairs and estates. Due to illiteracy, many women lost their properties by signing documents that they knew little about.[36] The sense of trust that used to exist between members of the same family has been lost. Times have changed and siblings rarely trust each other with their property.

Due to the loss of property, some Swahili Muslim women whose parents owned resources in the past, are now living a destitute life. For instance, in an area like Mikindani on the mainland, some have sold their dilapidated houses for a very low price and moved to live on the fringes of estates owned by up-country people. It should be noted that there are many Swahili in some regions in Mombasa district who may fall under the category of internally displaced people due to the Land Ordinance Acts

[35] 'up-country' is used to describe people who come from beyond the coastal hinterland.

[36] Mwinyihaji, Esha F., 'The Contribution of Islam toward Women's Emancipation: A case study of the Swahili Muslims in Mombasa District, Kenya', Unpublished M.Phil Thesis, Moi University, 2001, pages 142–143.

of 1932.[37] Many Swahili were displaced from their original homelands at that time, or pawned their lands and estates at very low prices to Indian entrepreneurs. Many Swahili became squatters, especially those who were illiterate. Today, the women who lead a secluded lifestyle are now working out strategies to survive in the public sphere.

Swahili Muslim women were also involved in petty trading. However, this was done within the confines of their homes. They sold cooked foodstuffs, which were cooked within the homes, and buyers went to their homes. Some Swahili Muslim women employed domestic helpers who hawked the foodstuffs for them in the streets, or sold them at the market places. Though these businesses appeared to be petty, some Swahili Muslim women were able to accrue enough wealth to purchase property, such as houses with rental premises, or to buy jewellery and *kangas* (Swah.: ladies' printed cotton wrap). The jewellery and *kangas* are still considered important for they can be pawned or sold at times of difficulty. Swahili people who were living in town, and were involved in selling foodstuffs, cooked the foodstuffs at home while their men established stalls to sell what their wives cooked.

The trend is changing for Swahili Muslim women living in the villages. These women no longer cook all of the foodstuffs at home, but cook outside their homes, especially by the roadside where there are many passers-by who are potential buyers. The selling of foodstuffs is no longer solely in their own hands; up-country people have also learnt the business and have forced these women to move out in order to sell their stuff. Therefore, one of the necessities for moving into the public sphere is to compete with their more enterprising up-country neighbours involved in the same businesses.

Another reason necessitating the appearance of Swahili Muslim women in the public sphere is to ensure enough income to supplement what their husbands earn. In some of the households observed, women are the sole breadwinners. Other Swahili Muslim women are engaged in these businesses in order to get enough money to buy what their husbands cannot buy for them, or to make their lives more comfortable. The Swahili Muslim women have opined that if they wait every day for what their husbands bring home, life will be very uncomfortable. This is the opinion of the uneducated women who live in the villages and also

[37] Kindy, Hyder, *Life and Politics in Mombasa*, Nairobi: East African Publishing House, 1972, page 190.

the opinion of the educated women who work in offices in town. Some women argue that they need to live in a good neighbourhood, have presentable furniture, be able to take their children to good schools and not to municipal schools where there is little teaching going on.

The other necessity for entrance into the public sphere is in order to get security from Non-Governmental Organizations (NGOs). Swahili Muslim women, like other women, have had difficulties securing loans from banks to start worthwhile business ventures. The role of NGOs such as Tototo Home Industries and Bamako Initiative was crucial. Microfinance through NGOs came to the rescue of women by encouraging them to work in groups.[38] For instance, Tototo Home Industries gave them training about different ways to advance women financially, such as poultry keeping and owning rental property. They also gave them credit facilities to set-up economic activities. This training has gone a long way to expose Swahili Muslim women to the public sphere. It has empowered them to take charge of their economic lives. Apart from starting saving schemes for different women's groups, these NGOs have also encouraged literacy programmes for elderly illiterate women. The major setback in these initiatives is the lack of repayment of loans by some of the women. Many women take loans, not to start a business, but to repay old debts. Whereas some women have managed to educate their children through such programmes, others have simply utilised the loans for daily needs like food.

Swahili Muslim women have shown an amazing capacity for mobilization in their various women's groups. For example, they are usually the majority at political rallies organized by male candidates, especially where *Taarab* musicians are entertaining at such events. In the past, these women have not tried to be candidates, but have simply voted for men, taking into account the favourite candidate of the family patriarch.[39] This shows that Swahili Muslim women have been used as steps by men to climb up to political leadership.

Challenges Facing Swahili Muslim Women

One of the challenges facing Swahili Muslim women's entry into the public sphere is that of contestation. The study, conducted in Mombasa, reveals that the public sphere is not just there for women to take. There is competition with the men who are already there. The Swahili Muslim women

[38] Kambua, Changamwe, 13th May 2007.
[39] Munira Abeid, Spaki, 15th May 2007; Mishi Abdul, Kisauni, 15th May 2007.

also have to struggle to get a place using the means that are in vogue, for instance, the requirement of parliamentary contestants in Kisauni constituency to have policies touching on the squatter problem, regardless of whether they are male or female.[40] Through a series of workshops that took place in Nairobi, women were equipped with such resources as to how to formulate policies, state their visions and what they can accomplish. The aspiring Swahili Muslim women contestants were among those who attended. These workshops served as venues of political enlightenment, but were not sufficient by themselves to propel Swahili Muslim women into political positions. The women expressed a lot of zeal in the initial stages of campaigning but lost momentum as more powerful politicians gained popularity with the public.

Religion is another challenge. On religion, there are several reasons advanced as to why *sharīʿa* is against Muslim women's participation in the public sphere. That is the way *sharīʿa* has been revealed and people are to follow it.[41] The following reasons are advanced:

- Women lack the necessary knowledge about public life
- Female participation leads to the mixing of the sexes (*ikhtilāf* and *khalwa*)[42]
- Female biological cycle and life cycle will cloud their judgement
- Women can never be heads of state
- Females need to travel with a *maḥram*[43]

There is always the quotation of *sūrat al-Nisāʾ* (4): 34 that men are protectors of women. Different scholars have different interpretations of the verse. This is a verse that is quoted whenever the issue of leadership arises and it is meant to put women in their rightful position of submission to men. There is also the verse on *ḥijāb* (*sūrat al-Aḥzāb* (33): 33).

To further support the point is the *ḥadīth* on Persia: that a society led by women will never prosper.[44] This *ḥadīth* is the subject of debate in Islamic public discourses as a weak *ḥadīth*, following its chain of transmission. These are scriptural matters that are given to the masses who take

[40] Mishi Abdul, Kisauni, 15th May 2007.
[41] Fatma Sufi, Munawarah, 26th May 2007; Amina Zuberi, Fort Jesus, 25th March 2008.
[42] *ikhtilāf* Arab.: controversial questions; *khalwa* Arab.: seclusion.
[43] *maḥram* Arab.: close kin with whom marriage is forbidden.
[44] Bukhari: Volume 9:219.

them as being absolute whilst not being given an understanding of the issues. Both ordinary and professional women among the Swahili tend to group activities into categories as *ḥalāl* (lawful) or *ḥarām* (unlawful) questions. Some of the religious teachings reinforce the already-existing customs such as male leadership and early marriages. There is a *ḥadīth* that three things should not be delayed: prayers, burying a dead person and for a maiden to get married. Amina Zuberi sought an official position from the Council of Imams and Preachers of Kenya on Muslim women and leadership; however she got no response from them.[45]

There is a lot of ambiguity concerning the political leadership of Swahili Muslim women, centred on Islam. Yet there is no direct or implicit reference to it in *sharīʿa*. The current Swahili Muslim women's activism is based on the need for the collaboration of both men and women in the public sphere in order to achieve development.

Customs are also cited as being a restraint to public participation. I have grouped the two together because Islam has been associated with Swahili culture for a long time. The recent presence of Muslim reformists and their classification of certain things as *bidʿa* (Arab.: innovation) has led to attempts to distinguish between religion and culture.[46] Swahili Muslim women cannot lead men, or women cannot make good leaders according to local custom. Leadership is something reserved for men, according to Swahili customs. Another aspect of customs is early marriage, where the person getting married is not consulted. Men talk and finalize the affairs of women in an absolute manner. Educated women may have a say in the choice of a husband; what about those who do not go beyond primary school in their education?

There seems to be a division among women at various levels. Firstly there are urban and rural Swahili Muslim women. The urban women consider themselves to be more modernized and this can be seen in the type of houses they live in and also in the fuel used for cooking, namely gas, electricity and charcoal. Rural dwellers live in simple Swahili houses without proper demarcation of rooms in the house, as sitting room or dining room; a house of nine rooms may have only one bathroom and one toilet. They mostly use firewood and charcoal as fuel for cooking.

---

45 Amina Zuberi, Fort Jesus, 20th March 2008.

46 Munira Abeid, Spaki, 15th May 2007; Mishi Abdul, Kisauni, 15th May 2007; Maimuna Salim, Shanzu, 20th March 2008; Maimuna Omar Waziri, Junda, 19th March 2008.

Then there is another distinction based on educational status. The more educated tend to move to urban centres, and if they have a high income, they live in affluent areas, guarded by security guards and dogs. They hardly mix with village women, unless they are relatives, and then only on special occasions. Visits by relatives from the village to the town are always interpreted in terms of "what do they want from 'us' ", not just to enquire about their well-being. The world of the educated women revolves around home-work-school-home. If they make visits to the village, it is to their immediate parents. We can say that economic achievement among women further reinforces the barrier of dialogue among Swahili Muslim women. They lose touch with reality and tend to judge other people's lack of similar achievement as laziness, without reflecting on the whole picture. Changes in the Kenyan economy as a whole have had an impact on whether Swahili Muslim women remain in the private sphere or are forced to participate in the public sphere in order to survive.[47]

Wariness concerning secular education as a whole has its roots in the fact that it was initially offered by missionaries. This led to the fear that if a Swahili Muslim woman attended a mission school, she would be converted to Christianity and would marry a Christian. So parents thought that it was safer to only send their boys to school, as the risk was greater with girls. The issue of education has been perceived by Muslims in general as marginalizing since 1907 when the seat of government was moved from Mombasa to up-country Nairobi. Prior to that, literacy existed at the coast for a long time. Girls have inherited secular education marginality three times over: from 'traditions' in parents' preference to educate boys rather than girls; from 'religion' because secular education was perceived as bad due to the mixing of boys and girls in schools, plus the notion that girls should be 'protected'; and from the 'colonial' one which affects all Muslims, both male and female.

Alliances are formed, and a dependency culture develops, among the Swahili Muslim women, either in groups, or individually, with aspiring contestants of a parliamentary seat. The politicians expect to get votes from them by promising either to help them in their projects or by giving bribes. However, it is also noted that these bribes are short-lived and come once every five years. 2007 was an election year in Kenya, and Swahili Muslim women in the study area were very excited about the 'boon' to

47 Kresse, 2007, page 56.

come in the election months. They eagerly waited for politicians to arrive so that they could 'harvest' their bribes. Some informants expressed the opinion that Swahili Muslim women are losers in the end as those who benefit a lot are those seen in the politicians' homes throughout the year. Again, Swahili Muslim women form their own alliances to assist them in their day-to-day affairs; the women's groups are examples of these. The rurally based include Mwangaza, Kisauni, Likoni and Mikindani, among others. We also have religious Women's organizations such as Muslim Women's Action Group and the women's wing of Changamwe Muslim Youth. The religious groups lack able leadership and apt management, as observed in one informal talk. An example was given of Malindi Educational Development Association (MEDA), a group in Malindi, north coast of Kenya, that received 36 million shillings. This is because they have set targets for their manager, whose work is to formulate policies, initiate projects and maintain them by soliciting for funds. Such activities are not found in these women's religious organizations. They lack long-term goals and ways to achieve them.

Money is an important factor as to whether women can mobilize people to become public leaders, especially in politics. It is a requirement that you spend money in order to get returns. Swahili Muslim women are known to like receiving small handouts during the election process, so they are targeted. Then Swahili Muslim women contestants have to have money as a resource to buy their way in. As well as efforts by Kenya Anti-corruption Commission to do away with a bribe culture, there are many placards condemning the practice. The effort still has a long way to go. People engage in politics to become rich quickly because parliamentarians raise their salaries whenever they like.

Conclusion

The entry of Swahili Muslim women into the public sphere is multifaceted. In order for them to make meaningful lives for themselves and their families, Swahili Muslim women have to adapt to the changes that face them. Economic needs have overshadowed the cultural and religious restrictions affecting them. They are gradually carving out a place in the public sphere. Most Swahili Muslim women's supremacy as heads of their households is silently acknowledged. Their major entrance into political leadership remains a future objective that they are determined to achieve. The 2007 elections provided the civic candidacy of Swahili

Muslim women with three seats. The parliamentary contestants did not succeed, but they made a mark showing that they are ready to take up the responsibility. These women are optimistic that the future looks bright for them, and their initial venture served as a lesson for them. They have learnt that *sharīʿa* provides room for their active engagement in leadership. They have already been successful in sensitizing their community to the current pandemic of HIV/AIDS. In the non-political leadership ranks, Swahili Muslim women have made significant progress. They need proper guidance on governance and effective ways to propel them into the public sphere.

CHAPTER NINE

WOMEN'S VIEWS ON THE ROLE OF KADHI'S COURTS: A CASE STUDY OF KENDU BAY, KENYA

Rebecca Osiro

Introduction

At the start of the 20th century, during the early years of the British colonial era in East Africa, Muslims began to move to more rural settings in the interior, with the development of trading centres away from the railway line. This led to the need for appropriate leadership. This chapter examines how Muslim women in one such remote rural community on the shores of Lake Victoria have interacted with Kadhi's Courts.

The existence of Kadhi's courts in the coastal strip of Kenya had been ensured under the agreement between the Sultan of Zanzibar and the British to "preserve an Islamic way of life".[1] However, during the British colonial period, beyond the coastal strip, Kadhi's courts were only established in areas with a significant Muslim presence such as Isiolo in Eastern Province and Mumias in Western Kenya.[2] The British developed a triple court system, with Native courts and Islamic courts as well a legal system modelled on British common law.

In the run-up to independence in 1963, an agreement was drawn up between the Sultan of Zanzibar, the Prime Minister of Kenya and the British Secretary of State which ensured that Kadhi's courts should continue on the coastal strip "to the determination of questions of Muslim law relating to personal status (for example, marriage, divorce and inheritance) in proceedings in which all parties profess the Muslim religion".[3]

---

[1] An-Na'im, A. A. (ed.), *Islamic Family Law In A Changing World: A Global Resource Resource Book*, London: Zed Books, 2002, page 40.

[2] Chesworth, John A., 'Kadhi's Courts in Kenya: Reactions and Responses', in Tayob A., and J. Wandera (eds.), *Constitutional Review in Kenya and Kadhis Courts*, Cape Town: Centre for Contemporary Islam, 2011, pages 3–17, page 5.

[3] Clause two of the exchange of letters between the Prime Ministers of Kenya and Zanzibar dated 8th October 1963. See Chesworth 2011, page 5.

In addition, the triple court system was codified in 1963. However, in 1967, Kenya abolished formal traditional courts, whilst retaining the common law courts and Islamic courts. The Islamic courts carried out their administrative functions only for Muslims, dispensing decisions on family issues such as personal status, marriage, divorce, property inheritance and succession. As the need arose for the Muslims to have legal and religious leadership, the constitution was amended to allow Kadhis to operate beyond the initially stipulated Ten Mile Strip along the coast, to urban centres in the country's interior.[4]

The area under study, Kendu Bay, is a small rural town situated on the shores of Lake Victoria in the western part of Kenya. It is about one hundred and twenty kilometres south of Kisumu, the administrative headquarters of Nyanza, one of the eight provinces in the country. The Kadhi's court is located in Kisumu and the poor infrastructure of Nyanza province makes it relatively inaccessible. It is partly for this reason that the Muslims in Kenya feel marginalized on a religious basis.[5]

Previous studies have examined women's use of Kadhi's courts on the coast, notably Susan F. Hirsch and E. E. Stiles' 1998 study,[6] which observed that women frequented the courts more than men. This chapter, by studying women from a remote rural location, seeks to discover whether these women are able to access Kadhi's courts and to benefit from them. This research was carried out as the place of Kadhi's courts in the Constitution of Kenya was being hotly debated throughout the nation.

The research was conducted through a series of in-depth interviews in Kendu Bay and environs as well as in Kisumu. Those who were interviewed for the research are identified by initials; the location and the month of the interview is also given, together with the sequential number of the interview.

---

[4] Anderson, J. N. D., *Islamic Law in Africa*, London: Frank Cass & Co. Ltd., 1970, pages 81, 107.

[5] Said, A. S., 'An outline history of Islam in Nyanza Province', in M. Bakari & S. S. Ahmed (eds.), *Islam in Kenya: proceedings of the National Seminar on Contemporary Islam in Kenya*, Nairobi: MEWA, 1995, pages 19–27.

[6] Hirsch, Susan F., *Pronouncing and Preserving: Gender and the Discourses of Disputing in African Islamic Court*, Chicago: University of Chicago Press, 1998; Stiles, E. E., 'A Kadhi and His Court: Marriage, Divorce, and Zanzibar's Islamic Legal Tradition' (A doctoral dissertation), St. Louis, Missouri, UMI, 2002.

The Community and Origins of Kendu Bay town

Today Kendu Bay is a cosmopolitan town. The Luo are the dominant ethnic group followed by a significant minority, the Gwe,[7] who have been assimilated by the Luo. Swahili culture prevails, due to intermarriage and trade between the coastal and the local communities. The western part of Kendu Bay town, towards Lake Victoria (the old town), where most of the Muslim population live, is a mixture of small huts of corrugated iron and grass thatched roofs served by a dusty road and paths.

Islam arrived in the community with the coming of an Arab trader, Nyasoro, who arrived by boat in the bay in 1902 and built a house on the shore. In 1904 a mosque was built in the town where the Islamic court was established, at a strategic point close to the shore.[8] It was there that a group of eight elders, referred to as *Kamba Nane* (Swah: eight strings), volunteered their leadership to the Muslim community, led by Nyasoro and his Gwe counterpart, Kherala Madoro, who were the first Muslims in the area.

In 1906, the first Christian missionary, Arthur Carscallen, a missionary from the British Adventist Mission,[9] arrived in Kendu Bay, staying with Nyasoro for the first few days after his arrival. Once he was settled he joined the locals in their courts from where he disseminated Christian teaching. He was still remembered by the local people in Kendu Bay, who knew him as *Bwana Kaskal*.[10] Carscallen's missionary work was carried out along the shores of Lake Victoria. He established a training centre at Gendia, about four kilometres south of Kendu Bay town, and also several schools. He was involved in the translation of parts of the New Testament (*St. Matthew's Gospel*) into the Luo language, teaching and converting local people to Christianity.[11] Carscallen is depicted as 'a missionary, an

---

[7] The Gwe are a sub group of the Luhya.

[8] Initially, a grass thatched Mosque was erected at Miti Mbili, about twenty kilometres south of Kendu Bay town. The building served for prayers as well as a court.

[9] Mahon, J., 'What Happened in 1906?', Souvenir Special 100 Years of Mission 1906–2006, *Messenger: Journal of the Seventh-day Adventist Church in the United Kingdom and Ireland* Volume 111.17, 2006, pages 3–11. Arthur Asa Carscallen (1879–1964) was a Canadian and a Seventh Day Adventist who had gone to Britain as a *colporteur* and was then chosen as the first missionary to be sent abroad by the new British Adventist Mission.

[10] Osiro, R. A., 'Polygamy Among Muslim Women in Kendu Bay and Kiboswa, Nyanza Province, Kenya', MA Dissertation, St. Paul's United Theological College, Limuru (unpublished), 2006, page 9.

[11] Neufeld, D., *Seventh Day Adventist Encyclopedia*, Washington: Review and Herald Publishers Association, 1976, pages 731–732.

administrator and linguist'.[12] The fact that his missionary and administrative roles are mentioned separately might fit well with the oral literature that a kind of 'Christian law' existed alongside the natives' family law.

With Carscallen's arrival, three types of legal system became operational in the area, that is, customary, Islamic and Christian forms that regulated issues that pertained to family life.[13]

Mixed Identity

The women who were interviewed for the research identified themselves as being members of the larger Muslim community. Phrases such as 'we Muslims...' or 'in Islam...we...' pointed out to their being part of a whole. They were members of a socially recognised group. The identity was either by birth or by incorporation through marriages that took place within an inter-religious context. The Muslim men mostly married women from Christian backgrounds. Out of eleven women interviewed, nine had converted to Islam at the time of their marriages. The incorporated women were perceived as 'the other', being seen as having a lack of knowledge in matters of *dini* (Swah: religion).

The feeling was strongly shared among different categories of women. One who was a Muslim by birth commented:

> ...There are some who do not know *dini* but claim to be Muslims. Just like the family where my daughter is married.[14]

One from a Christian background lamented:

> ...Muslim men do not marry their Muslim girls. They go for women from mission families who do not know the law of *dini*. I came from a mission background because my father was a Catholic. It is the women of my calibre who are married by Muslim men, brought here and dumped like imbeciles who cannot articulate issues. Their fellow Muslims would not allow them to do that because they know the law.... Muslim men should be stopped from marrying girls from mission homes...[15]

Identity also crossed socio-ethnic lines; Islamic cultural identity manifested itself in matters of dress, such as the wearing of veils and headscarves within the town, while those on the outskirts of the town applied

---

[12] Neufeld, 1976, page 239.

[13] Osiro, 2006, pages 8–9.

[14] NS, Kendu Bay, April 07, 2007 (The daughter was married to a family that lived on the periphery of the town).

[15] MW, Kosele, April 09, 2007.

simple head scarves or moved within their homesteads without covering their heads. The variation in dress-code was influenced by the type of daily chores the women engaged in. Muslim women in the towns were basically involved in petty businesses while their counterparts on the periphery of the town were actively engaged in farming in addition to household duties that were defined along cultural lines. Women from non-Muslim backgrounds were ill-prepared in matters of Islamic legal duties and rights prior to marriage. Even after marriage, the women were more concerned with raising their families and making a living than understanding prescriptions provided in Muslim Family Law. These sentiments were shared strongly by women from the outskirts of Kendu Bay town who are part of the Kendu Bay Muslim community.

A middle-aged woman was more specific in her concern, and poured out feelings that were held by her fellow women as well:

> Although I had been in Islam for long, I did not know exactly what *mahr* [Arab.: dower; Swah.: *mahari*—bridewealth] meant because no one explained it to me. Once you are married here, you don't get to know things because there is no time for it. You saw us come from the fields to prepare lunch after which we go back until five or six in the evening. After that, you are busy with the kitchen work.[16]

Consequently, their integration into the wider Islamic community was not fully realised. The availability and willingness of teachers in matters of religion did not seem to suit the women's busy daily schedules even though they desired to attain or realise the religious set norms. The qualifications of the teachers could also be questioned, taking into account the observation of one of the informants that anyone could be approached to solemnise marriage as long as he could read the Qur'ān.[17] An elderly informant emphasized the need to educate the women in Islamic legal provisions in order to establish stable families. In her words:

> It is said that you should seek *'ilm* [Arab.: knowledge] up to China. How can they know Islam if they do not learn?[18]

Examples were manifested in the way women born in Muslim families abhorred the lifestyle on the periphery of the town. Owing to the immense responsibility that rested on her shoulders, an informant born

16 ASA, Kosele, April 06, 2007.
17 AST, Kosele, April 08, 2007.
18 MW, Kendu Bay, April 10, 2007.

and brought up among a majority-Muslim population until the time of her marriage commented:

> If as a mother-in-law you do not have any source of income, how would you take care of your daughter-in-law? It is hard. Both of you end up working throughout the day, and that is why the women do not have time for *madrasa* [Swah.: Qur'ānic school]. If you are a *kibarua* [Swah.: casual worker], you use what you have earned to feed your entire household. Whatever you bring home, you give to your daughter-in-law to prepare.[19]

In contrast, the women born in non-Muslim families easily adapted to the lifestyle that was highly esteemed in town. Of the seven women interviewed within the town setting, only one was born in a Muslim family. Yet a feeling of social elevation could be deduced from their detestation of the kind of religious life their counterparts on the periphery of the town led. This was illustrated by comments such as:

> If you observed our fellow Muslims who live on the town's periphery ... closely, you will find that they do not know ways of *dini* well ... They marry without contracting *nikāḥ* [Arab.: marriage contract with two witnesses] ... If you go to their homes, you will find that sisters are married to one husband.[20]

Although what was considered rural and less religious was only eleven kilometres away from the town setting, the town embodies a clear picture of 'high culture' as described by Kurt Beck with reference to Muslims in the Nile Valley and small market towns of Sudan.[21] There were, however, mixed thoughts from those considered to belong to the 'low culture' as to whether they were lacking in ways of religion.

Clifford Geertz observed cultural diversity in two different countries i.e. Morocco and Indonesia,[22] yet in Kendu Bay, the sharp variation existed within a short distance of less than eleven kilometres. One informant[23] portrayed a kind of filtering of aspects of religion that were acceptable to her, as opposed to other aspects where she held to the cultural norms.

---

[19] MW, Kosele, April 08, 2007.

[20] MW, Kendu Bay, April 10, 2007.

[21] Beck, K., 'Tribesmen, Townsmen and the Struggle over a Proper Lifestyle in Northern Kordofan', in *Kordofan Invaded*, Stiansen, Endre U. & Michael Kevane (eds.), Leiden: Brill, 1998, pages 255–264.

[22] Geertz, C., *Islam Observed: Religious Development in Morocco and Indonesia*, Chicago: University of Chicago Press, 1968, pages 1–22.

[23] ASH, Kendu Bay, April 04, 2007.

For example, she commended religious laws that she generalised as being positive to women but abhorred the practical realities that negated the same.

Issues Affecting Marriages

Mahr

Mahr [Arab.: dower; Swah.: *mahari*—bridewealth] was one of the aspects in the contracting of marriage which was least observed in a practical sense. It was found that only a few women who were made aware of their rights asked for it, but only at the time of divorce. This could have been an overstatement, but a cross-section of informants[24] had had their *mahr* given in part or received nothing. It was absurd that despite the clarity in remittance of *mahr* in the Qur'ān and *sharīʿa*, it hardly came into realisation. This was true even in cases involving *mahr al-mithl*[25] where future payment is postulated. In accord with other women interviewed, an informant was categorical in her statement:

> First of all, *mahr* is never given, it is only pronounced so that things can go on. Once you are joined *nikāḥ* (marriage has been solemnized), that is the end of it. The few women who are enlightened about *nikāḥ* can ask for it and be given but only in cases of *ṭalāq*. There is no *mahr* in marriages that do not break up.[26]

Such strong statements on practical realities negate what Doi states of *mahr* as being the Muslim woman's economic right.[27] Far from the non-realisation of economic right, the irony was that women who married on the periphery of the town were bound by cultural constrictions to persevere in their marriages and rarely divorced. When their marital status

---

[24] MJ, Kendu Bay, April 02, 2007 (did not receive *mahr*); ASH, April 05, 2007; MW, Kosele, April 08, 2007 and MW, Kosele, April 09, 2007 (received their *mahr* in part) while ASH, Kendu Bay, 04, 2007; MW, Kosele, April 08, 2007; ASH, Kendu Bay, 04, 2007; ASH, Kendu Bay, 05, 2007; NSH, Kendu Bay, 07, 2007 and MW, Kosele, April 09, 2007 testify of women who were never given any *mahr*.

[25] *Mahr al-mithl*: "*mahr* of the like", i.e. unspecified dower, in which the amount is not exactly laid down, but the bridegroom gives a bridal gift befitting the wealth, family and qualities of the bride. It also applied in all cases in which nothing definite about the *mahr* was agreed upon in the contract, Gibb, H. A. R. & Kramers, J. H., *Shorter Encyclopaedia of Islam*, Leiden: Brill, 1953, page 315.

[26] MW, Kosele, April 09, 2007.

[27] Doi, A. R. I., *Women in Shari'ah*, London: Ta-Ha Publishers Ltd., 1996, pages 154–162.

became too difficult for them to bear, they separated informally (not as stipulated in Islamic Law) but later re-united with their husbands without observance of any religious laws. It was in this regard that an informant exclaimed:

> Here women do not go to the Kadhi for help. When the situation gets too difficult for them, they take off to their places of birth. They stay for some time then they decide to come back hoping that the situation will have improved.[28]

Since the Muslim community in Kenya and, by extension, East Africa, mostly applied Shāfiʿi *madhhab*, a woman who had not been given *mahr* had the right to refuse consummation of the marriage and the marriage could be annulled.[29] Nevertheless, Muslim women were restricted, either by ignorance, or through strong cultural norms that were still cherished by people. Hisae Nakanishi's article[30] similarly portrays women's ignorance of Islamic law in the post-revolutionary Iran. She quotes a woman lawyer who emphasized that 'only women who are knowledgeable about women's rights and prenuptial agreements are able to stipulate various conditions for their marriage...'[31]

Within Luo culture, the bride price was paid to the bride's parents, and was regarded as a form of recompense for raising their daughter. Culturally it was regarded as inappropriate for a woman to 'extort' money from a man who was not related to her by blood. Where it did occur it was construed as a form of prostitution and such a woman was viewed with contempt by society. It is possible that the cultural view of bride price instilled an aspect of shame into the women so that even the few who had the opportunity to state their requests in the contract, refrained from asking for a befitting *mahr*.

---

[28] ASA, Kosele, April 06, 2007.

[29] Doi, 1996, page 161.

[30] Nakanishi, H., 'Power, Ideology, and Women's Consciousness in Post-revolutionary Iran', in *Women in Muslim Societies: Diversity Within Unity*, Bodman, H. L. and N. Tobidi (eds.), London: Lynne Rienner Publishers, 1998, pages 83–100.

[31] Nakanishi, 1998, page 93.

Bāṭil (*Invalid*) *Marriages*

Traditionally, *sūrat al-Nisāʾ* (4): 3[32] has been perceived as giving Muslim men freedom to marry up to four wives. Amina Wadud-Muhsin[33] and Asma Barlas,[34] among other scholars, echoed reformist Muḥammad ʿAbdu's sentiments on the subject[35] in view of *sūrat al-Nisāʾ* (4): 129.[36] In Kendu Bay, marriage to more than four wives was a common occurrence, partly due to Luo culture, which does not restrict the number of wives.[37] One of the women interviewed[38] was a fifth wife and had obtained a valid document for the marriage. She noted that there were eight more wives after her and implied that she would not be surprised if another had been added the night before. One might be excused if one questioned the validity or authenticity of such a document. Was the religious law bent to suit the socio-cultural context? Anthropologist Talal Asad offers a solution in his view of Islam as a discursive tradition. The discourses on the ground seek to instruct practitioners as to the correct form and purpose of given practice that has a history.[39] Where histories exist, for example the Islamic history from the formative period in the light of the ancestral history of the local people, whatever seems more appealing takes precedence over the other. The locals' concerns and practices (local features) then become part of the discourse.

Wadud argues against the limitation of justice on the man's ability to provide material support equally among the wives. She questions justice in terms of quality of time, affection, spiritual, moral and intellectual

[32] If you fear that you will not deal fairly with the orphan girls, you may marry whichever [other] women seem good to you, two, three, or four. If you fear that you cannot be equitable [to them], then marry only one, or your slave(s): that is more likely to make you avoid bias.

[33] Wadud, M. A., *Qur'ān and Woman. Reading the Sacred Text from a Woman's Perspective*, Kuala Lumpur: Penerbit Faraj Bakti, 1994, pages 82–84.

[34] Barlas, S., *Believing Women in Islam: Understanding Patriarchal Interpretations of the Qur'an*, Austin: University of Texas Press, 2002, pages 189–192.

[35] Esposito, L. J. &, N. J. Delong, *Marriage in Muslim Family Law*: (Second Edition), New York: Syracuse University Press, 2001, page 48.

[36] 'You will never be able to treat your wives with equal fairness, however much you desire to do so,...'

[37] Brett Shadle has conducted extensive research on marriage disputes in Gusiiland, which is in South Nyanza, not very distant from Kendu Bay. However as it mainly concerns the Gusii people and their cultural practices it is less relevant to the cultural issues facing Luos in Kendu Bay. Shadle, Brett L., 'Bridewealth and Female Consent: Marriage Disputes in African Courts, Gusiiland, Kenya', *Journal of African History* 44, 2003, pages 241–262.

[38] MW, Kosele, April 09, 2007.

[39] Asad, T., *The Idea of an anthropology of Islam*, Washington, D.C.: Center for Contemporary Arab Studies, Georgetown University, 1986.

support.[40] In the area of research, however, justice is not even based on material support to the wives, but primarily on the man's ability to pay dower to her parents. Among families who lived in the outskirts of the rural market town, the men apportioned pieces of land to their wives who in turn toiled on farms for sustainability. The workload was so much that the women hardly found time to attend *madrasa* classes instituted for an introduction to, or for advancement in religious instruction. An informant[41] noted that the women seldom found time even to learn how to say *ṣalāt* (Swah.: prayer) correctly, following the *rakʿa* (Arab.: unit of prayer) because of the lack of training. Wadud could have had in mind the time that the man spent with each of the wives but, in the area of research, spouses who spent time together in public were viewed negatively. The issue of 'quality' was almost out of the question. Asma and Wadud rejected control or fulfilment of sexual desire by the men and women respectively as being reasons for polygynous marriages but these reasons were aired by some of the informants in the area of research. One stated categorically that polygynous marriage was actually derivative of perverse pleasure. Such sentiments bring to the fore the factors or personalities that influence the local concerns and practices that pervade the religious discourse. They also raise the question as to whether these concerns and practices cut across the gender divide.

Consanguine Relations

History holds Caliph 'Uthmān ibn ʿAffān as having earned the nickname 'Master of the Two Lights' for marrying the Prophet's two daughters, Ruqayya and Umm Kulthūm, but he never had both sisters as wives at the same time. His marriage to Umm Kulthūm took place after the death of Ruqayya.[42] The marriage to uterine sisters therefore adhered to the prohibition in *sūrat al-Nisāʾ* (4): 23,[43] that forbids marriage to two sisters at the same time.

The inclusion of a wife's aunt and niece probably would not exclude a wife's half sister, just as one of my informants explained. Another informant, however, justified her position in that the sister with whom she

[40] Wadud, 1994, page 83.
[41] MW, Kosele, April 08, 2007
[42] Fry, George C. & J. R. King, *A Survey of the Muslim Faith*, Michigan, Grand Rapids: Baker Book House, 1980, page 131.
[43] 'You are forbidden to take as wives ... two sisters simultaneously, ...'

shared a marriage was not related to her by a uterine but by a consanguine relationship. Even though they were daughters of the same father they belonged to different mothers as their mothers were co-wives. This justification appears wanting in the light of Qur'ānic exposition; the guiding principle can be summarised as:

> It is prohibited to have as wives two women who, if one of them were a male, would be prohibited to each other.[44]

However, she could be excused for being content as to the legality of her marriage taking into account that uterine sisters were in wedlock 'at one and the same time' within the neighbourhood. Sixteen out of the seventeen informants shared similar sentiments, with some being more specific. For example:

> My fourth co-wife is the one who came to greet you before I came here to talk to you. She is my younger sister.[45]
>
> ... But here you can find sisters married by one husband and all the children are given equal treatment.[46]
>
> Almost all the younger sisters who came to baby sit their elder sisters' children are married by the fathers of those children.[47]

Inasmuch as the office of the Kadhi was central to the Muslim faithful in the area of research, one would understand that such instances would drive the informants to develop ambivalent feeling towards the office, particularly when such arrangements were backed up by documents which were generally considered as legal.

What might be the driving force behind these marriages? The informant who shared with her half-sister in marriage narrated how her sister coerced her into the marriage. She managed to convince their father, who reluctantly gave permission for the proposed marriage of his younger daughter. His older daughter had only one son in her marriage which, according to her, was tantamount to being childless. According to the tradition of the people in Kendu Bay, a barren wife would look for a co-wife from her area of birth who would bear children in her stead. The older sister and second wife in the marriage applied a cultural practice that compelled her younger sister to join her in the marriage. In her narration she said:

---

44 Footnote 27, *Tahfhīm al-Qur'ān*, A. A. Mawdūdī, p. 157.
45 ASA, Kosele, April 06, 2007.
46 AST, Kosele, April 08, 2007.
47 MW, Kosele, April 09, 2007.

> After her request was turned down and she knew that she had no way out, she came home one evening, wailing from a distance as if someone had died.
>
> She wailed so much that the villagers converged at her home... She was crying until tears rolled down her cheeks because she had been denied her request. She implied that her own family had abandoned her by refusing her status where she was married. The family knew that she did not have a child, but refused to let her husband take her sister (myself) who would dignify her. My father however stood his ground but his elder brother softened his stance [and] told my father that it was a taboo for me to marry elsewhere. That I had no option but to be married by my sister's husband. That my sister had already blocked my way by her wails and I ended up being married here against my will.[48]

Joining her sister in marriage was the only option for the younger sister's future stability and well being in the society. Her elder sister had colluded with her elderly husband in the scheme. Farther from cultural claims, one wonders whether lust could have been one of the factors behind such marriages. The young woman had been living with her elder sister when she acted as 'nanny' to the children, whenever her school sessions were over. Moreover, she stated that now after many years of marriage and having entered into marriage contracts with other women, the man was making advances to her young niece, who was living with her. She had to send the primary school girl back to her parents' home, in order to avoid a possible repeat of history. During one of the heated arguments that she engaged in with her husband on the issue, he retorted that she could not bar him from marrying her niece.[49]

Clear and specific sentiments came from the informant who shared with her uterine sister in a marriage. She recalled, "I was not aware that as she grew up, *Jaduon'g*[50] got interested in her and I only realised that when she was heavy with child". The husband had voluntarily spoken of his intention to marry the younger sister. In an interview with him, the man was aware that sororal polygamy was against religious as well as cultural norms but he had been driven by lust into a romantic relationship with his sister-in-law. He however concluded that the issue was between him and God for he had made his decision and no one could reverse the

48 MW, Kosele, April 09, 2007.

49 MW, Kosele, April 09, 2007.

50 *Jaduon'g*: A Luo word for elders, also as a term of respect. The second meaning applies in the text.

process or nullify the marriage. Lust might be the driving force behind most, if not all, marriages but it would not be the only or main rationale given for a marriage.

Sentiments from the area of research, however, point out that marriage to the uterine sisters was precipitated through cultural demeanour or lust. In as much as culture did not allow for marriage to uterine sisters, it definitely provided a fertile ground for its enactment. That the act of the wailing of an older sister surpassed religious stipulations as well as social implications[51] indicates how flexible the society was to a cultural disposition.

According to the narration of Athar Ḥusain, Caliph 'Uthmān agonised at the death of Ruqaiyya not only because he had lost a beloved wife, but because his connection with the Prophet's family had been severed. He had therefore received a tripartite consolation from the Prophet. Apart from being treated as one of the victors of the Badr[52] war even though he did not participate in it, he was given part of the spoils and offered marriage to the Prophet's second daughter, Umm Kulthūm.[53]

With functionalist Emile Durkheim's characterisation of social facts in mind, although the contracting of a marriage on the premise that a sister wailed did not appear to be a common social fact, it was made compulsory by being transmitted amidst protests by the other party.[54] It surpassed religious stipulation and endured both time and space. Culture surpassed the borders of gender here as the 'balancing wheel' depicted male and female on either side of the tussle. Culture and religion become intertwined when social facts that are common cross each other. An example of a social fact that seemed to strongly inform the cultural context was manifested in marriage contracts that involved widows.

---

[51] The younger sister was asthmatic, a second reason for which her father was not willing to let her be married in a polygamous family. The father's first reason was the manner in which Muslim men married many wives for this meant that his daughter would not have a spouse who would give her the undivided attention which she needed in her situation.

[52] Badr: The Battle of Badr (625) is significant for the victory that Muhammad and his followers attained against those who were considered as wanting in faith. It is one of the most significant events in history among Muslims. Hughes, 1978, page 30.

[53] Husain, S. A., *The Glorious Caliphate*, Lucknow-India: Islamic Research and Publications—Series No. 73, 1974, pages 93–94.

[54] Shorter, Aylward, *African Culture—An Overview: Social-Cultural Anthropology*, Nairobi: Paulines Publications Africa, 1998, pages 9–14.

Re-Marriages

Ideally, a re-marriage, specifically in widowhood, was neither the preserve of the Muslim faithful in the area of research nor of the universal Muslim community but was also permissible among most Christian communities. To the Muslims, a woman is free to marry another man upon completion of the *ʿidda* (Arab.: period of retreat); in divorce this is a period of three months; in widowhood, the woman's confinement for three months and ten days is required.[55] The woman is expected to engage in a new marriage contract with the fulfilment of all legal requirements. The cultural heritage of the local people[56] in Kendu Bay, however, upholds the practice of widow inheritance, where the widow is re-married to her brother-in-law, similar to levirate[57] marriages in the Old Testament. The practice was so deeply rooted in the community that re-marriages upon the death of male spouses are usually contracted along cultural lines, with care for the widows and continuation of lineage not being the central objectives. One of the women interviewed had been re-married by her brother-in-law,[58] while another's husband had married his sister-in-law[59] upon the death of his brother. A third widow's marriage was like an intricate puzzle that could not be solved. She had been re-married to either her brother-in-law or to a young man who worked on the farm of her father-in-law. Family members volunteered contradicting information in regard to her marriage. It was clear that the husband passed away leaving her with their first born daughter, still a baby. As the young farm man was complimented for agreeing to marry the widow, the other party was proud of a brother-in-law with whom the widow bore a son and another daughter. Giving her case as an example, a third family member offered information that introduced another element concerning the paternity of the two younger children.[60]

---

[55] *sūrat al-Baqara* (2): 228, 229, 230 and 340.

[56] There are also communities from other parts of the country such as the coastal region. There are notable individuals from Tanzania and Uganda who also form part of the Muslim community in Kendu Bay.

[57] Levirate marriage: A form of marriage prescribed by the Law of Moses in which a man was required to marry the widow of a brother who died with no male heir. The term levirate means "husband's brother". The purpose of the law was to provide an heir for the dead brother, thereby preserving his name and estate. The law also was designed to provide for the welfare of the widows (Deuteronomy 25:5–10).

[58] MW, Kendu Bay, April 10, 2007.

[59] ASH, Kendu Bay, April 05, 2007.

[60] MW, Kosele, April 09, 2007.

What was commonly relayed by the three was that *nikāḥ* was followed. It meant that the re-marriage was considered as legal according to religious stipulations. The three also concurred that neither was *mahr* given to the young woman nor was dowry paid to her parents, in relation to the re-marriage, because the formalities could not be repeated. It was a clear indication of cultural practice enduring to inform the religious discourse. In this area, the representative of the Kadhi solemnized marriages either upon the completion of payment of *mahr* and dowry, or promise from the bridegroom to pay the same. Such promises would be written down and signed by the bridegroom and his father, guardian or representative of the father. The widow stayed within her late husband's homestead and carried out chores within the family.

Some of the informants who had been separated from their spouses were faced with the difficulty of suing for divorce because of the irregularities that surrounded the contract of the marriage. Even though apostasy was a strong reason for divorce, the nature of marriage at the time it was contracted dictated the nature of its dissolution. Not even the estranged wife who still professed Islamic faith could approach the representative office of the Kadhi for assistance, since the marriage was not solemnized through the office. "We could not even talk of *talaka* (Swah.: divorce) because we were not married according to the laws of *dini* (Swah.: religion)", she said.[61] Other informants echoed similar sentiments which ran in consonance with Islamic values, as Abdelhamid Chirane and Manazir Ahsan state that faith is the determining factor for the recognition of Islamic marriages.[62] It appeared as though the marriage contract was subjected to more scrutiny at the time of divorce. The process could have also been made more difficult by the parties' failure to contact religious leaders at the beginning of their marital life. One informant apportioned the blame by stating, "I blame the office of the Kadhi for not being proactive. Even when it was known that someone was suffering, the office kept quiet until it was prompted".[63]

The informants noted that it was not easy for women to enter into *ṣāḥiḥ* marriages (Arab.: valid, or completely lawful) upon divorce or widowhood due to cultural and social expectations from the community. The few women who pressed for their religious rights were perceived negatively by those who integrated culture into their religious practices. On the other

---

[61] FA, Kendu Bay, April 02, 2007.

[62] King, M. (ed.), *God's Law versus State Law: Construction of an Islamic Identity in Western Europe*, London: Grey Seal Books, 1995, pages 16–18, 25–26.

[63] ANK, April 04, 2007.

hand, if the women entered into marriage contracts that were either *bāṭil* (invalid) or *fāsid* (irregular), they were viewed with contempt by religious leaders and the few who were informed about religious stipulations.

Abdelhamid Chirane, Manazir Ahsan, Shabbir Akhtar, Haleh Afshar and Zaki Badawi, among other scholars, note the difficulty in the process of integrating religious values in a non-Muslim society.[64] Although they write of Muslim families in Europe, the difficulties are similar to those that affect Muslims in Kendu Bay. The latter are equally a minority group with varied cultural virtues and a social setting whose obligations at times stand against Islamic rules. Such norms included leviratic and sororal marriages. The latter case, however, took place upon the death or a substitute for an older sister if she could not bear children or did not bring forth a son.[65] It was not unusual, however, to come across consanguine marriages which were not necessarily due to the demise of, or as a substitute for, but in addition to an older sister. A Muslim elder and former government official concurs with Kyewalyanga that "Luo rules of exogamy prohibit any Luo to marry a person who is a *wat* i.e. who is a cognate relative".[66]

Retaining Kadhi's Courts in the Constitution

The call for a review of the Constitution is therefore both real and relevant to the people if such details were to be taken care of. It would be in consonance with the proposed constitutional principles which, according to Constitution of Kenya Review Commission (CKRC) Draft Constitution of 2002, were to cater for the marginalised communities of which the Muslims claim to be one. However, the draft constitution was not specific about the various social and cultural intricacies that were real and practical issues to the diversity within which the faith community exists. Ahmed Issack Hassan, Commissioner, CKRC 2002, noted the recognition of the *Shīʿa* Muslims in the proposed appointment of Kadhis. The positive gesture, however, would cater for sectarian divide but not the differences embedded in their socio-cultural settings.

Under the tentative recommendations of the CKRC Draft Constitution, there is a provision for a 'female assistant to the Kadhi's Court to assist

64 King, 1995.

65 Kyewalyanga, F-X. S., *Marriage customs in East Africa: With special reference to selected tribes of Kenya: Akamba, Bantu Kavirondo, Gusii, Kipsigis, Luo, Nandi, and Teita*, Hohenschäftlarn: Renner Publication, 1978, pages 19–26.

66 Kyewalyanga, 1978, pages 20–34.

in dealing with the more delicate and intimate issues affecting women litigants in the court'. The provision would still limit such a woman for she would be holding administrative but not judicial authority. It is categorically stated in the Draft that she would 'not deputise for or act in the place of the Kadhi'. Nevertheless it should be welcomed as a positive move directed towards enacting justice for the female gender in the corridors of law. It would also help the office of the Kadhi, to some extent, in getting to the bottom of the issues that affect Muslim women. The Muslim women in Kendu Bay, however, would have wished to have women in the representative units of the office of the Kadhi, at the grass-roots level. An informant clearly spelled out her desire:

> I wish we had a woman representative to work closely with the *muʿallim* (Arab.: teacher) here. She could offer more assistance to the women because there are issues that you cannot share with the *muʿallim* because he is a man.[67]

Such female representatives would function at the level of Area Magistrate where the said-*muʿallim* dispensed his duties.

The commissioner for the CKRC Draft Constitution also alluded to the codification of Muslim Family Law into legislation in Kenya, an appeal that he put across as one of the indicators that showed the Muslims as a marginalised community.[68] The proposed legislation would impact on the people's lives if the proposed codification took into consideration the intra-Muslim contexts. A Senior Resident Magistrate at the Kisumu Law Courts aired similar views to those of the commissioner. He felt that an Islamic Judge should be assigned judicial duties at the High Court instead of having a Kadhi, which to him meant a religious leader rather than a judge. He qualified his sentiments by proposing that Islamic law be introduced into the public universities as electives so that there would be judges who were conversant with Islamic laws and who could dispense their duties inclusive of issues that concerned Muslims. It pointed to judges who could discharge their duties regardless of their religious affiliations, even in cases where both parties professed Islam. "Cases should come from Kadhi's Courts to the High Court and not to the Chief Kadhi", he said. "Kadhis should have minimal intervention in judicial cases, only at Lower Court levels, but equality should be maintained at high levels of legal jurisdiction".[69] The Magistrate agreed with women informants that

67 LA, Kosele, October 14, 2007.
68 CKRC, 2002.
69 MB, Kisumu, October 16, 2007.

women representatives be deployed at the community level where the Muslim Community, or *muʿallim*, operated.

Conclusion

Despite the complex cultural and social issues that surround the contracting of marriages among Muslims in Kendu Bay, the women aired strong feelings that Kadhi's Courts should remain in the constitution. It was evident from the research findings that women acknowledged the importance of having their marriages solemnized by Kadhis or their representatives, hence the significance of Kadhi's Courts. As one of the informants stated: "The office of the Kadhi is essential to the Muslim community here in Kendu Bay specifically in their marriage contracts". Out of the seventeen women interviewed, only three had stayed in marriages that had not been solemnized by the office of the Kadhi or its representative.

The new Constitution was approved in August 2010 with the Kadhi's Courts clauses retained in much the same form as previously. The new clause 170. (5) states:

> The jurisdiction of a Kadhi's court shall be limited to the determination of questions of Muslim law relating to personal status, marriage, divorce or inheritance in proceedings in which all the parties profess the Muslim religion and submit to the jurisdiction of the Kadhi's courts.

Through this research we have seen that the Muslim women interviewed in Kendu Bay and its environs have found themselves disempowered due to a number of reasons. Many of the women coming from a non-Muslim background have not understood their rights within a Muslim marriage, leaving them disadvantaged, with their marriages not being recognised by the Kadhi's Courts. Cultural practices have been followed which are at odds with Islamic practices, leaving the women in a difficult position, with many marriages being considered as invalid, again leaving women with a loss of rights. The physical distance of the Muslim community in Kendu Bay from the Kadhi's Court in Kisumu, together with the uncertainty of the availability of the Kadhi's representative, again reduces the opportunities for the women to gain their rights.

PART FOUR

TANZANIA: "CALLS FOR THE RE-INTRODUCTION OF *SHARĪ'A*"

Map 6 Map of Tanzania: Showing principal places referred to in Part Four

CHAPTER TEN

DEMAND FOR THE RE-INTRODUCTION OF KADHI'S COURTS ON THE TANZANIAN MAINLAND: A RELIGIOUS, SOCIAL AND POLITICAL ANALYSIS

William Andrew Kopwe

Introduction

The demand for *sharīʿa* implementation on the Tanzanian mainland is a social reality.[1] This chapter is part of ongoing doctoral research on *sharīʿa* implementation in the country. *Sharīʿa* debates in the country revolve around the issue of Kadhi's courts.[2] Currently, Islamic personal law is in operation in the country, dispensed by the Magistrates' courts. However, for several reasons, Muslims in general are not satisfied with the current practice of the administration of Islamic law by secular courts. Hence, Muslims are demanding a separate system of Kadhi's courts, as was the case during colonial times when the courts were not only recognized, but also funded by the Government.[3]

---

[1] When Tanganyika united with Zanzibar in 1964 some matters were agreed to be non-union matters. This included judicial systems, allowing for the continued existence of Kadhi's courts in Zanzibar. Therefore, the debate on Kadhi's courts is found mainly on the Tanzanian mainland.

[2] There has been a debate among Tanzanians as to whether Kadhi's courts are tantamount to *sharīʿa* or not. However, Lodhi and Westerlund are of the opinion that "The proposals of Bakwata [*Baraza Kuu la Waislam Tanzania* (The Supreme Council of Muslims in Tanzania)] in 1987 to reinstate separate Islamic courts is only one example which demonstrates that the question of the position of *sharīʿa* in Tanzania is still a burning issue", Lodhi, Abdulaziz & David Westerlund, 'Tanzania', in *Islam Outside the Arab World*, D. Westerlund & I. Svanberg (eds.), Richmond: Curzon, 1999, pages 97–110, page 104. This shows that demand for Kadhi's courts is more or less the demand for *sharīʿa* implementation in the country, in particular for personal law. On the other hand our interviews with sheikhs in Tanga, Dodoma and Arusha confirmed that Kadhi's courts are part of *sharīʿa* since they adjudicate cases in accordance with *sharīʿa*. However, they insisted that their demand for their re-introduction does not mean that they need total *sharīʿa* implementation in the country, rather they need these independent courts for personal cases only.

[3] Interview with: Sheikh Mataka, 31st January 2007, Dar-es-Salaam and Sheikh Zuberi, 14th February 2008, Dodoma. Both of these sheikhs are members of the Muslim council of scholars (*ʿulamāʾ*).

Meanwhile, Christians feel that re-introducing Kadhi's courts as a Government institution would introduce *sharīʿa* into the domain of the overall administration of justice. This would infringe the constitution and obliterate the state's secularity. Furthermore, in general, Christians feel that running the courts at the Government's cost will cause taxpayers' money to be used by one religious group.[4] This situation challenges both the secular nature of the state and the religio-socio-political sphere of the country. This chapter analyses the challenges posed by the demand for a separate system of Kadhi's courts, and the relations of Kadhi's courts to *sharīʿa* debates in the country.[5]

The research for this chapter was carried out between April 2006 and July 2008. In-depth interviews were conducted with key actors in various parts of the country. Additional information was found through research in the Tanzania National Archives and contemporary media reports.

History of Kadhi's Courts in the Country

The concept and practice of Kadhi's courts is not new on the Tanzanian mainland. Although there is no precise date when the courts were officially established in the country, Muslim scholars state that the history of Kadhi's courts in Tanzania goes back as far as the coming of Islam into the country.[6] This is supported by the account of Ibn Baṭṭūṭa (1304–c. 1370) when he travelled to East Africa. Visiting the states along the coast, Mogadishu (Somalia), Mombasa (Kenya) and Kilwa (Tanzania), he found that the Muslims were followers of the Shāfiʿī madhhab (Arab.: School of Law) and that there were *qāḍī* (Arab.: judge) and *faqīh* (Arab.: one who can give legal judgement) present in all the city states he visited.[7]

In a television broadcast,[8] Sheikh Ali Basalehe, who is a spokesperson for a coalition of Muslim communities in Tanzania, referred to the use of the term Kadhi in the Swahili Bible to show that the concept and the

4 *Daily News* (Tanzanian daily newspaper, in English.), Wednesday, 30th August 2006.

5 Because of the sensitivity of the debate, some of the interviewees' names are either withheld or they are given pseudonyms.

6 Interview with Sheikh Mataka, 30th January 2007, Dar-es-Salaam.

7 S. Hamdun & N. King *Ibn Battuta in Black Africa*, Princeton: Markus Wiener Publishers, 2003, pages 17–25.

8 This was in a television interview carried out by the Channel Ten TV station in the *Je tutafika'* (Swah.: Will we arrive?) programme which was discussing the issue of Kadhi's courts' re-introduction in the country. In this programme, the Sheikhs were called as Muslim scholars, for expert opinions.

word Kadhi were present in Tanzania before European colonialism in the country. Missionaries used the existing indigenous concepts and Swahili words, like Kadhi, in translating the Bible into Swahili. Thus, in Matthew 5:25 the Swahili 1952 Union Version of the Bible[9] says:

> *Patana na mshitaki wako upesi, wakati uwapo pamoja naye njiani; yule mshitaki asije akakupeleka kwa kadhi, na kadhi akakupeleka kwa askari, ukatupwa gerezani.*
>
> (Come to terms quickly with your accuser while you are on the way to court with him, or your accuser may hand you over to the judge [*kadhi*], and the judge [*kadhi*] to the guard, and you will be thrown into prison.)[10]

The term Kadhi in the Swahili Bible is a translation of the New Testament Greek *kritēs* and of the English word Judge. Kadhi appears 27 times in the Swahili Union Version Bible. In every instance it has been used to depict approximately the same meaning as Matthew 5:25.[11]

Apart from that, during the period of German colonialism (1890–1918) there was a double-tier system of courts: Islamic religious courts and secular courts.[12] The German Colonial Government took the existence of Kadhi's courts for granted. In 1919 Tanganyika became a League of Nations Mandated Territory; because of the nature of British Indirect rule, it was important for the British to establish laws which would help the indigenous people to rule more effectively. Therefore, the British Colonial Government officially recognized the native courts by instituting the 'Courts Ordinance', enacted by H. Byatt, the Governor of the Tanganyika Territory, on 14th December 1920.[13] By this, the British Colonial Government legally recognized the operation of Kadhi's courts in the coastal area. Hence, Kadhi's courts were treated as one of the Native

---

[9] The Union Version was the first Bible in Swahili with a text agreed by all Christian denominations. Earlier Bibles in Swahili include those in Zanzibar Swahili by Universities' Mission to Central Africa (1895), in Mombasa Swahili by Church Missionary Society (1914) and Röhl (1937), who avoided words with an Arabic root, Chesworth, John A., The Use of Scripture in Swahili Tracts by Muslims and Christians in East Africa, doctoral thesis University of Birmingham, 2008, http://etheses.bham.ac.uk/150/. It is worth noting that Röhl uses *mwenye hukumu* [the one who gives judgement] rather than *kadhi*.

[10] The English translation is from the *New Revised Standard Version*, Oxford: Oxford University Press, 1995.

[11] *Itifaki ya Biblia: Orodha ya maneno yote ya Agano la Kale na Agano Jipya na Madondoo Yake*, Dodoma: Central Tanganyika Press (Swahili Bible Concordance), 1990.

[12] Shivji, Issa. G. (ed.), *Constitutional and Legal System of Tanzania: A Civics Sourcebook*, Dar-es-Salaam: Mkuki na Nyota Publishers Ltd, 2004, page 19.

[13] Tanzania National Archives Acc. AB 2587: Native law and Customs 1919–1922.

Courts just like other tribal courts, but limited to Muslims' personal cases only.

When Tanganyika gained independence in 1961, the country was full of factions due to ethnicity, religion, political parties, economic imbalance and educational differences among Tanganyikans. Therefore, the great task ahead for the Government leaders was to create unity in the country. Mpangala comments that one of methods used to unite the country was the abolition of native courts.[14] During its 1963 session, from the 11th–26th June, the National Assembly abolished the Law of Native Courts. Since Kadhi's courts were amongst the native courts, they were abolished and their duties were subsumed into the Magistrates' court. However, section 7(3) of the Magistrates' Court Act of 1963, which was revised in 1984, ensured that the magistrates who presided over cases pertaining to native laws judged justly, with the assistance of court assessors.

Muslims in the country were strongly disturbed by this merger. From 1967 to 1970 there were strong debates in the Parliament about it, resulting in the 1971 Marriage Act which officially recognized several types of marriage, including religious marriage. Furthermore, the Government ordered magistrates to be instructed in Islamic laws to ensure that they would be able to dispense justice in accordance with Islamic law.[15]

The Current Debate on the Re-Introduction of Kadhi's Courts

The current *sharīʿa* debate in Tanzania is about Kadhi's courts. Muslims want the Government, through an act of Parliament, to institute Kadhi's courts as a court distinct from the magistrates' court. Shivji gives a reason for this, that "The decisions of these [magistrates'] courts deviate to some degree from the strict rules of traditional Islamic law in matters such as marriage, divorce, succession, inheritance, guardianship, and *waqf*"(Arab.: inalienable religious endowment).[16] The debate is mainly fuelled by two factors: firstly, that many Muslims want Kadhi's courts to be a Government institution, and secondly, that Muslims want Kadhi's courts to be funded by the Government. They want it to be like it was during colonial times

[14] Mpangala, Gaudens, *Peace, Conflicts, and Democratization Process in the Great Lakes Region: The Experience of Tanzania*, Dar es Salaam, 1999, page 3. http://www.fiuc.org/iaup/esap/publications/dar/mpangala1.pdf,

[15] See also An-Na'im, A. A. (ed), *Islamic Family Law In A Changing World: A Global Resource Book*, London: Zed Books, 2002, pages 39–53; 57–61.

[16] Shivji, 2004, page 20.

and similar to what is currently done in some other East African countries such as Kenya and Zanzibar.[17] If this were the case, Kadhi's courts would be acting on behalf of the Government by settling issues pertaining to Muslims, who are citizens of this country.[18]

Demand for Kadhi's courts was given impetus by the Union of Muslim Youth (UMY) who published a ten-year development plan in 1984. Sigvard von Sicard comments that "It was their [the UMY's] insistence which made BAKWATA request the re-introduction of Kadhi's courts in 1987".[19]

The agenda again came into the public sphere in 1998, when Augustine Lyatonga Mrema,[20] an opposition party Member of Parliament (MP), brought the agenda to Parliament for the creation of a Kadhi's Courts Law. The demand was revitalized by Thomas Ngawaiya,[21] an MP from an opposition party, who was supported by Mohammed Ramiya, a Chama cha Mapinduzi (CCM) MP. This support made the House seriously consider the issue by appointing a Committee to deal with it. It is interesting to note here that those people who introduced the demand in the House were all Christians, apart from Ramiya, who joined them later.

The debate gained impetus from the ruling party's (CCM) 2005 election manifesto. CCM pledged that its Government would follow up measures already introduced to improve the judicial system, including finding a solution to the issue of re-establishing Kadhi's courts in Tanzania mainland.[22] However, today, many Tanzanians are suspicious of the promise, considering that it was merely political propaganda, because the CCM statement is vague. The manifesto does not elucidate how the issue would be dealt with. It is perceived that CCM used it to attract Muslims to the party, in order to get their votes.

It was because of this that when the debate between Christians and Muslims on this issue heated up, creating a volatile situation, the

---

[17] Though Zanzibar is part of the United Republic of Tanzania, there are some matters, like Kadhi's courts, where Zanzibar has its own policies.

[18] Interview with a member of BAKWATA executive council, 31st January 2007, Dar-es-Salaam (name withheld).

[19] Sicard, von S., 'Tanzania', In *Encyclopaedia of Islam* 2nd Edition, P. Bearman, T. Bilquis, C. E. Bosworth, E. van Donzel and W. P. Heinrichs (eds.), Volume 10 Fas. 165–166, Leiden: Brill, 1998, pages 194–196.

[20] Augustine Mrema left CCM in 1995 and in 1998 he was a member of the National Convention for Construction and Reform-Mageuzi (NCCR-Mageuzi); subsequently he joined the Tanzania Labour Party (TLP).

[21] Ngawaiya is no longer a member of an opposition party; subsequently he returned to the ruling party, Chama Cha Mapinduzi (CCM). *Chama cha Mapinduzi* can literally be translated as the 'revolutionary party'.

[22] CCM 'Election Manifesto', Dodoma, 2005, page 132.

minister for legal and constitutional affairs offered the Government's stand on the issue. The minister addressed a press conference on 4th August 2006. She was quoted as saying that, in the Manifesto, CCM did not articulate how the issue of Kadhi's courts was going to be resolved. Hence she urged people to be calm while the Government finds appropriate means of resolving the problem.[23]

The above statement by the CCM minister indicates the politicization of the issue. CCM was aware that some of the opposition parties, such as the Tanzania Labour Party (TLP), capitalized on the Muslim demand in order to win people's support in the election. Therefore, the inclusion of such an abstract statement can be seen as a counter-attack to the opposition parties.

Aside from the issue of Kadhi's courts re-introduction being hijacked by politicians, numerous reasons have been given by Muslims in the country for their demand to be met. Here the major arguments are presented:

> A Sufi Sheikh in Arusha argues that if the Government allows the Hindus to cremate their deceased loved ones in accordance with their beliefs, why shouldn't the Government allow Muslims to exercise their religious rites through Kadhi's courts. He argues that if the constitution grants freedom of worship and religious practices to its citizens, it should do so equally to all religious groups.[24]

The interview with Sheikh Mataka, the chairman of BAKWATA Executive Council, revealed that, although Islamic law is currently dispensed by the Magistrates' courts, there are still several deficiencies noted. The most significant one is that those magistrates do not have authority to adjudicate cases by Islamic law. For one to be a judge who judges according to Islamic laws, one has first and foremost to be a devoted Muslim. However, there are a lot of magistrates who are not Muslims. According to Sheikh Mataka, those people who are not Muslims dispense Islamic law without commitment and conviction for the sanctity of the law. On the other hand, in order for one to be an accepted judge in Islamic law, one has to be a *man* of integrity. He went on to say that, in the Magistrates' courts, some magistrates are women, others fornicators, others are alcoholics, and some even take bribes; these are characters who are against Islam.[25]

---

[23] *Mwananchi* (Tanzanian daily newspaper, in Swahili.), 5th August 2006.

[24] An interview carried out on 27th August 2007 in Arusha.

[25] In the discussion Mataka emphasized that a Kadhi is supposed to be a man and not a woman, and that women are not allowed to be judges in an Islamic court (Interview carried out on 31st January 2007, Dar-es-Salaam).

Apart from that, there are several magistrates who do not have a mastery of Islamic laws. Therefore, often, when it comes to the issue of inheritance, these magistrates send their clients to sheikhs who arrange the inheritance for them. Then they go back to the magistrate for an official judgement to be made by the court.[26] A discussion with an advocate in Arusha revealed that at the University of Dar-es-Salaam, where most of the lawyers in Tanzania study, Islamic law is taught as an elective course. Therefore not all of the lawyers have knowledge of Islamic law.[27] This argument is supported by a lawyer who says that he knows many magistrates who are not well-versed in Islamic law. He also says that since not all of the Islamic laws are written in the books of law it sometimes becomes difficult for one to judge rightly according to Islamic law.[28]

Various Responses to Kadhi's Courts' Re-Introduction

The agenda for the re-introduction of Kadhi's courts in the country was received with a diversity of perceptions. There have been inter- and intra-religious heterogeneous views from within and without Islam and Christianity regarding the attitude of the Government toward re-introduction of Kadhi's courts. The theory of religious economy is relevant to this study.[29]

The current demand for the re-introduction of Kadhi's courts has been so strong because of religious resurgence which is a result of religious globalization. Muslims in the country are undergoing a strong revival, which calls people back to a pristine form of Islam. Various Muslim groups in the country feel that they have an obligation to find ways to rightly manifest their religion. Moreover, there are several Muslim discourses regarding their status concerning participation in the socio-political domain, and opportunities for appointment as civil servants in the country. This has been made explicit in the numerous grievances presented to the

[26] Interview with Sheikh Mataka, 31st January 2007, Dar-es-Salaam.

[27] Discussion with Advocate Ezra Mwaluko on 8th March 2007, Arusha.

[28] Interview with Kenny, 15th June 2007, Bayreuth, Germany. This lawyer is a Tanzanian who was doing his PhD in the University of Bayreuth, where we were able to conduct an interview with him, during his summer school.

[29] This theory was coined by Peter Berger (1963). Berger used the model of 'market place' to explain the relationship between religious groups in a secular state. Berger, P., *Invitation to Sociology*, New York: Doubleday, 1963, page 79.

Government by scholars who are Muslims, Islamic religious scholars, Muslim-owned media, and official Muslim umbrella bodies.[30]

Politicians have also hijacked the agenda of Kadhi's courts and want to manipulate it for their own political ends. Meanwhile, there is a strong religious market (society) competition in this country; different religious groups strive for influence in society. As a result, every move in the public sphere which seems to be religious is looked at with suspicion. Sometimes the doubts posed by different religious groups are genuine and sometimes they are just suspicions and prejudices.

However, Tanzania's Constitution, in Article 19 stipulates that:

> 19.—(1) Every person has the right to the freedom to have conscience, or faith, and choice in matters of religion, including the freedom to change his religion or faith.
> (2) Protection of rights referred to in this Article shall be in accordance with the provisions prescribed by the laws which are of importance to a democratic society for security and peace in the society, integrity of the society and the national coercion [*sic*].
> (3) In this Article reference to the term "religion" shall be construed as including reference to religious denominations, and cognate expressions shall be construed accordingly.[31]

This can be seen as allowing this kind of religious market i.e. a free market, in the sense that people are free to follow the religion of their choice and are also free to disseminate their beliefs. This text causes a lot of complications and challenges in the religious arena of the country because, all the time, religious groups and the Government take refuge in the Constitution to defend their agendas. This is what is expressed in the following responses to Kadhi's courts by different groups in the country.

---

[30] The Dar-es-Salaam University Muslim Trusteeship (DUMT) is a good example. See also BAKWATA's letter to President Benjamin William Mkapa (www.igs.net/~kassim/nyaraka/barua_halmashauri.htm accessed on 23.05.2008).

[31] Constitution of the United Republic of Tanzania, 1997, Right of freedom of religion Act No. 1 of 1984 Art. 6; Act No. 4 of 1992 Art. 9; Act No. 1 of 2005 Art. 6. Note Section 2 previous to 2005 read "Without prejudice to the relevant laws of the United Republic the profession of religion, worship and propagation of religion shall be free and a private affair of an individual; and the affairs and management of religious bodies shall not be part of the activities of the State authority". (http://www.judiciary.go.tz/downloads/constitution.pdf accessed on 20.03.2012)

Response of the National Muslim Council of Tanzania (BAKWATA)

As for BAKWATA, which is at the forefront of the demand, its stand is openly expressed by the Mufti. The Mufti of Tanzania, who is the official spokesman of BAKWATA, expressed his sentiments by accusing non-Muslims in the country, saying that those who dispute the re-introduction of Kadhi's courts have bad intentions towards Islam.

Furthermore, Sheikh Mataka commented that the resistance of Christians to the re-introduction of Kadhi's courts is due to their intolerance of Muslim affairs and activities in the country. The chairman said that:

> Muslims in the country have been very tolerant of the extra privileges that Christians get from the Government. Among such privileges are, for example, people resting on Saturdays and Sundays. This allows a Christian to pray in his or her church. Meanwhile, work continues for Muslims except for a few hours on Fridays which Muslims utilize for their prayers. Another privilege is that 1st January is a public holiday, based on the Christian calendar; however, the first day of the Muslim year, is not a public holiday. These are some of the many privileges which Christians enjoy in the country, while Muslims are forced to tolerate such a situation.[32]

Sheikh Mataka urges Christians in the country to be tolerant of the issue of the re-introduction of Kadhi's courts, because that is what Muslims do concerning many privileges that Christians get from the Government.

In an interview with Sheikh Mubaraka of the Shīʿa, Bilal Muslim Agency of Tanzania, Tanga branch, he revealed that Kadhi's courts are an important alternative for *sharīʿa* implementation in the country. For him, *sharīʿa* implementation in the country is supposed to be a gradual process. His argument is that when Muslims are trained to abide by Muslims' personal laws, they will be able to live by the will of God, which automatically helps them not to commit other crimes. That is because the same fear of God in the personal law will spontaneously exert a fear of breaking other laws. Hence in a secular country like Tanzania, Kadhi's courts may be an alternative for the whole *sharīʿa*.[33]

---

[32] Interview with Sheikh Mataka, 31st January 2007, Dar-es-Salaam.

[33] Interview carried out on 8th February 2008, Tanga. Sheikh Mubaraka is an experienced person in the issue of Kadhi's courts, because he worked as a secretary to the Chief Kadhi in Kenya for several years.

The Government's Response

The history of the demand for Kadhi's courts' re-introduction in the country shows that the Government had started to act upon the issue ever since its genesis in the Parliament in 1998. Following this agenda, the Parliament delegated the issue to its Committee for Constitutional, Legal and Administration Affairs. According to the report of the Committee, the job was not finished during the Parliamentary session in 1998. However in 2002 the issue was carefully dealt with by the Committee.

The Parliamentary Committee met from 4th to 6th August 2004 in Dodoma to discuss the findings of their research on the issue of the re-introduction of Kadhi's courts in the country. The report, which was published in October 2004, *Taarifa ya Kamati ya Katiba, sheria na utawala kuhusu uanzishwaji wa Mfumo wa Mahakama/taasisi ya Kadhi Tanzania Bara* (Report of the Committee for Constitutional, Legal and Administration Affairs concerning the introduction of System of Courts/ the institution of Kadhis in Tanzania Mainland), shows that the majority of Muslims in the country are in favour. Therefore, the Committee suggested that the Government should explore the possibilities for re-introducing Kadhi's courts. However, the Committee cautioned that the matter should be administered carefully and in such a way that it does not divide people along religious lines. In order to successfully put this institution in place, the Committee gave several suggestions. Selected suggestions drawn from the report of the Committee are:

- The court should deal only with personal issues of Muslims which would include marriage, inheritance, divorce, Islamic foundations [Arab.: *waqf*; Swah.: *wakfu*] and the interpretation of Islamic laws such as giving statements on the timing of Ramadan and reconciliation of disputes between Muslims.
- The Government should establish Departments of Islamic Law in the law schools in the country.
- Citizens should be educated on the structure and functions of Kadhi's courts, so as to remove the fear which is believed to result from the feeling that instituting Kadhi's courts is tantamount to the full implementation of *sharīʿa,* including penal law, which would turn Tanzania into a Muslim state.

- The structure of the court should follow a descending order of: Court of Appeal, High Court, Grand Kadhi's court, Regional Kadhi's courts, District Kadhi's courts and Primary Kadhi's courts.[34]

The current Government's position was given by the Minister for Legal and Constitutional Affairs. According to the minister, the Government is of the opinion that Kadhi's courts are an important institution for Muslim affairs in the country. That is why CCM included the issue in its election manifesto, in order to find a way forward to achieve the improvement of Muslims' well-being in the country. Also, according to the minister, the Government is still gathering evidence from the experiences of countries where Kadhi's courts are in operation and from those countries where Kadhi's courts are not in operation. The minister further said that in order for the Government to resolve the issue correctly, it will seek the views of the majority in different institutions, while also taking into consideration the constitution, the different operating laws in the country and various customs of Tanzania.

The Government's decision to gather evidence of the experience of Kadhi's courts from countries outside Tanzania surprised many Muslims in the country. Sheikhs Basalehe and Mataka, for instance, do not see any reason for the Government to do other research on the issue, considering that the Committee appointed by the Parliament had finished its job and given its suggestions. According to Basalehe and Mataka, Muslims in the country were waiting for the implementation of the suggestions by the Committee.[35] The report given by the Parliamentary Committee shows that the members of the Committee made enquiries about the operation of Kadhi's courts in selected African countries with the intention of finding out whether those countries have Kadhi's courts system and how they operate. The countries visited included Kenya, Uganda, Mozambique and South Africa.[36]

---

[34] The report was originally in Swahili, the English translation is by the author.

[35] This was in a television interview carried out by the Channel Ten TV station in the *Je tutafika'* programme which was discussing the issue of Kadhi's courts' re-introduction in the country.

[36] Channel Ten TV interview with Sheikhs Basalehe and Mataka.

The Response of Muslims Outside BAKWATA

The response of Muslims outside BAKWATA shows that there is no united view on the issue, causing suspicions and the accusations of the CCM Government, BAKWATA and Christians in the country. Though there is no official statement from these Muslims, because they lack a legally registered umbrella body for their representation, their voice should not be taken as insignificant, since they are part of the greater Muslim *umma* (Swah.: community) in Tanzania.

This group of Muslims has mainly two views. Either, that the Kadhi's courts should be there and be managed by the Muslim community, or, that they should not be there at all. Two important reasons are given by these Muslims. Firstly, they have fears that, if Kadhis are financially supported by the Government, they will not be independent. Hence they will not make decisions for the good of the Muslims in the country. Most of the decisions will be dictated by the Government. To use a common saying, "He who pays the piper chooses the tune". Hence it will be the Government, which pays the Kadhis, which will impose the decisions of the Kadhi and Kadhi's courts in general. As a result, Muslim matters will be decided by the secular, non-religious, Government, a situation which Muslims deem as disempowering Muslims in the country, because the Kadhis will implement the Government's policies.[37]

Also, these Muslims suspect that the idea of the re-introduction of Kadhi's courts in the country is a plan by the CCM Government to control Muslims. They say that the Government has failed to control Muslims through BAKWATA, because many Muslims nowadays do not trust BAKWATA, an instrument which they regard as being used by the Government to control Muslims. For them, Kadhi's courts, which will be controlled by the Government, are of no help to the Muslims. They give the example of Zanzibar, where Kadhi's courts are in operation. They say the Kadhis in Zanzibar do not have any significance to the Muslims, because they are controlled by the Government.

On the other hand, a Muslim organization called Khidmat Dawaat L'Islamiyat Center (Center for the Service of Islamic *Daʿwa* (Arab.: calling people to Islam)) wrote a letter to the CCM national leadership to express its views concerning the re-introduction of Kadhi's courts in the country.

[37] *An-Nuur* (Tanzanian weekly newspaper, in Swahili.) no. 997, 22nd–28th September 2006.

The unsigned letter is ascribed to a person identifying himself as the secretary general of the organization, Ustadh A.S. Mkambaku. The views expressed in the letter reflect those of Anṣār al-Sunna Muslims. The letter indicates that those Muslims who are represented by this organization categorically denounce the idea of the re-introduction of Kadhi's courts in the country, because the court will be under the auspices of BAKWATA, an organization that they are against, because they regard it as a puppet of CCM. The letter also indirectly shows that, since the Kadhi's courts will be limited to only personal cases, they are of no importance, because other issues like adultery, theft and other crimes are not to be judged according to Islamic law. The group represented by this organization says that the Kadhi's courts are not their most pressing demand. Their actual demand is the equal division of power in the country between Muslims and Christians. Analysis of the reasons given by the organization, that Kadhi's courts will not be important for Muslims since they will not have control over non-personal cases, may lead to a conclusion that the organization is 'for' the implementation of total *sharīʿa*.

According to the letter, BAKWATA insists on the re-introduction of Kadhi's courts, because BAKWATA Sheikhs will then have an assurance of employment. Surprisingly enough, the letter supports the Christians' stance of rejecting the re-introduction of the courts because the court will be financed by taxpayers, using money paid by both Christians and Muslims.

In a TV interview with Channel Ten television, Sheikh Yahya Hussein, founder and leader of *Baraza la Kujisomea Qur'an Tanzania* (BALUKTA, Tanzania Council of Qurʾān Reading) said that the abolition of Kadhi's courts had been an idea instigated by the then Minister for Legal Affairs. This Minister was from the Ahmadiyya community, which is considered by Sunni Muslims to be a non-authentic Muslim group. Hence, for him, Kadhi's courts were not an important thing, because they do not recognize the Ahmadiyya community.

In a similar vein, Sheikh Hussein commented that, currently, arbitration of marriage problems and other *fatāwā* (legal statements by a *muftī*) are offered by BAKWATA, which is an umbrella organization representing Muslim organizations; however, not all Muslims in the country recognize BAKWATA as representing them. Therefore Kadhi's courts, for him, are important because their introduction is a way by which Muslims can get rid of BAKWATA hegemony.

There is yet another Muslim perspective. Our interview with a representative of the Ahmadiyya Muslim community in Tanga shows that they are categorically against Kadhi's courts. They say that they are not 'for'

Kadhi's courts because other mainline Muslims do not recognize them as real Muslims. It is only because of Government secularism and the constitutional provision of the freedom of worship in the country that they can sustain their presence in the country. Therefore, they know that if Kadhi's courts are instituted, most of the *fatāwā* which a Kadhi offers will be against them. Also, they fear that the Kadhi's courts will intensify the existing discrimination which they suffer from 'mainline' Muslims.[38]

All of the above views from Muslims of different affiliations show that there is little uniformity in the stance among Muslims regarding Kadhi's courts.

Christians' Response to the Re-Introduction of Kadhi's Courts

Generally, Christians, as individuals, are not against the re-introduction of Kadhi's courts in the country, on condition that Kadhi's courts should not to be managed and funded by the Government. Their concern is that if the Kadhi's courts are governmentally instituted, other religious groups in the country may demand similar special favours from the Government. According to these Christians, it would be better for the Government to abstain from the issue of re-introduction of Kadhi's courts in the country. Rather, the issue should be left in the hands of the Muslim community.[39]

The Roman Catholic, Lutheran, Anglican and Pentecostal churches in Tanzania categorically denounce the re-introduction of Kadhi's courts in the country. These churches, at different times, have offered their statements on the issue. They all reject the idea of bringing the issue of Kadhi's courts as a bill of law to the Parliament for discussion. Objections to the infringement of the country's Constitution and the issue of the Government's financial support of Kadhi's courts have been a common denominator in all statements.

During the period of research the Roman Catholic Church did not make an official statement on the issue. A telephone interview with a University teacher, who is also a Roman Catholic priest, provided me with information that the church has yet to publish: their suggestions to

38 Interview with Abdallah Ramadhani, 11th February 2008, Tanga.

39 Interview with Habakkuk, 28th May 2007, Arusha (A theologian who teaches in the Christian university, Tumaini University College, owned by the Evangelical Lutheran Church in Tanzania).

the Government about the issue of Kadhi's courts.[40] However, the Roman Catholic Church expressed their doubts on the issue when they invited President Kikwete to the Tanzania Episcopal Conference meeting on 27th June 2006. In their speech to the President, the bishops said that they had carefully scrutinized the CCM manifesto for the 2005 election and saw that there are some areas in which the Government should be very careful in their implementation, so as to avoid endangering the nation's unity. For these bishops, the issue of Kadhi's courts should be resolved while taking the nation's constitution and legal system into consideration. Unlike other churches, the Roman Catholic Church suggested that the Government should incorporate the views of the majority in the country.

The Evangelical Lutheran Church in Tanzania summarizes their stance by saying that re-introduction of the Kadhi's courts in the country is a dangerous undertaking for peace, unity and solidarity of the nation. Furthermore, the entrenchment of the court would weaken the country's constitution, which explicitly shows that religion and politics should not be mixed. Therefore, the church says, Parliament should refute the idea of reintroducing Kadhi's courts in the country.

The Anglican Church's stance is set out in their statement of August 2006.The Anglican Church says that, in order to avoid an infringement of the nation's constitution, the re-introduction of Kadhi's courts should be left to the Muslim community to decide on their own. However, they insist that the court should not interfere with the national legal system. If that court is to be established, it should be under the Muslim community and its institutions.[41]

Our interview with Mwaki, a bishop in the Tanzania Assemblies of God (TAG), one of the Pentecostal Churches in Tanzania, showed that the Pentecostal churches do not support the re-introduction of Kadhi's courts. According to him, the Church wants Muslims to institute Kadhi's courts as their own institution and considers that the Government should not be involved.[42]

---

40 Telephone interview carried out with the lecturer in January 2008 (name withheld).

41 See the Anglican statement on the issue of Kadhi's courts, *Kanisa la Anglikana Tanzania Agosti 2006, Tamko la Maaskofu wa Kanisa Anglikana Tanzania Kuhusu Hoja ya Mahakama ya Kadhi Tanzania Bara* (Anglican Church of Tanzania August 2006, Statement of the Bishops of the Anglican Church of Tanzania concerning the proposal for Kadhi's Courts in mainland Tanzania), pages 2, 4 (Unpublished document).

42 Interview with Mwaki, 22nd May 2007, Tanga (the Bishop of the Tanzania Assemblies of God church in Tanga).

The General Secretary of the Christian Council of Tanzania (CCT) felt that Christians do not object to the operation of Kadhi's courts in the country, as long as the Government does not become involved in their operation.[43]

Christian-Muslim Mistrust over the Issue of Kadhi's Courts

Colonialism in Tanzania left a legacy which resulted in great socio-political disparity between Christians and Muslims in the country. This state of affairs is seen clearly in the levels of education among people of the two religions. Muslims feel that the Christians were favoured by the colonial Governments, especially in education.[44] This more-or-less shaped Christian-Muslim socio-political positions in the post-colonial Governments. In post-colonial Governments the number of Muslims with Government portfolios has been relatively smaller than that of their Christian counterparts. This disparity has been a Muslim grievance for several decades now and some Muslims condemn Christians in post-colonial Governments for conspiring to keep Muslims' education levels low. The late Kighoma Ali Malima, who was Minister of education during part of Ali Hassan Mwinyi's regime (1985–1995), can be seen as an example of this attitude.[45]

On the other hand, Christians reciprocate Muslim grievances with remarks that Muslims are striving for power in order to transform Tanzania into an Islamic state. Hence, Christians have become so cautious that they scrutinize Muslims who become national leaders. This results in more suspicion and accusations between the two communities. It was because of such a context that the re-introduction of Kadhi's courts was allegedly attributed to the current president, Jakaya Mrisho Kikwete,

[43] Interview with Leonard Mtaita, 16th February 2008, Dar-es-Salaam (General Secretary of the Christian Council of Tanzania).

[44] See Mohamed Said 'Intricacies and Intrigues in Tanzania: The Question of Muslim Stagnation in Education', *Change* 1993. http://www.igs.net/~kassim/nyaraka/Elimu2.html.

[45] Kighoma Malima was the first Muslim Minister of Education in the country after independence. Malima wrote a secret letter to President Mwinyi, which by chance fell into the hands of the media, saying that, after he assumed the position as the Minister of Education, he realized that his predecessors, who were Christians, purposely barred Muslim children from joining higher education in the country. The letter by Malima caused a lot of debate among Christians and Muslims. But the issue was quietly settled by the Government, and it also resulted in Malima losing his position.

who is a Muslim. One of the interviewees asserted that Muslims' demands and grievances usually surface strongly every time a Muslim president is in power.[46] Other interviewees related several incidents which occurred during the regime of Ali Hassan Mwinyi (who was the first Muslim president) and compared them with what is happening with the incumbent president. Some of the things that happened during Mwinyi's presidency included: the Government's attempt to join the Organization of Islamic Conferences (OIC); the wrecking of pork shops in Dar-es-Salaam in 1993; and the rapid increase of mosque building along main roads all over the country. Also during this time, the country witnessed growing Islamic fundamentalism and public polemical preaching, which created hostility between Christians and Muslims. These events were regarded, by some, as indicators that Muslims were on their way to make Tanzania an Islamic state.[47]

Now, with the demand for the re-establishment of Kadhi's courts, some Christians accuse Kikwete of masterminding the move to make Tanzania an Islamic state. However, nobody can substantiate this allegation. The history of Kadhi's courts shows that this demand has been a latent issue ever since their abolition in 1963.[48] Some measures have been taken by the Government to appease Muslims following their agitations. A good example of such measures is the Marriage Law amendment of 1971 which gives provision for religious marriage.

After a long period of silence, President Kikwete addressed the issue on 11th November 2007, during the installation of the Head of the Evangelical Lutheran Church in Tanzania (ELCT). In this address, which was covered by almost all the media in Tanzania, Kikwete publicly made it clear that the Kadhi's courts agenda, found in the CCM 2005 general election manifesto, was not initiated by him. He defended himself, saying that the argument was brought to Parliament by a member from an opposition party. He insisted that the agenda was not even a CCM agenda.

Kikwete, in the same address, said that the Kadhi's courts agenda was put into the CCM 2005 general election manifesto during Benjamin Mkapa's regime, a whole year ahead of the elections. This was prepared when Kikwete had not even been nominated as a CCM presidential candidate. President Kikwete said, according to the principles, guidelines and

[46] An interview conducted on 27th August 2007 in Arusha (name withheld).
[47] Interview with Bukuzi, 30th May 2007, Arusha.
[48] Interview with Sheikh Mataka, 30th January 2007, Dar-es-Salaam.

regulations of CCM, no presidential candidate is involved in the preparation of the party's election manifesto on an individual basis.

Kikwete also said that, as a presidential candidate, he adopted a manifesto in which Kadhi's courts was one of the agenda items. The manifesto was prepared by a special commission and was handed over to him by William Mkapa, the then president and national chairman of CCM.[49]

Therefore, Kikwete concluded, he did not in any way try to inveigle the issue into the party's agenda; neither did he engineer the issue into his Government. However, he said, since his party's election manifesto has Kadhi's courts as one of its agenda items, his Government will find amicable ways to resolve the issue. He promised that the Government will offer a solution without infringing the country's constitution and without being biased to any religious group.

During his response, Kikwete admitted that there is growing hostility among Christians and Muslims in the country following the debate on the re-introduction of Kadhi's courts in the country. Kikwete's confession of the present fragile situation, and his defence of not being the mastermind of the issue of Kadhi's courts, shows that Christians and Muslims in Tanzania look at each other with suspicion and mistrust. This results from the debate about the re-introduction of Kadhi's courts, especially concerning the Government's involvement in the issue.

The President's statement was strongly criticized by Augustine Lyatonga Mrema, the chairman of the Tanzania Labour Party, who, whilst a Member of Parliament, had brought the issue to the House.[50] Mrema criticized the president as having 'jumped on the bandwagon' although he did not know its direction. He said that the Government should have sought his advice before it indulged itself in resolving the issue because he was the one who initiated the agenda. He further said that "the fact that President Jakaya Kikwete approved the 2005 CCM election manifesto, which brought him to power, means there is no way he can distance himself from it and equally from the Kadhi's courts".[51]

An analysis of Kikwete's defence against the allegations of him being the mastermind of the demand for Kadhi's courts in the country reveals that he was not only defending himself, but also answering Christians who allege his involvement. Two things indicate this, firstly, his choice to

---

[49] *The Guardian*, Tanzanian Newspaper of 13th November 2007.

[50] Mrema said this during a press conference on 12th November 2007, just one day after Kikwete's statement.

[51] *The Guardian*, Newspaper of 13th November 2007.

address the issue during the installation of the head of ELCT. He could have done this on any other day, but his choice of this day might be because he knew that many Christians would be listening carefully. Hence, his message could reach a larger Christian audience in the country.[52]

Secondly, Kikwete attributed the issue of Kadhi's courts to Christian politicians. He reminded people that the genesis of the issue can be traced back to a Christian, Augustine Mrema. He can be seen as further confirming this by attributing the origin of the issue in the CCM general election manifesto to another Christian, William Mkapa, the then president and party chairman.

Although Kikwete did not openly defend himself by claiming that his religious affiliation does not influence the philosophy of his politics, his speech seemed to address the accusation. He did this by referring to the on-going allegations that he played a part in engineering the demand for Kadhi's courts through his party, because he is a Muslim.

As was stated earlier, suspicions and accusations between Christians and Muslims on the issue of Kadhi's courts go beyond the involvement of a Muslim President. In fact, the underlying issue here is the whole attitude of Christians toward the issue. Our research revealed that most people think that the re-introduction of Kadhi's courts is a covert plan of Muslims towards fully-fledged *sharīʿa* implementation in the country. On the other hand, most of the Church leaders who were interviewed expressed their sentiments that Muslims want to use the country's resources in disguise, using the issue of Kadhi's courts. Hence, they insisted that the Kadhi's courts issue should be left to the Muslim community for its implementation and management.

Meanwhile, some Muslims, especially some of the leaders like the Mufti, suspect that Christians have a hidden motive which aims to impinge on Muslims' freedom of worship. To some Muslims, this state of affairs is just a perpetuation of the perceived conspiracy by the post-colonial Christian-oriented Government to hinder Muslims' rights in the country. It was because of such attitudes that the Mufti of Tanzania publicly condemned those who questioned the re-introduction of Kadhi's courts in the country. According to the Mufti, opponents of the re-introduction of Kadhi's courts are those people who do not have good will toward Islam in Tanzania.

---

52 The Evangelical Lutheran Church in Tanzania is the second largest denomination in the country after the Roman Catholic Church. ELCT has significant influence in the country because there are many Government officials who are members of this church.

Therefore, as has been stated by President Kikwete, accusations, suspicions, and prejudices characterize the issue of Kadhi's courts' re-introduction. This condition needs the Government's special attention. The Government has to properly address it to avoid misunderstandings and conflicts among Christians and Muslims. Since the two communities are not homogeneous, the Government has to be as careful as possible in its decisions on this case, since the issue has already proved to have provoked a wide variety of views from both within and outside religious groups in the country.

Challenges of Kadhi's Courts' Re-Introduction

Several socio-political challenges are posed by the demand for the re-introduction of Kadhi's courts in the country. Some challenges are from within Islam and others are from outside. The most serious challenge is posed to the Government. Though Tanzania has a secular Government, it has the responsibility to protect the rights of its people. Muslims in this country form a very important group of citizens. It would be very unwise decision-making if the Government fails to take into account the demands and grievances of its constituents.[53] This does not imply that the Government should infringe the constitution. However, the Government should find every possible way to solve the problems facing different groups, both for the sake of peace and tranquillity of the country, and for its future.

This state of affairs puts CCM in a predicament. On the one hand, the Muslims in the country demand fulfilment of what they were promised by CCM in the manifesto; on the other hand, the country's legal and religious pluralism makes Christians and other non-Muslims hang on to the constitution to denounce the establishment of Kadhi's courts in the country as a Governmental institution.

However, the Government is not responsible to its Muslim constituency alone. The Government has equal responsibility to all religious groups in the country. Christians' and other non-Muslims' complaints about Kadhi's courts should not be taken lightly. This is a challenge which calls for the Government to clear all doubts about Kadhi's courts' entrenchment from among non-Muslims in the country. Non-Muslims should be given

---

53 Interview with Mpemba, 22nd May 2007, Tanga.

convincing reasons as to why their money should be used for running what is regarded by them as a religious institution, which caters for one religious group only. Also, the Government should give enough reasons why Kadhi's courts are not going to be a religious institution but a Governmental institution. The Government should not forget that Christians, non-Muslims and Muslims outside BAKWATA also constitute very critical, influential and powerful groups of voters who have the potential to affect elections. The great challenge ahead of the Government is how to satisfy all religious groups on this issue, while remaining neutral.

Constitutionalism is another serious challenge to Kadhi's courts. Article 19 of the Constitution of the country states that:

> [Section 1] Every person has the right to freedom of thought or conscience, belief or faith, and choice in matters of religion, including the freedom to change his religion or faith.

Citizens are at liberty to follow beliefs of their choice as long as they do not impinge on the country's laws. This is a challenge to the Kadhi's courts project. The first challenge is that section one of article 19 of the constitution stipulates that people are allowed to follow the religion of their choice; hence Muslims have constitutional rights to exercise their religion *de jure*. This is enough reason for the Government to grant Kadhi's courts to Muslims. Doing so will allow Muslims in the country to practise their religious duties rightly. Hindering Kadhi's courts is tantamount to barring Muslims from fulfilling their religious duties. Prior to 2005, section two of the same article stipulated:

> Without prejudice to the relevant laws of the United Republic the profession of religion, worship and propagation of religion shall be free and a private affair of an individual; and the affairs and management of religious bodies shall not be part of the activities of the State authority.

This could be seen as being a major hindrance to Kadhi's courts being a Government institution. However, this section was deleted by Act No. 1 of 2005 Art. 6. and the present Section 2 was substituted, which states:

> Protection of rights referred to in this Article shall be in accordance with the provisions prescribed by the laws which are of importance to a democratic society for security and peace in the society, integrity of the society and the national coercion [*sic*].

The new section cannot be regarded as being a bar to Kadhi's courts becoming a Government institution in as far as they are "in accordance with the provisions prescribed by the laws...".

State secularism challenges instituting Kadhi's courts as a Governmental organization, because to do so means bringing religion into the public sphere. Doing so would contravene the country's constitution which stipulates that religion is a private matter. Apart from that, to do so opens doors for other religious groups to demand that their religious issues and practices also be given special positions or to be institutionalized in the Government. This could result in anarchy in the country.

Furthermore, in the October 2004 report by the Parliamentary Committee, it says that some of Muslims' personal issues like marriage, inheritance, divorce and *wakfu* are not administered correctly in accordance with the Qurʾān. Hence Kadhi's courts should be instituted to cater for these needs. However, these needs are not the only things which are mentioned in the Qurʾān. If the Government creates a court to cater for those things, it means that the Government could be forced into the position of having to create a court for other things which are mentioned in the Qurʾān. But what about the many things which are mentioned in the religious scriptures of other religions? Will it be possible for the state to create courts to cater for things mentioned in other religious scriptures and their ethical codes?

The above challenges raise various concerns. Firstly, the issue of the re-introduction of Kadhi's courts should be solved by prudence and not through legal ways. In this country, we have witnessed several issues being resolved by prudence. We can cite the issue of the Presidential position whereby Christian and Muslim presidents have alternated. This is neither a constitutional nor a legal requirement, but it is prudently done so as to create harmony and tranquillity in the country.[54] Also, we have many things in Christian-Muslim relations which are done not because of law but because of amicability and good relations between the two communities. One example is the popular tradition of some Christians asking Muslims to slaughter their animals for meat; Christians do so because they want their Muslim brothers and sisters not to be offended when they are invited by Christians for a meal.[55] Also, Christians do not want to offend Muslims when they go to buy meat in shops. Therefore the Kadhi's courts issue can be resolved by using that kind of philosophy.

---

[54] Interview with Tumaini University Lecturer, 3rd March 2007 (name withheld).

[55] Most butchers throughout Tanzania are Muslims; during the 1990s the Anglican Bishop of the Diocese of Central Tanganyika (Dodoma Region) attempted to run a 'Christian Butchery' but this lost money and was soon discontinued.

Secondly, the argument calls for a review of the constitution. The constitution should be amended to incorporate new challenges in the country. The Government should be very careful in doing so, because incorporating religious issues in the constitution is very dangerous since the Government cannot satisfy all the religious groups in the country.

Furthermore, one of the lawyers interviewed commented that religious following is emotional. It is dangerous to build your laws on emotions, because emotions change constantly. A person can suggest one religious thing today and deny it tomorrow. Therefore that state of affairs may lead to instability in the country.[56]

Another solution is for people to abide by the constitution and leave religious matters to the private sphere. Muslims in the country should institute and manage Kadhi's courts within their religious circles. Alternatively, the Government should find more ways than are presently being followed in our Law Schools to enhance magistrates' understanding of Islamic laws, in order to rightly adjudicate Muslim personal issues.

Another challenge to Kadhi's courts is the issue of factionalism in Islam. Re-introduction of Kadhi's courts in the country is challenged not only by factors outside Islam but also from within Islam. Denominationalism and factionalism within Islam have proved to be big drawbacks for the institution of Kadhi's courts in the country. Some groups, such as Anṣār al-Sunna Muslims, do not support Kadhi's courts. As we have seen earlier, for them, Kadhi's courts are part of BAKWATA's covert agenda to create job opportunities for their Sheikhs, and as a mechanism to control other Muslims who do not recognize BAKWATA. According to them, this has been facilitated by the CCM Government, which is regarded as a Christian dominated Government, whose aim is to inhibit the development of Islam in the country. Their main argument here is that if BAKWATA was serious in fulfilling Allāh's will, it would have agitated for full *sharīʿa* implementation in the country. For them, *sharīʿa* is not only for personal cases in Muslims' lives, but for the totality of Muslim life. Hence, to only demand Kadhi's courts, is to reduce *sharīʿa* to personal issues only. Though these groups do not mention what sort of *sharīʿa* may best fit the country, their historical background shows that they are for the *salafiyya*[57] understanding of *sharīʿa*, which identifies itself with the pristine Islam that advocates strict *sharīʿa* law.

---

[56] Interview with Kenny, 15th June 2007, Bayreuth, Germany.

[57] *Salafiyya* movement advocating a return to the ways of the early generations of Muslims.

Disloyalty to BAKWATA also poses a great challenge to Kadhi's courts' implementation. This is the reason behind BAKWATA's need of Government backing in the re-introduction of Kadhi's courts. BAKWATA wants the Government to enforce the power and authority of the Kadhis, and the courts at large, over all Muslim denominations and factions. But, if the Government agrees with this move, the Government will have become biased to one Muslim faction in the country. This may cause intra-Muslim conflict in Tanzania.

The challenge becomes more intense due to the fact that BAKWATA has been alleged, by Muslims who are not under its patronage, to be an appendage of the CCM Government.[58] For them, BAKWATA was founded by the Government in order to control and contain Muslims who were regarded as rebels. So, for them, there is no doubt that the CCM adopted the Kadhi's courts agenda in its 2005 general election manifesto in order to help BAKWATA to continue to control Muslims in the country. This was possible because some of the CCM Executive Committee members are active BAKWATA members as well. Therefore, the denial of Kadhi's courts by Muslims outside BAKWATA is a denial of both CCM and BAKWATA.[59]

Simultaneously, the above argument, regarding loyalty to BAKWATA, projects further difficulties as to the pragmatism of re-introducing Kadhi's courts. Several Muslims interviewed, especially young Muslim women,[60] expressed the sentiments that they prefer a magistrate's court to a Kadhi's court. Women want equal rights in marriage and inheritance, just like non-Muslim women. Their views should not be taken for granted because such views challenge the practicality of the Kadhi's court.[61] Such responses

[58] For a description of the origins of BAKWATA and its links with TANU, see: 'Islam and Politics in Tanzania', Mohamed Said, http://www.igs.net/~kassim/nyaraka/islam_and_politics_in_tz.html.

[59] For Kassim, BAKWATA has been a big stumbling block to Muslims' development in the country (Interview with Kassim, Dar-es-Salaam).

[60] A group interview of five women was conducted in Tanga city during late 2007. One of the interviewees was a woman of about sixty years. To her, Kadhi's courts and Islamic law in general are crucial for Muslim women's justice. But this was different from the view of young women who took Islamic law as a law which cannot fit the current Tanzanian context. Although they did not deny it, because it is the law of God, they said they would not opt for it because to them it is difficult to abide by, especially at this time when living expenses are so high, which compels them to find different means of earning their daily livelihood.

[61] This view is not different from that of the late chairwoman of *Umoja wa Wanawake wa Tanzania* (UWT, The Union of Women of Tanzania), Mrs. Sophia Kawawa, who in 1988 came under fire after having publicly criticized Islamic rules that she felt were oppressive to women. Kawawa said that polygyny should be forbidden and women should have the same rights of inheritance as men.

pose the question as to how many Muslims in Tanzania actually want their cases to be adjudicated according to Muslim personal law. Moreover, the distribution of Kadhi's courts in the country poses another serious challenge to the issue. Historically, the court was considered to be a native court which had a geographical limitation, the 'coastal-strip', which, in an agreement of 1890, the Sultan of Zanzibar allowed the Germans to hold, with the understanding that Islamic Law should continue to be upheld. Now, given the fact that Muslims are distributed all over Tanzania, the court should also be distributed to satisfactorily cater for all Muslims in the country. The Parliamentary Committee proposed that Kadhi's courts should be placed in all areas where there is a magistrate's primary court. This means that the Government is creating another court system which will need to be financed, by almost the same amount, as the present court system.

Apart from the financial challenges facing Kadhi's courts, our discussion with a BAKWATA Executive Committee member showed that even if the Government re-introduces Kadhi's courts today, it won't be easy for the Muslim community to immediately implement their re-introduction because, currently, there are not enough Muslim jurists in the country. Therefore it will take time for the Muslims to educate sufficient jurists.[62]

Conclusion

We have seen that the demand for *sharīʿa* implementation is a social reality in mainland Tanzania. This reality is expressed by the current demand for the re-introduction of Kadhi's courts in the country. Kadhi's courts were in place before independence and in early post-independent Tanganyika, and Muslims have been demanding their re-instatement ever since their abolition by Parliament in 1963.

The issue has surfaced strongly following a religious resurgence among Muslim youths. The demand gained impetus from some political parties, including CCM, which mentioned Kadhi's courts in their election manifesto, giving the impression that the issue had been manipulated for political popularity. Nevertheless, CCM seems to be in a predicament as to how to resolve the issue, which has caused a volatile atmosphere among Christians and Muslims in the country.

---

62 Informal talks with Sheikh Mataka in January 2007, Dar-es-Salaam.

This research discovered that, since Christians and Muslims are not homogeneous societies, there have been a variety of views on the issue in inter- and intra-denominational domains and inter- and intra-religious domains both in Christianity and Islam.

Christians suspect that the demand for Kadhi's courts is just a ploy of Muslims towards gaining full *sharīʿa* implementation in the country. They view the demand as an infringement of the country's constitution and object to the use of taxpayers' money on one religious group. Hence, Christians, under their umbrella organizations, have exhorted the Government to abstain from taking Kadhi's courts' re-introduction as a national issue, but rather to view it is as a Muslim undertaking which should be resolved by Muslims themselves.

While Muslims, under BAKWATA's auspices, insist on the re-introduction of Kadhi's courts in Tanzania as something distinct from total *sharīʿa* implementation, it appears that some Muslims outside BAKWATA want total *sharīʿa* application in the country. It is because of this that those Muslims oppose the idea of re-introduction of Kadhi's courts in the country, since the judicial limit of the court implies that not all Islamic laws will be implemented by the court. These Muslims put more emphasis on equal opportunities for both Muslims and Christians in the socio-political arena, placing blame on BAKWATA for its failure to fight for the Muslims in this country.

This study has found that most Tanzanians are ignorant of the concepts of Kadhi and Kadhi's courts. It has discovered that there is a lot of confusion among Tanzanians in the Swahili use of the term Kadhi. Hence, there is a need for the study of the term in Swahili and in Arabic and of its legal use in a Tanzanian context.

It is our conviction that the demand for Kadhi's courts is not the sole cause of suspicions and accusations between Muslims and Christians in the country. Historically, there have been ambivalent relations between them, since the days of colonial rule. Muslims in the country have many grievances, including backwardness in education as compared to Christians, and they demand equal representation in the Government and civil services in the country.

The Muslims' demand for Kadhi's courts in the country is a genuine one. The Government should take it seriously, and should stop using the issue of Kadhi's courts as a political tool and start finding new avenues toward a solution of the issue.

Finally, this chapter poses one critical challenge: if the Government allows Kadhi's courts to be implemented in the country, would this be a panacea for the Muslims' grievances in the country? This is a challenge which requires further research.

CHAPTER ELEVEN

"CHAOS WILL NEVER HAVE A CHANCE": *SHARĪʿA* DEBATES AND TOLERANCE IN A PROVINCIAL TANZANIAN TOWN

Bernadin Mfumbusa

Introduction

Tanzania emerged from three decades of single party rule in 1992. Until then, two slogans: *zidumu fikra za mwenyekiti wa chama cha mapinduzi* (Swah.: long live ideas of the chairman of the ruling party) and *chama kushika hatamu* (Swah.: the ruling party is supreme), marked the limits of the acceptable discourses. Only discourses that agreed with the ruling party ideology were allowed to filter into the public sphere. The former Vice-President of the United Republic, Alhaj Aboud Jumbe, suggested that the doctrine of the 'supremacy of the ruling party' silenced alternative voices.[1]

People were reduced to singing praises in favour of the ruling elite, thus creating a spurious sense of national consensus. As a result, the democratic opening-up in the early 1990s released pent-up ethnic, religious, and racial tensions. Indians, who came to Tanzania originally as indentured labourers at the end of the 19th century, became overnight *gabacholi* (Swah.: thieves) in the eyes of some nationalists espousing a philosophy of indigenization (Swah.: *uzawa*).[2] For decades the Indians had enjoyed a monopoly over the urban commercial sector. The Supreme Muslim Council of Tanzania (known by its Swahili acronym BAKWATA), the sole custodian of the Muslims' interests, became 'a word of insult' in some Muslim quarters.[3] A plethora of organizations emerged claiming to be true representatives of the Muslims. Nestor Luanda estimated the

[1] Jumbe, Aboud, *The Partnership: Tanganyika—Zanzibar Union: 30 Turbulent Years*, Dar es Salaam: Amana Publishers, 1994.

[2] Wijsen, Frans & Bernadin Mfumbusa, *Seeds of Conflict: Religious Tensions in Tanzania*, Nairobi: Paulines Publications, 2004.

[3] Said, Mohammed, *The Life and Times of Abdulwahid Sykes (1924–1968): The Untold Story of the Muslim Struggle against British Colonialism in Tanganyika*, London: Minerva Press, 1998, page 303.

existence of more than one hundred Muslim organizations in the country in the mid-1990s.[4] Muslims in Tanzania nurse a number of grievances and demands. The grievances include the small number of Muslims in universities and the large number of Muslims among criminals and loiterers. The demands include the re-establishment of Kadhi's Courts, which had been abolished in 1963, and for Tanzania to join the Organization of Islamic Conferences (OIC). The grievances and demands were outlined in a letter to the President of the United Republic in 1999 which represented a rhetorical escalation, in a country where differences and disagreements were usually smothered by what Maddox and Giblin call "rhetoric about peace and unity".[5]

Evolution of the *Sharīʿa* Debate

The banning of the East African Muslim Welfare Society (EAMWS) in 1968 was a watershed in the *sharīʿa* debates in Tanzania. The ban is still seen as the government's attempt to undermine Islam in Tanzania.[6] Forty years after its creation, BAKWATA, which replaced EAMWS, is yet to receive total acceptance among Muslims. Said has suggested that referring to a Muslim as BAKWATA is 'like calling a Christian a disciple of Judas Iscariot'.[7] The publication of a 'White Paper on Marriage' in 1969, resulting in the Marriage Act, 1970, is another factor in the debates. The Act incorporates aspects of Islamic personal law, namely, matters of inheritance and divorce, as part of the jurisdiction of the primary court system. Other rather violent moments in the *sharīʿa* debates include the 1993 pork butchers' shops' crisis and the Mwembechai crisis of 1998. The ruling party, Chama cha Mapinduzi's (CCM) 2005 election manifesto, which sought to re-introduce Kadhi's Courts into the country, introduced a new twist to the contemporary debates.

---

[4] Luanda, N. Nestor, 'Christianity and Islam Contending for the Throne on the Tanzanian Mainland', in *Challenges to the Nation-State in Africa*, O. Olukoshi Adebayo & Liisa Laakso (eds), Uppsala: Nordiska Afrikainstitutet, 1996, page 172.

[5] Maddox, Gregory H. & Giblin, James L. (eds), *In Search of a Nation: Histories of Authority and Dissidence in Tanzania*, Dar es Salaam: Kapsal Educational Publisher, 2005, page 1.

[6] Imtiyaz, S. Yusuf, 'Islam and African Socialism: A Study of the Interactions between Islam and Ujamaa in Tanzania', (Unpublished dissertation), University Microfilms International (UMI), Ann Arbor, Michigan 1990; Said, 1998; Jumbe, 1994.

[7] Said, 1998.

Sharīʿa debates in Tanzania have followed three trends. Before 1985 the discourses focused on the interplay between religion, *ujamaa* policy and the state. These discourses occurred at an academic level and were largely dominated by foreign scholars intrigued by the relationship between *ujamaa* policy, on the one hand, and religion on the other.[8] The post-1985 discourses revolve around Muslim sectarian grievances and demands.[9] And there are discourses addressing issues affecting Muslims and Christians in various communities across the country. These are micro-level, grassroots' discourses whose themes range from mundane issues like killing a goat in 'a *ḥalāl* (Arab.: lawful) way', or the extent to which a Muslim family can get involved with Christian neighbours 'keeping pigs', the activities of Christian NGOs who are involved in proselytizing, as well as the occurrence of intermarriage, especially where Muslim girls are married to Christian men. These are touchy issues.

When the Portuguese arrived in the coastal town of Kilwa, in the 15th century, an established Muslim community existed which was deeply suspicious of the Portuguese missionary intentions. The Portuguese failed to establish a beachhead due to the Muslims' resistance. During the German rule (1885–1916), coastal Muslims were co-opted into administration as local leaders, namely, *akidas* (Swah.: headmen) and *jumbes* (Swah.: headmen) because of their ability to read and write. Sometimes, this has been cited as a factor in the fast spread of Islam in hinterland Tanzania. By the end of British colonialism in 1961, however, the mission school system had transformed the country's educational landscape in favour of Christians. Three ethnic groups that had early contact with the missionary school systems, the Chagga, the Haya and the Nyakyusa, were better educated than the rest of the population. These three ethnic groups are predominantly Christian. In 1959, the All Muslim National Union of Tanganyika (AMNUT), aware of the imbalances between Christians and Muslims, especially in the education sector, submitted a memorandum to the colonial Government, calling for independence to be postponed until

---

8 Sivalon, John, *Kanisa Katoliki na Siasa ya Tanzania: 1953 mpaka 1985*, Ndanda: Mission Press, 1985; Rasmussen, Lissi, *Christian-Muslim Relations in Africa: The Case of Northern Nigeria and Tanzania Compared*, New York: St. Martin's Press, 1993; Ludwig, Frieder, 'After Ujamaa: Is Religious Revivalism a Threat to Tanzania's Stability?' in *Questioning the Secular State*, David Westerlund (ed.), London: Hurst & Company, 1996, pages 216–236.

9 Jumbe, 1994; Said, 1998; Njozi, M. Hamza, *The Mwembechai Killings and the Political Future of Tanzania*, Ottawa: Globalink Communications, 2000; Mbogoni, Lawrence E. Y., *The Cross Vs the Crescent: Religion and Politics in Tanzania from the 1880s to the 1990s*, Dar es Salaam: Mkuki & Nyota Publishers, 2004.

Muslims had attained equal status with Christians in education.[10] AMNUT feared that Christians would use their educational advantage to dominate administrative and professional sectors after independence. In 1962, the government addressed the question of various imbalances in the country in a press release that said in part:

> There is no quick way to cancel out the present difference between our African and non-African citizens; there is no easy way to remove the existing disparity in education between Christians and Muslims, or between the educated few and the majority of the people, there is no short cut by which the Masai and the Wagogo can become Wahaya, Wachagga and Wanyakyusa.[11]

At the time the Europeans were generally wealthier than Africans and Asians. The legacy of European opulence lives on in the form of neighbourhoods known as '*uzunguni*' (Swah.: European quarter) in most towns. Such neighbourhoods are usually posher than the rest of the town. Indians dominated the urban retail sector and the European expatriates dominated the bureaucracy. The contemporary *sharīʿa* debates began in 1989 with Zanzibar's ill-fated attempt to join the Organization of Islamic Conferences (OIC).

A Theoretical Framework

Christian-Muslim relations in sub-Saharan Africa have been characterized as harmonious.[12] Families are often made up of members belonging to different religious affiliations, which encourages mutual understanding and tolerance. Also, people remain committed to their ethnic identity, in terms of staying in touch with ancestral spirits, even after conversion to Islam or Christianity. Ali Mazrui has attributed harmony in Africa to the African Tradition Religion's capacity to tolerate and accommodate alternative religious cultures, "the African Traditional Religion ecumenalism".[13] Harmony among people in Tanzania is also attributed to deliberate government policies like adoption of common symbols such as the *uhuru* (Swah.: freedom) torch which is raced through all regions, every year, as a

[10] Omari, Cuthbert. K., 'The Management of Tribal and Religious Diversity', in *Mwalimu: The Influence of Nyerere*, C. Legum & G. Mmari (eds.), Dar es Salaam: Mkuki & Nyota, 1995 pages 25–31.

[11] Said, 1998.

[12] Ludwig, 1996, page 216.

[13] Mazrui, Ali A., *The African Condition: A Political Diagnosis*, London: Heinemann, 1980.

symbol of unity. *Ujamaa* ideology that stressed socio-economic egalitarianism is another factor that encouraged unity.[14] Lately, however, elements of African Traditional Religions that united people are weakening due to an onslaught from Muslim groups like the Anṣār al-Sunna. The policies that cemented unity, such as compulsory national service for all advanced secondary school leavers, have been abandoned. National symbols, such as the national anthem, are trivialized in some quarters as nothing more than elements of Christian hegemony.[15]

The statistics on the ratio of Muslims and Christians are a matter of sometimes acrimonious dispute. *Muslim News International* of July 1963, for example, put the percentage of Muslims at between 65–70 percent of the population two years after independence.[16] The first post-colonial national population census in 1967, which was the last to address the religious identity question, registered Christians at 32 percent and Muslims 30 percent.[17] In the early 1970s, the number of Christians was estimated at 44 percent and Muslims 32 percent.[18] Westerlund, presenting government policy, put the number of Christians, Muslims and the adherents of the African Traditional Religions (ATR) at a third of the population each.[19] Other estimates show that Muslims make up 45 percent of the population and Christians 39 percent.[20] In 2006 President Jakaya Kikwete estimated the number of Muslims and Christians as 40 percent each.[21]

Four questions have guided this study: (1) to what extent have African Traditional Religions acted as a bridge between Muslims and Christians? (2) How does marginalization (or victimization) rhetoric play out in the grassroots' communities like Kondoa? (3) Do victim-making narratives work to strengthen identity politics among Muslims of Kondoa Municipality? (4) To what extent do *sharīʿa* related narratives in Kondoa reflect the national recorded patterns?

---

[14] Omari, 1995.
[15] Njozi, 2000.
[16] Nimtz, August H., *Islam and Politics in East Africa: The Sufi Order in Tanzania*, Minneapolis: University of Minnesota Press, 1980.
[17] Mohammed Saeed [*sic*], 'Islam and Politics in Tanzania', Muslim Writers Association, http://www.igs.net/~kassim/nyaraka/islam_and_politics_in_tz.html (accessed 11.08.07).
[18] Rasmussen, 1993, page 2.
[19] Westerlund, David, *Ujamaa na Dini: A Study of Some Aspects of Society and Religion in Tanzania, 1961–1977*. Stockholm: Acta Universitas Stockhomiensis, 1977.
[20] Jumbe, 1994.
[21] Thompson, John, 'Tanzanian president offers formula for West-Islam peace', *BU Today* 2006, http://www.bu.edu/phpbin/news-cms/news (accessed 11.10.2007).

Kondoa: Description of the Case

Kondoa is one of the five districts of the Dodoma Region of Tanzania, which is located in the semi-arid, central region of Tanzania. People are mostly peasants, eking out a meagre living through the cultivation of seasonal crops like millet, cassava, and maize. The ethnic fabric of the district is complex.[22] The Rangi is the largest ethnic group; others are the Alawi (Wasi), Burungi, and Sandawe. Like most towns, Kondoa has attracted many people from other parts of the country, coming with their own customs and beliefs. The town lies on an ancient caravan route that ran from the coastal towns of Bagamoyo and Tanga. The route was used by Arab traders in the 18th and 19th centuries, which means that Kondoa had had contact with Islamic culture for at least two centuries by the time Christian missionaries first arrived. As a result of the intensive exchange between the coast and the inland trading settlements, Kondoa developed into an important Muslim settlement; "33 of the 147 headmen in its vicinity were said to be Muslims in 1913".[23] *Sunnī* Islam is the dominant religion, abiding by the *shāfiʿī madhhab* (Arab.: School of Law). However, the influence of Islamic reform movements is increasing amongst the *Sunnīs*. The *sunnī* Muslim community is experiencing tensions with the arrival of new groups like the Anṣār al-Sunna (also known as *wahhābī* or *al-mujāhidūn*) in the 1980s. The Anṣār al-Sunna (Arab.: the followers of the traditions of the prophet) own mosques and challenge the BAKWATA-Muslims (*sunnī* Muslims will be identified as BAKWATA-Muslims and Anṣār al-Sunna) on matters of practice and tradition. The Anṣār al-Sunna is the fastest-spreading brand of Islam in Kondoa within *sunnī* Islam. Another *sunnī* group is *Tablīghī Jamāʿat* (Arab.: *Jamāʿat al-Tablīgh*, Society for spreading faith), which is largely focussed on propagating Islam (Arab.: *daʿwa*) amongst Muslims. The *Tablīghī Jamāʿat* is a dynamic and fast-growing

---

[22] On the pre-modern history of Kondoa and its environment: Johnston, H. H. & F. J. Bagshawe, 'The Peoples of the Happy Valley. (East Africa). Part I', *Journal of the Royal African Society*, Vol. 24, 1924, pages 25–33; Bagshawe, F. J., 'The Peoples of the Happy Valley. (East Africa). The Aboriginal Races of Kondoa Irangi. Part II: The Kangeju', *Journal of the Royal African Society*, Vol. 24, 1925, pages 117–130; Bagshawe, F. J., 'The Peoples of the Happy Valley. (East Africa).: The Aboriginal Races of Kondoa Irangi. Part III (Continued)'; *Journal of the Royal African Society*, Vol. 24, 1925, pages 328–347; Bagshawe, F. J., 'The Peoples of the Happy Valley. (East Africa).: The Aboriginal Races of Kondoa Irangi. Part IV: The Goroa and Their Kindred Hamitic Tribes, the Wambulu, or Erokh, the Wasi, or Alawa, and the Burungi'; *Journal of the Royal African Society*, Vol. 25, 1925, pages 59–74.

[23] Iliffe, John, *A Modern History of Tanganyika*, Cambridge: Cambridge University Press, 1999, p. 213.

transnational Islamic reform movement originating in colonial India. Finally, a *Shīʿa* community was established in the 1990s, made up of ethnic Rangi people. The community is unique as Shīʿism in Tanzania is largely dominated by Asians and is limited to major urban centres like Arusha, Dar es Salaam and Mwanza. The diversity of the Muslim community makes agreements among Muslims on many issues like Kadhi's courts difficult to achieve. The proliferation of religious groups, movements, and churches is redefining the religious demography of Kondoa. The Roman Catholics were the first Christian group to be established in the area in 1907, while the Anglicans and Lutherans arrived in the 1960s and 1970s respectively. The Pentecostals, also known as the 'Born Again Christian Movement', have become a strong phenomenon since the 1990s. Pentecostal churches include: Calvary Assemblies of God (CAG), Tanzania Assemblies of God (TAG), and Tanzania Full Gospel Church. The changing religious demography is resulting in sectarian social institutions such as orphanages, kindergartens and schools. Some of the institutions, especially a Christian NGO, 'Compassion International', which targets Muslim children, is becoming a centre of controversy.

Methodology

This chapter is based on a qualitative analysis of a sample of 20 interviews, part of a two-year study in Kondoa. The interviews were conducted in September 2006 and September 2007 with interviewees coming from different demographic backgrounds. There were Muslims and Christians, religious leaders and laity, male and female, the young as well as the old. A semi-structured interview guide was used in all interviews. Interviews lasted from 20 to more than 60 minutes. Most of the interviews were recorded, transcribed and translated into English. The privacy of respondents is protected by using aliases, generic titles or first names. Interview transcripts were analysed by compiling responses to each question across the pool of interviews, taking into account demographic details. Thematic coding was used to tease out themes across the interview range.[24] The themes discussed in the findings have been derived from a careful analysis of a sample of interviews representing key segments of society in terms of demography.

---

[24] Miles, Matthew B. & A. Michael Huberman, *Qualitative Data Analysis* 2nd edit., London: Sage, 1994, page 9.

Findings

Despite numerous references to African Traditional Religions in academic literature, few people ever admit to be practitioners. The vast majority of Tanzanians identify themselves simply as either Muslims or Christians. Yet the interviews were peppered with allusions, practices, customs and beliefs associated with ancestor veneration in various forms such as *tambiko* (Swah.: invoking spirits), offering libations, and initiation ceremonies. The practices abound among both Muslims and Christians, notwithstanding the prohibition of *shirk* (Arab.: associating others with God) among the former, or the disavowal of pagan practices among the latter. The evidence that such practices are increasingly a source of tension is mounting. Persistence of traditional beliefs among Muslims has its roots in early conversion processes, whereby new converts were allowed great leeway in the manner in which they practised their new religion. Muslims didn't abjure traditional brew, consulting oracles, or offering sacrifices to ancestors. A *shīʿa* cleric offered a graphic description of the early Muslims:

> Muslim converts were given a name and taught the ABCs of Islam like saying: 'Bismillah Rahman Rahim'. The converts were allowed to drink alcohol or partake in offering sacrifices... even during the Holy month of Ramadan when some wanted to drink alcohol they were allowed to do so. Sheikhs, however, insisted that children attend Qur'ānic schools without fail. Thus older people continued to drink and enjoy their traditional ways while their children and grandchildren mastered proper teachings of Islam...[25]

This approach has led to the situation whereby older Muslims are tolerant and accommodating, while the younger ones are averse to traditional ways. What mattered initially was the numbers of people purporting to be Muslims, rather than the quality of their belief or practice. Muslim missionaries had a long-term view of the conversion process. The first generation could be allowed to be nominal Muslims while the offspring were introduced to a stricter version of Islam. As a result, many Muslims remain committed to aspects of ATR. The visibility of ATR, however, remains low due to the absence of symbols such as temples. Also, the absence of strong Traditional Religion movements, such as the *Aladura* of Nigeria, has meant that its presence in public life is limited. Nevertheless, during bereavements, natural calamities, and illnesses, people have recourse to sacrifices to appease angry spirits over and above observing Islamic

[25] Personal interview with Hussein, 4th September 2007.

rituals. Calamities and bad fortune are often blamed on unhappy spirits (Swah.: *mizimu*). People invoke ancestral blessings in times of travelling, as shown by a popular blessing *Ukalwata wa satu na wa mundi* (Rangi: may you tread on a python's skin and a sheep's skin), which are considered sacred totems among the Rangi. The blessing is usually made over close friends and relatives about to embark on long trips. The invocation of 'python' and 'sheep', even at a metaphorical level, is a testimony to the durability of the African traditional beliefs among practising Muslims. Such practices, taken for granted for generations as part of an ethnic identity, are now being questioned and discouraged on religious grounds by the Anṣār al-Sunna, as they see such practices as un-Islamic survivals from the past.

Anṣār al-Sunna

The arrival of Anṣār al-Sunna in the 1980s heralded divisions among Kondoa Muslims. One Swahili word, *mapokeo* (traditions) has become emblematic of disagreements among Muslims. The Anṣār al-Sunna accuse Bakwata-*sunnīs* of abiding by traditions. Although members of Anṣār al-Sunna and BAKWATA groups play down their differences, they don't see eye to eye on a number of issues. Some of the differences mentioned by a senior BAKWATA Muslim cleric include Anṣār al-Sunna not celebrating the *mawlid* (birthday) of the Prophet and not recognizing the companions (Swah.: *maswahaba*) of the Prophet who fought to introduce religion in Saudi Arabia. Sometimes there is even a hint of suggestion that the Anṣār al-Sunna may be heretics.[26] Other differences may seem to be cosmetic but they are important. The Anṣār al-Sunna demand that their women-folks cover themselves from head to toe. This practice is not common among the BAKWATA *sunnī* Muslims. The burial ceremonies also differ radically in the two groups. The BAKWATA-Muslims cover graves with a piece of clothing during burials so that people cannot spy what is happening when a body is being laid to rest. The Anṣār al-Sunna do not cover graves during burials. While the Anṣār al-Sunna abide by a printed calendar, the other Muslims depend on a lunar one. Naturally, this has implications for practices like the celebration of *ʿīd al-aḍḥā* (Arab.: Muslim festival at end of Hajj) in Tanzania. The Anṣār al-Sunna celebrate on the same day that it is celebrated in Mecca while the BAKWATA-*sunnī* groups celebrate

26 Personal interview with Mohammed, 4th September 2006.

ʿīd al-aḍḥā on a different day. These differences lead to controversy, year in, year out.

Kadhi's Court

The proposed Kadhi's court, so far, has not generated much interest in Kondoa. Muslims are keenly aware of its religious import. Yet some say it brings nothing new to the manner in which they have practised their religion until now. Some Muslim leaders suggest that the Kadhi's Court is not a grassroots' agenda but rather has been imposed from 'above'. A Bakwata-*sunnī* cleric summarized the situation in the following words:

> After independence we were advised that we ought to have one court system... people could choose whether they wanted their personal matters decided in a customary or a religious court... there existed a Marriage Board, an Inheritance Board, and a Divorce Board... now someone 'from above' has discovered that something is amiss... the Kadhi's courts must come back... Muslims must handle their own affairs in their proper courts.[27]

The re-introduction of Kadhi's courts in Kondoa lacks the urgency manifest in newspaper reports. Mostly Muslim interviewees were happy with the status quo. A local *Shīʿa* Muslim said: "We have always managed our affairs without any problem; I don't see why change now".[28] Usually Muslims have recourse to Mosque councils to solve their personal matters related to *waqf*, inheritance, and divorce. According to some, economic motivation underlies the clamour for the introduction of Kadhi's courts as some sheikhs want to join the government payroll.[29] The financing of the Kadhi's court is a moot point. Many people, mostly Christians, say it is unfair to use taxpayers' money to run a religious institution in a country with a secular Constitution. A female pastor with the Anglican Church said setting up and running a Kadhi's court must remain a prerogative of Muslims, not the government. A certain apprehension exists in some circles that once the government pays for the operation of the court, it might eventually interfere with the politics of its running. A troubling precedence exists. BAKWATA's current pariah status in some Muslim quarters is due to the perception that it was a government creation. Some feel the same might taint a government-supported Kadhi's court in future.

---

27 Personal Interview with Swalehe, 4th September 2007.
28 Personal interview with Hussein, 4th September 2007.
29 Personal interview with Hussein, 4th September 2007.

Lately, a new dimension in the Kadhi's court debate has emerged. In 2005 the ruling party, *Chama cha Mapinduzi* (CCM), promised to re-establish Kadhi's courts once re-elected. The matter has since divided the country along religious lines. Some Muslims want the party to live up to its promise while others feel that the country's secular Constitution should prevail over the ruling party's election manifesto. The President, a Muslim, is now distancing the party from the Kadhi's court agenda. Meanwhile, a moratorium has been imposed on the Kadhi's court debates pending a report of a Law Commission set up to give advice to the government on the matter.

Christian NGOs

Some Christian NGOs are a source of unease in the Muslim community in Kondoa. 'Compassion', for example, operates four children's centres under the auspices of the Lutheran and Anglican Churches. According to its motto, the NGO seeks to release children from poverty in Jesus' name. Its activities revolve around a child sponsorship programme with funds coming from North America and Europe. The prerogatives of sponsors include, "exchanging letters and photos as well as fostering children's spiritual growth". The children receive education, health care, supplemental nutrition, and the guidance from committed Christian workers.[30] According to Anglican and Lutheran pastors involved in the project, more than 75 percent of the children receiving sponsorship in Kondoa are either Muslims or Roman Catholics. Children, irrespective of their religious affiliations, are exposed to the Bible as the source of moral teachings. Muslim clerics wonder why expose Muslim children to Christian values and not vice versa. A BAKWATA-*sunnī* sheikh summarized the feelings of many Muslims thus:

> Children are asked to sketch a church, draw a cross, or to pray in a certain Christian manner during meal times. If Compassion is committed to religious democracy, why not teach children some Islamic practices as well? Tell them to draw a Mosque and see what happens....[31]

Members of Muslim groups like *Shīʿia*, Anṣār al-Sunna and BAKWATA-*sunnī* share the view that 'Compassion' activities among children are not

[30] Compassion 'Releasing Children from poverty in Jesus' name', http://www.compassioncanada.ca (accessed 14.06.2007).
[31] Personal Interview with Mohammed, 6th September 2006.

acceptable as they are tantamount to a covert proselytization programme. An Anglican pastor overseeing the Compassion programme, however, was unmoved by Muslims' complaints, maintaining 'Compassion' would continue to draw from the Bible as the principle source of moral values. "No one is forced to join the programme. So those who feel they don't want their children to participate are free to take them away".[32]

Furthermore, some Muslim children are taken to distant boarding schools to pursue secondary education. Control over the children's religious upbringing is not guaranteed. There are more than 15 children from Kondoa now attending secondary schools in Dar es Salaam under the 'protection' of 'Compassion'.[33] The timing of 'Compassion' activities on Saturdays is a source of disagreement. Children meet to write letters to their personal sponsors, but this baffles both Catholics and Muslims who feel that children are spirited away from catechetical and Qur'ān studies which usually take place on Saturdays. Some Muslims feel that poverty and hunger are excuses to impose Christian values on Muslim children.

Meanwhile, the 'Compassion' programme is generating tension in polygamous Muslim families where some children get help but others don't. Children receiving help under the 'Compassion programme' are seen as rich, according to a Muslim cleric. If such children refuse to share the 'goodies' with the rest of the extended family, it becomes a problem. Why 'Compassion' targets children in a culture where male adults are breadwinners is a matter of debate. A *Shī'a* cleric sees this as a way of making children used to Christian religion, namely, through schooling them and giving them clothing and cooking oil, among other things. Sometimes *ḥadīth* are invoked to underline the Muslims' fear of 'Compassion' activities among the needy Muslim children. A *ḥadīth* related by a *Shī'a* cleric is typical:

> Jesus' preaching was met with limited success among the early Jews, according to the *ḥadīth*. Jesus opted to reach out to children instead. After some time the elders realized that the children were absorbing Jesus' teachings. The elders decided that Jesus should not see the children again. When Jesus came, the village elders said the children were not around. A chuckle, however, was heard from inside a nearby house. "Who is that?" Jesus asked. "Piglets", the elders replied. Frustrated, Jesus went his way. Meanwhile, the children had become real piglets.[34]

32 Personal Interview John in Kampala, 6th July 2007.
33 Personal Interview with Hilda, 10th September 2006.
34 Personal interview with Hussein, 4th September 2007.

Whether the *ḥadīth* is apocryphal or not, the anecdote drives home the Muslims' disquiet over 'Compassion' and its activities among Muslim children. Some Muslims wrote a letter to the President of the United Republic accusing the NGO of using poverty as an excuse to convert Muslim children. Most religious leaders interviewed, while aware of the existence of the letter, could not produce a copy. The furore notwithstanding, 'Compassion' is not contemplating a change of strategy. Citing an Ethiopian experience where 'Compassion' had an ill-fated programme in the 1990s, one leader said the resistance from the Muslims in Kondoa would slacken with time. 'Compassion', in the Ethiopian case, was forced by members of a Muslim community to stop the programme. Yet, three years after the forced departure, people came "begging for us to return".[35]

Places of Worship

Pentecostal churches located in Muslim neighbourhoods are a source of serious disputes. This has brought a new dimension to *sharīʿa* debates in the area. Until the mid-1980s, few symbols of Christianity existed in Kondoa town centre. The Catholic Church, the oldest in the area, is located four kilometres outside town. Mosques and *madrasa* (Swah.: Qurʾānic schools) are found in every corner of the town of 21,000 people. Kondoa town is sometimes called *kwa vabonde* (Swah.: the place of the Bondei). The Bondei are a Muslim coastal ethnic group that brought Islam to the area. As a metaphor, *kwa kabonde* means a place of Muslims. This sense of ownership is reflected in the sentiments of a local Muslim populace. A Muslim cleric summarized the feelings of many Muslims when he said: "Kondoa is like Somalia—one ethnic group, one religion".[36] This view may no longer reflect the demographic reality on the ground. Pentecostal churches are challenging the dominance of Islamic institutions. The Full Gospel Church, for example, occupies land on which once stood the first mosque in Kondoa.[37] A female preacher with the Full Gospel Church offered a graphic picture of her early days as a missionary in Kondoa, a decade ago:

[35] Personal interview with John in Kampala, 6th July 2007.

[36] Personal interview with Rashid, 4th September 2007.

[37] Kabia, Hilda. 'An examination of Muslim and Christian relations in Dodoma urban and Kondoa districts, Dodoma region, Tanzania', St. Paul's United Theological College in Limuru, Kenya. Unpublished MA dissertation, 2006.

> When we arrived with my husband here, there were no Pentecostals. We went from door to door, house to house, telling people why we came. When we moved into our current building an Arab neighbour gave us an ultimatum: 'I don't like the noise (prayers) you are making. I am giving you seven days to clear out or face the consequences.[38]

The *sharīʿa* debates are becoming increasingly centred around the debate over ownership of the town. 'To whom does Kondoa belong?' is central to the debates according to most narratives. Other Church leaders share similar experiences of harassment. Calvary Assemblies of God (CAG) has had a short but chequered history. Founded in 2004, it drew a motley congregation of about 30 people who met for prayers in a public building. The members, however, were banned from using the premises owned by the Kondoa Municipal Council. The congregation dispersed; it is now rebuilding in a rented house, in a Muslim neighbourhood. Sometimes the congregation is pelted with stones during prayer sessions.[39] The government's failure to assign appropriate places for houses of prayer is largely to blame for some of the tension. A senior BAKWATA Muslim cleric said:

> Now you see churches and mosques side by side, this is something new...when I make a call for prayers...there is a bell tolling inviting Christians to pray...now if I say, Jesus is not God, according to my belief and someone else says Jesus is God in his church next door...there is conflict....[40]

Tensions notwithstanding, the religious demography of Kondoa remains simple. Most Rangi people, the dominant ethnic group in the area, are either *sunnī* Muslims or Roman Catholics. The Pentecostals are a growing but recent phenomenon. The Full Gospel Church (FGC) is still run by its founder, who came from northwest Tanzania. Pejoratively, some refer to FGC as "the church of the young Haya man". Haya is one of the prominent Tanzanian ethnic groups from the north-west of the country, but the ethnic allusion is a sign of disrespect. Despite evidence of mounting tension, people say the extent of conflict and disagreements among Muslims and Christians in Kondoa 'is exaggerated'.[41]

---

[38] Personal interview with Sophia, 2nd September 2006.
[39] Personal interview with Peter, September 2007.
[40] Personal interview with Swalehe, 4th September 2007.
[41] Personal interview with Matthew, 2nd September 2006.

Hardening Sectarian Attitudes

For many generations, religion has been a matter of personal choice among people in Kondoa. Intermarriages are common; virtually all families have members belonging to different religious affiliations. In Kondoa, people of different religious or ethnic backgrounds are not corralled into exclusive neighbourhoods, something which has encouraged understanding and tolerance. Yet a hardening of sectarian attitudes is evident, especially among the younger generations. Many Muslim youths are falling under the spell of the Anṣār al-Sunna, the fastest-growing Muslim group. An Anṣār al-Sunna cleric enthused: "We are everywhere in town, in villages around and even in the hills".[42] Some Anṣār al-Sunna Muslim youths get training outside the country, in Kenya, Saudi Arabia, or the Sudan, bringing back new ideologies. According to a young Anṣār al-Sunna, newly back from a study trip to Lamu, Kenya, the rationale for going was to learn 'true Islam'. This implies BAKWATA-sunnīs abide by mere traditions (*mapokeo*). The so-called 'true Islam', however, often entails turning one's back on traditional practices, harbouring new attitudes towards other Muslims.

Public Rallies (mihadhara)

Public rallies (Swah.: *mihadhara*) organized by Muslim groups are a source of constant friction. Muslims tend to use 'the Bible' as the basis of their public preaching. Muslim preachers cite verses Christians are said to contradict. A popular Biblical reference that Muslim preachers use is Psalm 115, said to condemn idolatry. Christians are baffled by Muslims' public rallies' propensity to attack elements of their faith. A Pentecostal elder summarized the frustrations of many Christians: "If Muslims say Jesus is not God it is fine. If we use the Qur'ān to illustrate some of our teachings, Muslims call in the police saying we have insulted their religion".[43] This is a perennial problem. Kondoa Anglicans once asked a Muslim convert to offer witness in a public rally; Muslims were riled. The convert, who had been an *imām*, is alleged to have received five million Tanzanian shillings (about US$5,000) to convert to Christianity so as 'to destroy Islam'. Muslims organized a counter rally 'to correct the teachings of the Muslim convert', as one sheikh said. The basis of the rally's sermons was the Bible. "We showed them the truth using the Bible . . . we said look

---

42 Personal interview with Juma, 4th September 2007.
43 Personal interview with Shannel, 7th September 2006.

here alcohol is forbidden... look here eating pork is forbidden... look here idolatry is forbidden".[44] Apparently the preaching was based on the Old Testament book of Leviticus. Such tit-for-tat tactics guarantee hardening of feelings across the religious divide.

Muslims and Non-Muslims

The younger people increasingly appraise one another through the prism of religion. A member of Full Gospel Fellowship Church said, "When growing up in the 1970s, we lived with Muslims like brothers... there was no difference... now if I look at a Muslim I know there is difference...".[45] The sentiment is mutual. An Anṣār al-Sunna cleric summarized the changing sentiments towards Christians in the following words: "If my relative were to become a Christian then the bond of kinship will be broken... a *kāfir* cannot inherit my property or share in my life".[46] Tolerance is tested in many other ways. Some Christians interviewed said their Muslim landlords won't allow them to host prayer-meetings.

Generation Gap

Younger Muslims and Christians appear to be less amenable to dialogue. Members of Anṣār al-Sunna view Christians—even their relatives—with limited respect. Sentiments like "If you are Christian, you are *kāfir*," are becoming common. A convert to Pentecostalism shared a dim view of Muslim-Christian relations:

> when I was young we didn't think much of our religious differences... now people point at you and say *mlokole* (Swah.: Born Again Christian)... now Muslims have been made to understand that Christianity is something, which should be wiped out of the face of the earth.[47]

The older people have recourse to phrases like: "Rangi people have no religious quarrels" and "Rangi people are blood brothers". The changing sentiments reflect an influence of new religious ideologies.

Marginalization and Victimization

Confession-specific institutions like kindergartens and primary schools are proliferating. Until the mid-1980s, children attended the same kinder-

---

[44] Personal interview with Mohammed, 6th September 2006.
[45] Personal interview with Shannel, 7th September 2006.
[46] Personal interview with Juma, 4th September 2006.
[47] Personal interview with Shannel, 7th September 2006.

gartens or schools irrespective of gender, religion or race. The country's policy put an emphasis on integration. Now there are orphanages and kindergartens exclusive to either Muslims or Christians. Older Muslims said there has never been overt marginalization in non-Muslim institutions like schools. Up to 75% of the students of Catholic mission schools in the 1950s were said to be Muslims.[48] A senior BAKWATA cleric who attended a Catholic Middle School acknowledged the lack of forced conversions in the schools. Over-emphasis on Qur'ānic studies at a tender age, and failure by many Muslim parents to check truancy, appear to have exacerbated the problem of literacy among Muslims.[49]

Conclusion

Several issues have emerged in the study.

One: *sharīʿa* debates appear to heighten religious awareness and tension in Kondoa. Issues of ownership of the town, and belonging, are becoming a prominent part of the *sharīʿa* debates. As a *Shīʿa* sheikh said: "Kondoa, like Somalia, is a place of one ethnic group and one religion". The arrival of the Anṣār al-Sunna is challenging the orthodoxy of the BAKWATA (mainstream) *Sunnī* and *Shīʿa* Muslims. Increasingly, people see themselves first as members of a specific religious group rather members of an ethnic group.

Two: tendencies reflecting generational perspectives are evident. Older people are optimistic that chaos born of religious conflict is not inevitable. The conviction is based on the view that ethnic bonds are stronger than religious ones. Among the younger people, religious discourses betray signs of incremental radicalisations.

Three: the discourses in Kondoa lack victimization rhetoric, which has characterized much of the discourses in the public sphere. The grassroots' preoccupation is with day-to-day problems: proselytization, intermarriage, contents of public rallies and churches encroaching into Muslim neighbourhoods. As a sign of recognition of potential conflict, there is an inter-religious committee charged with nipping problems in the bud. Both Muslim and Christian leaders interviewed said the committee is important in resolving conflicts in the area. The identity politics is encouraged by the teaching and arrival of new groups or sub-groups rather victim-making narratives among Muslims of Kondoa Municipality.

---

[48] Personal interview with Alois, 5th September 2006.
[49] Personal interview with Mariamu, 5th September 2006.

Four: the *sharīʿa* narratives in Kondoa do reflect the national recorded patterns on issues like Kadhi's court, Organization of Islamic Conferences (OIC), Danish cartoons, and the Middle East conflict. Events like the Iraq war or the Hezbollah-Israel war are celebrated in graffiti.

Five: there is a marked divergence between the micro-level discourses which are preoccupied with quotidian issues and the macro-level discourses pervaded by victimization and marginalization rhetoric.

Finally: African Traditional Religions acts both as a bridge as well as a wedge. Older people across the religious divide share a lot in terms of common ethnic heritage and usage. The younger Muslims belonging to Anṣār al-Sunna and Christian Pentecostals frown at many traditional practices as being incompatible with their worldview.

From the foregoing, it is clear there are two dimensions in the Sharia debates in Tanzania. One dimension is the macro-national level discourses dominated by academicians, politicians, and the media. Here, themes include the need for Kadhi's courts in Tanzania, victimization of Muslims (in 1999 some Muslims presented a list of 12 grievances to then President William Benjamin Mkapa), wearing of hijab in schools and workplaces, and the question of who is the authentic representative of Muslims in the public sphere. There are hundreds of Muslim organizations in the country. Another dimension is the micro-level grassroots' level discourses. Themes such as locations of places of worships in contested sites, activities of Christian NGOs, and preaching of hatred often emerge. In general there is a dissonance between the macro-level discourses, which are politicized, and the micro-level discourses which touch on peoples' daily lives.

BIBLIOGRAPHY

Abdulaziz, M. H., *Muyaka: 19th century Swahili Popular Poetry*, Nairobi: Kenya Literature Bureau, 1979.

Abun-Nasr, Jamil, 'Islamisches Recht im nigerianischen Rechtssystem', in *Muslime in Nigeria: Religion und Gesellschaft im politischen Wandel seit den 1950er Jahren*, Abun-Nasr, Jamil (ed.), Münster-Hamburg: Lit-Verlag, 1993.

Abun-Nasr, Jamil M., *The Tijaniyya—a Sufi Order in the Modern World*, London: Oxford University Press, 1965.

Adeleye, M. O., 'Islam and Education', *The Islamic Quarterly*, vol. XXVII, no. 1, 1983, pages 140–150.

Adenaike, F. A. (ed.), *The Pioneers*, Ibadan: Syndicated Limited, 1991.

Adetona, L. A., 'The dynamics of Independent Shariah Panel in Lagos State, South-West of Nigeria'. *Journal of the Nigeria Association of Teachers of Arabic and Islamic Studies*, vol. 8, 2005.

Aguilar, M. I., *Being Oromo in Kenya*, Trenton: Africa World Press, 1998.

Ahmed, C., *Les Conversions à l'Islam Fondamentalisme*, Paris: L'Harmattan, 2008.

Ajulu, Rok, 'Politicized Ethnicity, Competitive Politics and Conflicts in Kenya: A Historical Perspective', *African Studies*, 61:2, 2002, pages 251–268.

Akintola, I. L., *Shariah in Nigeria: an Eschatological Desideratum*, Ijebu-Ode: Shebiotimo Publication, 2001.

Algar, Hamid, *Wahhabism: A Critical Essay*, Oneonta, New York: Islamic Publications International, 2002.

Alhassan, Idris Abdullahi, 'The role of the School of High Islamic Studies Sarkin Mangu Jos in advancing the spread of Islamic culture and Arabic language for the years 1989 to 2001', Arabic Studies, University of Jos, BA Thesis (unpublished), 2003.

Ali, Osman M. Osman, 'Death-related Beliefs and Practices, an Area of Conflict in a Multicultural Community: Rural Shendi', M.Sc Thesis, University of Khartoum, 1994.

——, 'The Dynamics of Interpretation of Textual Islam in Northern Sudan: Case Study among the Rural and Urban Population of Shendi Province', Ph.D. Thesis, University of Khartoum, 2004.

Al-Qaradawi, Y., *The Lawful and the Prohibited in Islam* (*Al-Halal Wal Haram Fil Islam*), New Delhi: Millat Book Centre, 1960.

al-Zakzaky, Ibraheem, 'Application of Shari'ah in the contemporary world: Lessons from some Muslim countries', Paper presented to the national Conference on the Application of Shari'ah organized by the Department of Islamic Law, Faculty of Law, Bayero University and RAMNAN Law Consult, Kano, Bayero University, 1st to 3rd December 1999.

Ambali, M. A., *The practice of Muslim family law in Nigeria*, Zaria: Tamaza Publishing Company Ltd. 1998.

Anderson, J. N. D., *Islamic Law in Africa*, London: Frank Cass & Co. Ltd., 1970.

Anglican Church of Tanzania, *Kanisa la Anglikana Tanzania Agosti 2006, Tamko la Maaskofu wa Kanisa Anglikana Tanzania Kuhusu Hoja ya Mahakama ya Kadhi Tanzania Bara* (Unpublished document), [Anglican Church of Tanzania August 2006, Statement of the Bishops of the Anglican Church of Tanzania concerning the proposal for Kadhi's Courts in mainland Tanzania], Dodoma: Anglican Church of Tanzania, 2006.

An-Na'im, A. A. (ed.), *Islamic Family Law in a Changing World: A Global Resource Book*, London, Zed Books, 2002.

——, *African Constitutionalism and the Role of Islam*, Philadelphia, Pa.: University of Pennsylvania Press, 2006.

An-Nuur (Tanzanian Newspaper in Swahili), no. 997, 22nd–28th September 2006.

Asad, T., *The Idea of an Anthropology of Islam*, Washington, D.C.: Center for Contemporary Arab Studies, Georgetown University, 1986.

Askew, K. M., 'Female Circles and Male Lines: Gender Dynamics along the Swahili Coast', *Africa Today*, Volume 46, Number 3/4, Summer/Autumn 1999, pages 67–102.

Assal, Munzoul A. M., 'Displaced Persons in Khartoum: Current realities and post-war scenarios, Report', Cairo: The Population Council, 2004.

Bagshawe, F. J., 'The Peoples of the Happy Valley (East Africa): The Aboriginal Races of Kondoa Irangi. Part II: The Kangeju', *Journal of the Royal African Society*, Vol. 24, 1925, pages 117–130.

——, 'The Peoples of the Happy Valley (East Africa): The Aboriginal Races of Kondoa Irangi. Part III (Continued)', *Journal of the Royal African Society*, Vol. 24, 1925, pages 328–347.

——, 'The Peoples of the Happy Valley (East Africa): The Aboriginal Races of Kondoa Irangi. Part IV: The Goroa and Their Kindred Hamitic Tribes, the Wambulu, or Erokh, the Wasi, or Alawa, and the Burungi', *Journal of the Royal African Society*, Vol. 25, 1925, pages 59–74.

Baraza Kuu la Waislam wa Tanzania (BAKWATA), 'Letter to President Benjamin William Mkapa', 1999, www.igs.net/~kassim/nyaraka/barua_halmashauri.html.

Bang, A., 'Intellectuals and Civil Servants: Early 20th Century Zanzibar Ulama and the Colonial State', in *Islam in East Africa: New Sources*, Biancamaria Scarcia Amoretti (ed.). Rome: Herder, 2001, pages 59–98.

Barlas, S., *Believing Women in Islam: Understanding Patriarchal Interpretations of the Qur'an*, Austin: University of Texas Press, 2002.

Bashīr, Bashīr M., *al-taḥawwulāt al-kubra fi'l-Sūdān 1989–2000* (The Major Transformations in Sudan between 1989 and 2000), Khartoum: Future Studies Centre, 2002, (Published in Arabic).

Beck, K., 'Tribesmen, Townsmen and the Struggle over a Proper Lifestyle in Northern Kordofan', In *Kordofan Invaded*, Stiansen, Endre U. & Michael Kevane (eds.), Leiden: Brill, 1998, pages 255–264.

Bellucci, S., M. Katumanga & E. Otenyo, ' "Political" education versus "Civic" Education in colonial and Independent Kenya', *Africa: Rivista trimestrale di studi e documentazione Dell'Instituto italiano per l'Africa e l'Oriente*, 62.1, 2007, pages 1–19.

Berger, P., *Invitation to Sociology*, New York: Doubleday, 1963.

Brigaglia, Andrea, 'Two Published Hausa Translations of the Qur'ān and Their Doctrinal Background', *Journal of Religion in Africa*, 35 (4), 2005, pages 424–449.

Burrill, E. S., R. L. Roberts & E. Thornberry (eds.), *Domestic Violence and the Law in Colonial and Postcolonial Africa*, Athens: Ohio University Press, 2010.

Chama Cha Mapinduzi (CCM), 'Election Manifesto', Dodoma: Chama Cha Mapinduzi, 2005.

Chesworth, J. A., 'Fundamentalism and Outreach Strategies in East Africa: Christian Evangelism and Muslim *Da'wa*', in *Muslim-Christian Encounters in Africa*, Benjamin F. Soares (ed.), Leiden: Brill, 2006, pages 159–186.

——, *The Use of Scripture in Swahili Tracts by Muslims and Christians in East Africa*, doctoral thesis University of Birmingham, 2008, http://etheses.bham.ac.uk/150/

——, 'The Church and Islam: *Vyama Vingi* (Multipartyism) and the Ufungamano Talks', in *Religion and Politics in Kenya*, B. Knighton (ed.), Basingstoke: Palgrave, 2009, pages 155–180.

——, 'Kadhi's Courts in Kenya: Reactions and Responses', in *Constitutional Review in Kenya and Kadhis Courts*, A. Tayob and J. Wandera (eds.), Cape Town: Centre for Contemporary Islam, 2011, pages 3–17.

Christelow, A., 'Persistence and Transformation in the Politics of Shari'a, Nigeria, 1947–2003: In Search of an Explanatory Framework', in *Muslim Family Law in sub-Saharan Africa. Colonial Legacies and Post-colonial Challenges*, S. Jeppie, E. Moosa & R. L. Roberts (eds.), Amsterdam: Amsterdam University Press, 2010, pages 247–272.

Clarke, P. B., 'Islam, Education and the Development Process in Nigeria', *Comparative Education*, vol. 14, no. 2, 1978, pages 133–141.
Compassion International, 'Releasing Children from poverty in Jesus' name', http://www.compassioncanada.ca.
Comprehensive Peace Agreement (CPA), between the National Congress Party NCP and the Sudan People's Liberation Movement/Army SPLM/A, 2005.
Constitution of Kenya Review Commission (CKRC), 'Draft Bill of the Constitution of Kenya Review Commission', CKRC: Nairobi, 2002, www.kenyaconstitution.org.
——, *The Final Report of the Constitution of Kenya Review Commission*, Nairobi: CKRC, 10th February 2005.
——, *Source Book for Civic Education: Referendum 2005*, Nairobi, CKRC, September 2005.
Constitution of the Special Commission for the Rights of Non-Muslims in the National Capital, Ministry of Presidency Affairs, Republic of Sudan, 2006.
Constitution of the United Republic of Tanzania, 1997, with amendments to 2005, http://www.judiciary.go.tz/downloads/constitution.pdf.
Cruise O'Brien, Donal, 'Coping with the Christians: The Muslim predicament in Kenya', in *Religion and Politics in East Africa*, Bernt Hansen & Michael Twaddle (eds.), Oxford: James Currey, 1995, pages 200–219.
Csapo, M., 'Religious, Social and Economic Factors Hindering the Education of Girls in Northern Nigeria', *Comparative Education*, vol. 17, no. 3, 1981, pages 311–319.
da Costa, Y., *The Honor of Women in Islam*, Washington: The Supreme Council of America, 2002.
Daily Nation (Kenyan Newspaper), 'Referendum for results by province', 23rd November 2005.
Danfulani, Chikas, 'The Re-implementation of Sharia in Northern Nigeria and the Education of Muslim Women 1999–2007', University of Bayreuth, 2012, available as an e-thesis via http://opus.ub.uni-bayreuth.de/opus4-ubbayreuth/frontdoor/index/index/docId/1134.
Danfulani, Umar, H. D., *The Sharia Issue and Christian-Muslim Relations in Contemporary Nigeria*, Stockholm: Almqvist & Wikdsell International, 2005.
Doi, A. R. I., *Shari'ah: The Islamic Law*, London: Ta Ha Publishers Ltd., 1984.
——, *Islam in Nigeria*, Zaria: Gaskiya Corporation Ltd., 1984.
——, *Women in Shari'ah*, London, Ta Ha Publishers, 1996.
Eickelman, Dale F., *Moroccan Islam: Tradition and Society in a Pilgrimage Centre*, Austin: University of Texas Press, 1976.
——, *The Middle East and Central Asia: An Anthropological Approach*, New Jersey: Prentice Hall, 1997.
Eisenstadt, S. N. & W. Schluchter, 'Introduction: Paths to Modernities—A Comparative View', *Daedalus* 127:3, 1998, pages 1–18.
Eltigani, Eltigani E., *War and Drought in Sudan, Essays on Population Displacement*, Gainesville: University Press of Florida, 1995.
El-Affendi, A., *Turabi's Revolution. Islam and Power in Sudan*, London: Grey Seal, 1991.
El-Zein, Abdul Hamid, 'Beyond Ideology and Theology: The Search for the Anthropology of Islam', *Annual Review of Anthropology*, vol. 6, 1977, pages 227–254.
Esposito, J. L., *The Oxford Dictionary of Islam*, New York: Oxford University Press, 2003.
Esposito, J. L. & N. J. Delong, *Marriage in Muslim Family Law* (Second Edition), New York, Syracuse University Press, 2001.
Fluehr-Lobban, C., *Islamic law and society in the Sudan*, London: Frank Cass, 1987.
Fratkin, E., 'The Problems of Pastoral Land Tenure System in Kenya: Demographic, Economic and Political Process among Maasai, Samburu, Boran and Rendille, 1950–1990', *Working Paper in African Studies*, No. 177, Boston: Africa Studies Center, 1994.
Fry, George C. & J. R. King, *A Survey of the Muslim Faith*, Grand Rapids, Michigan: Baker Book House, 1980.

Gbadamosi, T. G. O., *The growth of Islam among the Yoruba, 1841–1908*, London: Longman Group Limited, 1978.
Gecaga, M. G., 'Religious Movements and Democratization in Kenya: Between the Sacred and the Profane', in *Kenya: The Struggle for Democracy*, G. R. Murunga & S. W. Nasong'o (eds.), Dakar: Codesria Books, 2007, pages 58–89.
Geertz, C., *Islam Observed: Religious Development in Morocco and Indonesia*, Chicago: University of Chicago Press, 1968.
Gellner, Ernest, *Muslim Society*, Cambridge: Cambridge University Press, 1981.
Gibb, H. A. R. & Kramers, J. H., *Shorter Encyclopaedia of Islam*, Leiden: Brill, 1953.
Gilsenan, Michael, *Recognizing Islam: An Anthropologist's Introduction*, London: Croom Helm, 1984.
Gumi, Sheikh Abubakar with Ismaila A. Tsiga, *Where I stand*, Ibadan: Spectrum Books Limited, 1992.
Hallaq, W. B., *A History of Islamic Legal Theories. An Introduction to Sunnī uṣūl al-fiqh*, Cambridge: Cambridge University Press (CUP), 1997.
——, *The Origins and Evolution of Islamic Law*, Cambridge: CUP, 2005.
——, *Sharīʿa—Theory—Practice—Transformations*, Cambridge: CUP, 2009a.
——, *An Introduction to Islamic Law*, Cambridge: CUP, 2009b.
Hamdun, Said & Nöel King, *Ibn Battuta in Black Africa*, Princeton: Markus Wiener Publishers, 2003.
Hashim, Abdulkadir, 'Muslim State Relations in Kenya after the Referendum on the Constitution,' in *AASR Bulletin* 24, November 2005, pages 21–27.
——, 'Coping with Conflicts: Colonial Policy towards Muslim Personal Law in Kenya and Post-Colonial Court Practice,' in *Muslim Family Law In Sub-Saharan Africa: Colonial Legacies and Post-Colonial Challenges*, S. Jeppie, E. Moosa & R. L. Roberts (eds.), Amsterdam: Amsterdam University Press, 2010, pages 221–245.
Hasan, Yusuf Fadl, 'The Penetration of Islam in the Eastern Sudan', in *Islam in Tropical Africa*, ed. Lewis, I. M., London: Oxford University Press, 1966, pages 144–159.
Hempel, Lynn, 'What's it worth to you? The Questionable Value of Instrumentalist Approaches to Ethnic Identification', in *Ethnicity, Ethnic Conflict and Peace Process: Comparative Perspectives*, E. A. Tirykian (ed.), London: Sage, 2004.
Hirsch, S. F., 'Kadhi's Courts as Complex Sites of Resistance: The State, Islam, and Gender in Postcolonial Kenya', in M. Lazarus-Black & S. F. Hirsch (eds.), *Contested States: Law, Hegemony, and Resistance.* New York: Routledge, 1994, pages 207–230.
——, *Pronouncing and Preserving: Gender and the Discourses of Disputing in African Islamic Court*, Chicago: University of Chicago Press, 1998.
——, 'State Intervention in Muslim Family Law in Kenya and Tanzania: Applications of the Gender Concept', in *Muslim Family Law In Sub-Saharan Africa: Colonial Legacies And Post-Colonial Challenges*, S. Jeppie, E. Moosa & R. L. Roberts (eds.), Amsterdam: Amsterdam University Press, 2010, pages 305–329.
Hjort, Anders, *Savanna town: Rural Ties and Urban Opportunities in Northern Kenya*, Stockholm: Stockholm Studies of Social Anthropology, 1979.
Hock, Klaus, *Der Islam Komplex. Zur Christlichen Wahrnehmung des Islams und der christlich-islamischen Beziehungen in Nordnigeria während der Militärherrschaft Babangidas*, Hamburg: Lit Verlag, 1996.
Hoexter, M., S. N. Eisenstadt & N. Levtzion (eds.), *The Public Sphere in Muslims Societies*, Albany: State University of New York, 2002.
Horton, M. and Middleton, J., *The Swahili: the social landscape of a mercantile society*, Oxford: Blackwell, 2000.
Human Rights Watch, 'Behind the Red Line: Political Repression in the Sudan', 1996, www.hrw.org/legacy/reports/1996/Sudan.html.
Hughes, T. P., *A Dictionary of Islam*, London: W.H. Allen & Co., 1978.
Husain, S. A., *The Glorious Caliphate*, Lucknow: Islamic Research and Publications-Series No. 73, 1974.

Iliffe, John, *A Modern History of Tanganyika*, Cambridge: Cambridge University Press, 1999.

Imtiyaz, S. Yusuf, 'Islam and African Socialism: A Study of the Interactions between Islam and Ujamaa in Tanzania', (unpublished dissertation), University Microfilms International (UMI). Ann Arbor, Michigan, 1990.

Isiolo District Poverty Reduction Strategy Paper: Consultative Report for the Period 2001–2004, Nairobi: Ministry of Finance and Planning, 2001.

Itifaki ya Biblia: Orodha ya maneno yote ya Agano la Kale na Agano Jipya na Madondoo Yake, Dodoma: Central Tanganyika Press, (Swahili Bible Concordance), 1990.

Jama'atu Izalatil Bid'a Wa Ikamatis Sunnah (JIBWIS), *al-Jamā*ᶜ *fī Suṭūr* (the Society in a few sentences), JIBWIS-Headquarters-Jos-Nigeria, nd., (in Arabic).

——, 'Izala Constitution', JIBWIS-Headquarters-Jos-Nigeria, nd.

Janmohamed, K. K., *A history of Mombasa c. 1895–1939; some aspects of economic and social life in an East African port town during colonial rule*, unpublished PhD thesis, Northwestern University, 1978.

Jawad, H. A., *The Rights of women in Islam: An Authentic approach*, London: Macmillan Press, 1998.

Jeppie, S., E. Moosa & R. Roberts (eds.), *Muslim Family Law in Sub-Saharan Africa: Colonial Legacies and Post-Colonial Challenges*, Amsterdam: Amsterdam University Press, 2010.

Jewel, J. H. A., *Mombasa: The Friendly town*, Nairobi: East African Publishing House, 1976.

Johnson, S. *The history of the Yorubas*, Lagos: C.S.S. Bookshops, 1976.

Johnston, H. H. & F. J. Bagshawe, 'The Peoples of the Happy Valley (East Africa) Part I', *Journal of the Royal African Society*, Vol. 24, 1924, pages 25–33.

Jumbe, Aboud, *The Partnership: Tanganyika—Zanzibar Union 30 Turbulent Years*, Dar es Salaam: Amana Publishers, 1994.

Kabia, Hilda, 'An examination of Muslim and Christian relations in Dodoma urban and Kondoa districts, Dodoma region, Tanzania' (unpublished MA dissertation), St. Paul's United Theological College in Limuru, Kenya, 2006.

Kadouf, Hunud Abia, 'Religion and conflict in the Nuba Mountains', in *Religion and Conflict in Sudan*, Yusuf Fadl Hasan & Richard Gray (eds.), Nairobi: Paulines Publications Africa, 2002, pages 107–113.

Kane, Ousmane, *Muslim Modernity in Postcolonial Nigeria, A Study of the Society for the Removal of Innovation and Reinstatement of Tradition*, Leiden: Brill, 2003.

Karrar, Ali Salih, *The Sufi Brotherhoods in the Sudan*, London: Hurst & Company, 1992.

Kebbede, Girma (ed.), 'Introduction', in *Sudan's Predicament, Civil war, displacement and ecological degradation*, Aldershot: Ashgate, 1999.

Kenya Gazette, *The Proposed New Constitution of Kenya* (Special Issue), Supplement No. 63, Nairobi, 22nd August 2005.

Ketefe, Kayode, 'Forty-seven Percent of Nigerians are illiterates', *The Punch* (Nigerian Newspaper), Tuesday 20th June 2006, http://www.punchng.com/main/article04.

Khalil, Mohamed Ibrahim, 'Human Rights and Islamization of the Sudan Legal System', in: *Religion and Conflict in Sudan*, Yusuf Fadl Hasan & Richard Gray (eds.), Nairobi: Paulines Publications Africa, 2002, pages 58–71.

Khalil, Fatima, 'Women's Rights Under Sharia', in *Understanding Shari'a in Nigeria: proceedings of National seminar on Shari'a*, A. M. Yakubu, A. M. Kani & M. I. Junaid (eds.), Ibadan: Spectrum Books Limited, 2001.

Kim, C. C., *Islam Among the Swahili in East Africa*, Nairobi: Acton Publishers, 2004.

Kindy, Hyder, *Life and Politics in Mombasa*, Nairobi: East African Publishing House, 1972.

King, M. (ed.), *God's Law versus State Law: Construction of an Islamic Identity in Western Europe*, London: Grey Seal Books, 1995.

Kogelmann, Franz, 'The 'Sharia factor' in Nigeria's 2003 Elections', in *Muslim-Christian Encounters in Africa*, Benjamin F. Soares (ed.), Leiden: Brill, 2006, pages 256–274.

Köndgen, O., *Das islamisierte Strafrecht des Sudan. Von seiner Einführung 1983 bis Juli 1992*, Hamburg: Mitteilungen des Deutschen Orient-Instituts 43, 1992.

——, 'Sharia and national law in the Sudan', in *Sharia Incorporated. A Comparative Overview of the Legal Systems of Twelve Muslim Countries in Past and Present*, Otto, J. M. (ed.), Leiden: Leiden University Press, 2010, pages 181–230.

Kresse, Kai, *Philosophising in Mombasa: Knowledge, Islam and Intellectual Practice on the Swahili Coast*, Edinburgh: Edinburgh University Press Ltd, 2007.

Kubai, A., 'Christian-Muslim Relations in Kenya since Independence,' in *Interface between Research and Dialogue: Christian-Muslim Relations in Africa*, Klaus Hock (ed.). Münster: LIT, 2004, pages 32–65.

Kyewalyanga, F.-X. S., *Marriage customs in East Africa: With special reference to selected tribes of Kenya: Akamba, Bantu Kavirondo, Gusii, Kipsigis, Luo, Nandi, and Teita*, Hohenschäftlarn: Renner Publication, 1978.

Latin, David, 'The Sharia Debate and the origins of Nigeria's Second Republic', *The Journal of Modern African Studies*, Vol. 20, No. 3, 1982, pages 411–430.

Law Review Commission of Tanzania *Report on the Law of Succession*, Dar es Salaam, LRCT, 2004, http://www.lrct-tz.org/pdf/mirathi.pdf.

Layish, A. and G. R. Warburg, *The Reinstatement of Islamic Law in Sudan under Numayrī. An evaluation of a legal experiment in the light of its historical context, methodology, and repercussions*, Leiden: Brill, 2002.

League of Imams and Alfas, 'Memorandum submitted to Osun State House of Assembly on review of 1999 Constitution by the League of Imams and Alfas of Osun State on behalf of the Muslim Community of Osun State', December 1999.

Legesse, Asmarom, *Oromo Democracy: An Indigenous African Political System*, Trenton and Asmara: Red Sea Press, 2006.

Lodhi, Abdulaziz & David Westerlund, 'Tanzania', in *Islam Outside the Arab World*, David Westerlund & Ingvar Svanberg (eds.), Richmond: Curzon, 1999, pages 97–110.

Loimeier, Roman and Rüdiger Seesemann (eds.), *The Global Worlds of the Swahili*, Hamburg: LIT Verlag, 2006.

Loimeier, Roman, 'The Writings of Nasiru Kabara (Muḥammad al-Nāṣir al-Kabarī)', *Sudanic Africa*, vol. 2, 1991, pages 165–74.

——, *Islamic Reform and Political Change in Northern Nigeria*, Evanston: Northwestern University Press, 1997.

Luanda, N. Nestor, 'Christianity and Islam Contending for the Throne on the Tanzanian Mainland', in *Challenges to the Nation-State in Africa*, O. Olukoshi Adebayo & Liisa Laakso (eds.), Uppsala: Nordiska Afrikainstitutet, 1996, pages 168–182.

Ludwig, Frieder, 'After Ujamaa: Is Religious Revivalism a Threat to Tanzania's Stability?' in *Questioning the Secular State*, David Westerlund (ed.), London: Hurst & Company, 1996, pages 216–236.

——, 'Christian–Muslim Relations in Northern Nigeria since the Introduction of Shari'ah in 1999'. *Journal of the American Academy of Religion* 76, 2008, pages 602–637.

Lynch, Gabrielle, 'The Fruits of Perception: "Ethnic Politics" and the case of Kenya's Constitutional Referendum', *African Studies* 65, 2, December 2006, pages 233–268.

M'Inoti, Kathurima, 'Beyond the "Emergency" in the North Eastern Province: The Legal Regime under the N.E. Province and Contiguous Districts Regulations, 1966', in *Constitutional law and politics in Africa: A Case Study of Kenya*, K. Kibwana (ed.), Nairobi: Claripress, 1998, pages 315–338.

Maddox, Gregory H. & James L. Giblin, (eds.), *In Search of a Nation: Histories of Authority and Dissidence in Tanzania*, Dar es Salaam: Kapsal Educational Publisher, 2005.

Mahdi, Saadatu Shehu, '*Women's Rights under Sharia*', a presentation at a political briefing organized by the John D. and Catherine MacArthur Foundation in Abuja, Nigeria, February, 2002.

Mahmoud, Mohamed, 'When *Shari'a* Governs: The Impasse of Religious Relations in Sudan', *Islam and Christian-Muslim Relations*, Vol. 18, No. 2, 2007, pages 275–286.

Mahon, J., 'What Happened in 1906?', Souvenir Special 100 Years of Mission 1906–2006 *Messenger: Journal of the Seventh-day Adventist Church in the United Kingdom and Ireland* Volume 111.17, 2006.

Makinde, A. K., 'The Institution of Sharī'ah in Oyo and Osun States, Nigeria, 1890–2005', Ph.D thesis, University of Ibadan, Ibadan. 2007, http://www.sharia-in-africa.net/pages/publications/the-institution-of-sharia-in-oyo-and-osun-states-nigeria.php.

Makinde, Abdul-Fatah 'Kola & Ostien, Philip, 'Legal Pluralism in Colonial Lagos: The 1894 Petition of the Lagos Muslims to their British Colonial Masters', *Die Welt des Islams*, 52:1, 2012, pages 51–68.

Malik, S. H. A., 'The Shari'ah in the life of a Muslim', in *Islamic tenets and the Shari'ah*, I. A. B. Balogun (ed.), Ibadan: Sam Bookman Publishers, 2000.

Marjomaa, Risto, 'The Long struggle for the Shari'a in Northern Nigeria', *Studia Orientalia (Helsinki)* 103, 2006, pages 39–66.

Maxon, Robert M., *East Africa: Introductory History*, Nairobi: East African Educational Publishers, 1986.

Mazrui, Alamin M. & Ibrahim Noor Shariff, *The Swahili Idioms and Identity of an African People*, New Jersey: Africa World Press, 1994.

Mazrui, Ali A., *The African Condition: A Political Diagnosis*, London: Heinemann, 1980.

Mbogoni, Lawrence E. Y., *The Cross versus the Crescent: Religion and Politics in Tanzania from the 1880s to the 1990s*, Dar es Salaam: Mkuki na Nyota Publishers, 2004.

Middleton, John, *The World of the Swahili*, New Haven: Yale University Press, 1992.

Miles, Matthew B. & A. Michael Huberman, *Qualitative Data Analysis* 2nd edit., London: Sage, 1994.

Ministry of Information, *Information month 2000—democracy day*, Osogbo: Osun State Government Press, 2000.

Ministry of Presidency Affairs, *Constitution of the Special Commission for the Rights of Non-Muslims in the National Capital*, Khartoum: Ministry of Presidency Affairs, 2006.

S. Mirza & M. Strobel, (eds. trans.), *Three Swahili Women: Life histories from Mombasa*, Bloomington: Indiana University Press, 1989.

Mombasa District Council, *Mombasa District Development Plan*, 1989–1993, Mombasa: Mombasa District Council, 1988.

Mpangala, Gaudens, *Peace, Conflicts, and Democratization Process in the Great Lakes Region: The Experience of Tanzania*, Dar es salaam: Institute of Development Studies University of Dar es Salaam 1999, http://www.iiuc.org/iaup/esap/publications/dar/mpangala1.pdf.

Mungeam, G. H., *Kenya: Select Historical Documents 1884–1961*, Nairobi: EAEP, 1978.

Mwakimako, H., 'Christian-Muslim Relations in Kenya: A Catalogue of Events and Meanings,' *Islam and Christian Muslim Relations*, Vol 18, No. 2, April 2007, pages 287–307.

——, '*Kadhi* Court and Appointment of *Kadhi* in Kenya Colony' *in Religion Compass* 2/4, 2008, pages 424–443.

Mwinyihaji, Esha F., 'The Contribution of Islam toward Women's Emancipation: A case study of the Swahili Muslims in Mombasa District, Kenya', M.Phil Thesis (unpublished), Moi University, 2001.

——, *The Persistence of Divination Among the Swahili Muslims in Kenya: Beliefs and Practices*, Saarbrücken: LAP Lambert, 2010.

Nageeb, S. A., *New Spaces and Old Frontiers. Women, Social Spaces and Islamization in Sudan*, Lanham: Lexington Books, 2004.

Nakanishi, H., 'Power, Ideology, and Women's Consciousness in Post-revolutionary Iran', in *Women in Muslim Societies: Diversity Within Unity*, H. L. Bodman & N. Tobidi (eds.), London: Lynne Rienner Publishers, 1998, pages 83–100.

Nasong'o, S. W., *Contending Political Paradigms in Africa: Rationality and Politics of Democratization in Kenya and Zambia*, New York and London: Routledge, 2005.

Neufeld, D. K. (ed.), *Seventh Day Adventist Encyclopedia*, Washington: Review and Herald Publishers Association, 1976.

Nigerian National Planning Commission, *Meeting Everyone's Needs: National Economic Empowerment and Development Strategy*, Abuja: Nigerian National Planning Commission, 2004.

Nimtz, August H., *Islam and Politics in East Africa: The Sufi Order in Tanzania*, Minneapolis: University of Minnesota Press, 1980.

Njozi, M. Hamza, *The Mwembechai Killings and the Political Future of Tanzania*, Ottawa: Globalink Communications, 2000.

Noibi, D. O. S., *Islamic perspective*, Ijebu-ode: Shebiotimo Publishers, 1998.

O'Brien, Susan M., 'La Charia contestée: Démocratie, débat et diversité musulmane dans les 'état Charia' du Nigeria', *Politique Africaine* 106, 2007, pages 46–68.

Okunola, M. A., 'The relevance of Shari'ah to Nigeria', in *Islam in Africa*, N. Alkali, A. Adamu, A. Yadudu, R. Motem & H. Salihi (eds.), Ibadan: Spectrum Books Ltd. 1993, pages 23–35.

Oloo, A. G. R., 'The Contemporary Opposition in Kenya: Between Internal Traits and Manipulation', in *Kenya: The Struggle for Democracy*, G. R. Murunga & S. W. Nasong'o (eds.), Dakar: Codesria Books, 2007, pages 90–128.

Omari, Cuthbert K., 'The Management of Tribal and Religious Diversity', in *Mwalimu: The Influence of Nyerere*, C. Legum & G. Mmari (eds.), Dar es Salaam: Mkuki & Nyota, 1995, pages 25–31.

Omolo, Ken, 'Political Ethnicity in Democratisation Process in Kenya', *African Studies*, 61:2, 2002, pages 209–221.

Osiro, R. A., 'Polygamy Among Muslim Women in Kendu Bay and Kiboswa, Nyanza Province, Kenya', MA Dissertation (unpublished), St. Paul's United Theological College, Limuru, 2006.

Ostien, Philip, 'An opportunity missed by Nigerian Christians', in *Muslim Christian Encounters in Africa*, Benjamin F. Soares (ed.), Leiden: Brill, 2006, pages 221–255.

——, *Sharia Implementation in Northern Nigeria 1999–2006: A Sourcebook, 5 volumes*, Ibadan: Spectrum Books Ltd., 2007, http://www.sharia-in-africa.net/pages/publications/sharia-implementation-in-northern-nigeria.php.

——, 'Divine Law and Local Custom in Northern Nigerian Zina Trials,' *Die Welt des Islams* 49. 3–4, 2009, pages 429–465.

Ostien, Philip, Jamila M. Nasir & Franz Kogelmann (eds.), *Comparative Perspectives on Shari'ah in Nigeria*, Ibadan: Spectrum Books Limited, 2005.

Ostien, P. & A. Dekker, 'Sharia and national law in Nigeria', in *Sharia Incorporated*, Otto, J. M. (ed.) Leiden: Leiden University Press, 2010, pages 553–612.

Osun State Government, *Osun State so far*, Osogbo: Ministry of Information, 1992.

Özden, Melik, *Internally Displaced Persons: An overview of the right of internally displaced persons of the Guiding Principles adopted by the United Nations*, Part of a Series of the Human Rights Programme Of the Europe—Third World Centre (CETIM), 2007.

Paden, John N., *Muslim Civil Cultures and Conflict Resolution: The Challenge of Democratic Federalism in Nigeria*, Washington D.C.: Brookings Institute Press, 2006.

Peters, Ruud, *Islamic Criminal Law in Nigeria*, Ibadan: Spectrum Books Limited, 2003.

Quraishy, M., *Textbook of Islam Book* 2, Nairobi: The Islamic Foundation, 1987.

Rasmussen, Lissi, *Christian-Muslim Relations in Africa: The Case of Northern Nigeria and Tanzania Compared*, New York: St. Martin's Press, 1993.

Ruto P., M. Adan & I. Masinde, *Indigenous Democracy: Traditional Conflict Resolution Mechanisms—Pokot, Turkana, Samburu and Marakwet.* Nairobi: ITDG-East Africa, 2004.

——, *Conflicts in Northern Kenya: A Focus on the Internally Displaced conflict victims in Northern Kenya*, Nairobi: ITGA-EA & DTP Martin Karimi Publishers, 2003.

Ṣaḥīḥ al-Bukhārī, http://www.usc.edu/schools/college/crcc/engagement/resources/texts/muslim/hadith/bukhari

Ṣaḥīḥ al-Muslim, http://www.usc.edu/schools/college/crcc/engagement/resources/texts/muslim/hadith/muslim

Said, A. S., 'An outline history of Islam in Nyanza Province', in *Islam in Kenya: Proceedings of the National Seminar on Contemporary Islam in Kenya*, M. Bakari & S. S. Yahya (eds.), Nairobi, MEWA, 1995, pages 19–27.

Said [Saeed], M. 'Islam and Politics in Tanzania', Dar es Salaam: Muslim Writers Association, http://www.igs.net/~kassim/nyaraka/islam_and_politics_in_tz.html.

Said, Mohamed, 'Intricacies and Intrigues in Tanzania: The Question of Muslim Stagnation in Education', *Change* 1993. http://www.igs.net/~kassim/nyaraka/Elimu2.html.

——, *The Life and Times of Abdulwahid Sykes (1924–1968): The Untold Story of the Muslim Struggle against British Colonialism in Tanganyika*, London: Minerva Press, 1998.

Ṣāliḥ ʿAbd al-Qādir Ṣāliḥ, al-Shaykh, *Al-munaẓẓama al-siyāsa al-waḥīda alatī lahā athar ʿalā al-waḥda al-waṭanīya fi'l-sūdān* [The One Single Political Organization and its Impact on the National Unity in Sudan], npd, 1997.

Salih, M. A. Mohamed, 'Islamic NGOs in Africa: Promise and Peril of Islamic Voluntarism' in *Islamism and Its Enemies in the Horn of Africa*, Alex de Waal (ed.), London: Hurst & Company, 2004, pages 146–181.

Salim, Ahmed Idha, *Swahili Speaking Peoples of Kenya's Coast, 1895*–1945, Nairobi: East Africa Publishing House, 1973.

Sanneh, Lamin, 'Preface: Religion and Conflict in Sudan', in *Religion and Conflict in Sudan*, Yusuf Fadl Hasan & Richard Gray (eds.), Paulines Publications Africa, Nairobi, 2002.

Sanni, A., 'The Sharīᶜa Conundrum in Nigeria and the Zamfara Model: The Role of Nigerian Muslim Youth in the Historical Context', *Journal of Muslim Minority Affairs*, Vol. 27, No. 1, 2007, pages 117–132.

Schacht, J., *An Introduction to Islamic Law*, Oxford: Clarendon Press, 1964.

Schrijver, P. (ed.), *Islam in Contemporary Sub-Saharan Africa*, Leiden: African Studies Centre, 2006.

Shadle, Brett L., 'Bridewealth and Female Consent: Marriage Disputes in African Courts, Gusiiland, Kenya', *Journal of African History* 44, 2003, pages 241–262.

Shivji, Issa G. (ed.), *Constitutional and Legal System of Tanzania: A Civics Sourcebook*, Dar-es-Salaam: Mkuki na Nyota Publishers Ltd, 2004.

Shorter, Aylward, *African Culture-An Overview: Social-Cultural Anthropology*, Nairobi: Paulines Publications Africa, 1998.

Sicard, von S., 'Tanzania', In *Encyclopedia of Islam* 2nd Edition, (eds.) P. Bearman, T. Bilquis, C. E. Bosworth, E. van Donzel & W. P. Heinrichs, Volume 10 Fas. 165–166, Leiden: Brill, 1998, pages 194–196.

Sidahmed, Abdel Salam, 'The Unholy War: Jihad and the Conflict in Sudan', in *Religion and Conflict in Sudan*, Yusuf Fadl Hasan & Richard Gray (eds.), Nairobi: Paulines Publications Africa, 2002, pages 83–96.

Sidahmed, A., *Politics and Islam in Contemporary Sudan*, London: Routledge, 1997.

Sivalon, John, *Kanisa Katoliki na Siasa ya Tanzania: 1953 mpaka 1985*, Ndanda: Mission Press, 1985.

Spaulding, Jay, 'Precolonial Islam in Eastern Sudan', in *The History of Islam in Africa*, Nehemia Levtzion & Randall L. Pouwels (eds.), Oxford: James Currey Ltd, 2000, pages 117–129.

Spear, Thomas P., *The Kaya Complex: A History of the Mijikenda Peoples of the Kenya Coast to 1900*, Nairobi: Kenya Literature Bureau, 1978.

Sperling, David C., 'The Coastal Hinterland and Interior of East Africa', in *The History of Islam in Africa*, Nehemia Levtzion & Randall L. Pouwels (eds.), Oxford: James Ltd., Oxford, 2000, pages 273–302.

Stambach, A., *Faith in Schools: Religion, Education, and American Evangelicals in East Africa*, Stanford: Stanford University Press, 2010.

Steeves, J., 'Beyond Democratic Consolidation in Kenya: Ethnicity, Leadership and "unbounded" politics', *African Identities*, Vol. 4, No. 2, 2006, pages 195–211.

Stiles, E. E., 'A Kadhi and His Court: Marriage, Divorce, and Zanzibar's Islamic Legal Tradition', (doctoral dissertation), St. Louis, Missouri, UMI, 2002.

——, 'When is a Divorce a Divorce? Determining Intention in Zanzibar's Islamic Courts', *Ethnology*, 42, 4, 2003, pages 273–288.

——, 'There is No Stranger to Marriage Here!' Muslim Women and Divorce in Rural Zanzibar', *Africa: Journal of the International Africa Institute*, 75, 4, 2005, pages 582–598.

——, 'Broken Edda and Marital Mistakes: Two Recent Disputes from an Islamic Court in Zanzibar,' in *Dispensing Justice in Islam: Qadis and their Judgements*, Masud, M. K., R. Peters & D. S. Powers (eds.), Leiden: Brill, 2006, pages 95–116.

——, *An Islamic Court in Context: An Ethnographic Study of Judicial Reasoning*, London: Palgrave Macmillan, 2009.

Stockreiter, E. E., 'Child Marriage and Domestic Violence: Islamic and Colonial Discourses on Gender Relations and Female Status in Zanzibar, 1900–1950s', in *Domestic Violence and the Law in Colonial and Postcolonial Africa*, Burrill, E. S., R. L. Roberts & E. Thornberry (eds.) Athens, OH: Ohio University Press, 2010, pages 138–158.

——, 'Islamisches Recht und sozialer Wandel: Die Kadhi-Gerichte von Malindi, Kenya, und Zanzibar, Tanzania', *Stichproben. Wiener Zeitschrift für kritische Afrikastudien* 2/3, 2002, pages 35–61.

——, 'Tying and untying the knot: Kadhi's courts and the negotiation of social status in Zanzibar, 1900–63', PhD thesis (unpublished), SOAS, University of London, 2008.

Sudan.Net, *Major Sudanese Political Parties*, http://www.sudan.net/government/parties.html.

Suleiman, G. Ibrahim, 'Mallam Ibrahim El-Zakzaky and the Question of Shi'ism', Islamic Studies, B.A.-Dissertation (unpublished), University of Jos, 2005.

Sunan Abū Dawūd, http://www.usc.edu/schools/college/crcc/engagement/resources/texts/muslim/hadith/abudawud.

Tanzania National Archives, Acc. AB 2587: Native law and Customs 1919–1922, Dar es Salaam.

Tayob, A. & J. Wandera (eds.), *Constitutional Review in Kenya and Kadhis Courts*, Cape Town: Centre for Contemporary Islam, 2011.

The Draft Constitution of Kenya 2004, adopted by the National Constitutional Conference on the 15th March 2004.

Thompson, John, 'Tanzanian president offers formula for West-Islam peace', *BU Today*, 2006, http://www.bu.edu/phpbin/news-cms/news.

Tier, Akolda M., 'Mixed Civil, Sharia and Customary Jurisdictions and laws in an ethnic conflict setting: the case of Sudan', in *Religion and Conflict in Sudan*, Yusuf Fadl Hasan & Richard Gray (eds.), Nairobi: Pauline's Publications Africa, 2002, pages 72–82.

Udo, R. K. & Mommon, A. B. (eds.), *Nigeria: Giant in the tropics*, Lagos: Gabumo Publishing Comp. Ltd. 1993.

Ukah, Asonzeh, *The Redeemed Christian Church of God (RCCG), Nigeria: Local Identities and Global Process in African Pentecostalism* PhD, Dissertation (PDF version), Bayreuth: Bayreuth University, 2003, available as an e-thesis via http://opus.ub.uni-bayreuth.de/opus4-ubbayreuth/frontdoor/index/index/docId/59.

Umar, Muhammad S., 'Sufism and Anti-Sufism in Nigeria', MA-thesis (unpublished), 1988.

——, 'Islamic Revivalism Today: the case of Jama'atu Izalat Al-Bidah Wa-Iqamat Al-Sunna', Islamic Studies, BA-Thesis (unpublished), University of Jos, 1983.

——, 'Profiles of New Islamic Schools in Northern Nigeria', *The Maghreb Review*, Vol. 28, 2–3, 2003, pages 146–169.

United Republic of Tanzania Parliamentary Debates (Hansard), National Assembly Official report, Seventh meeting, 11th June to 26th June 1963.

Vikør, K. S., *Between God and the Sultan.* Reading the Sacred Text from a Woman's Perspective, London: Hurst & Company, 2005.

Voll, John O. 'The Eastern Sudan, 1822 to the Present', in *The History of Islam in Africa*, Nehemia Levtzion & Randall L. Pouwels (eds.), Oxford: James Currey Ltd., 2000, pages 153–167.

Wadud, M. A., *Qur'ān and Woman. Reading the Sacred Text from a Woman's Perspective*, Kuala Lumpur: Penerbit Faraj Bakti, 1994.

Wani Gore, Paul, 'The Socio-economic and demographic consequences of population displacement in Sudan', in *Current studies on the Sudan*, Medani Mohamed M. Ahmed (ed.), Khartoum: Omdurman Ahlia University, 1998.

Wario, H. A., *Debates on Kadhi's Courts and Christian-Muslim Relations in Isiolo Town, Kenya*, MPhil Thesis (unpublished), Moi University, 2010.

Weimann, G. J., *Islamic Criminal Law in Northern Nigeria*, Amsterdam: Amsterdam University Press, 2010.

——, 'Islamic Law and Muslim Governance in Northern Nigeria: Crimes Against Life, Limb and Property in *Shari'a* Judicial Practice', *Islamic Law and Society* 17, 3, 2010, pages 375–419.

Westerlund, David, *Ujamaa na Dini: A Study of Some Aspects of Society and Religion in Tanzania, 1961–1977*, Stockholm: Acta Universitas Stockhomiensis, 1977.

Westerlund, David & Ingvar Svanberg (eds.), *Islam Outside the Arab World*, Richmond: Curzon, 1999.

Wijsen, Frans & Bernadin Mfumbusa, *Seeds of Conflict: Religious Tensions in Tanzania*, Nairobi: Paulines Publications, 2004.

Yakubu, A. M., A. M. Kani & M. I. Junaid (eds.), *Understanding Shari'a in Nigeria: proceedings of National seminar on Shari'a*, Ibadan: Spectrum Books Limited, 2001.

Yusuf, H. B., 'Managing Muslim-Christian Conflicts in Northern Nigeria: A Case Study of Kaduna State', *Islam and Christian-Muslim Relations*, Vol. 18, No. 2, April 2007, pages 237–256.

CONTRIBUTORS

Salma Mohamed Abdalla completed her MSc in Political Science at University of Khartoum in 2008. She is a PhD candidate at the Bayreuth International Graduate School of African Studies, University of Bayreuth, Germany. The topic of her PhD thesis is "Coping with Water Scarcity: the Role of Zakat Institutions in Water Distribution in Khartoum".

She is a Junior Researcher, on Water Management in Khartoum International Research Project (WAMAKHAIR), and Internal Coordinator, Africa Good Governance Network.

Ramzi Ben Amara holds a Master's degree in Religious Studies from the University of Bayreuth, Germany. As a member of Bayreuth International Graduate School of African Studies he was awarded his PhD in 2011 for "The Izala-movement in Nigeria: Its Split, Relationship to Sufis and Perception of the Sharia-Implementation". He is currently engaged in post-doctoral research at the University of Cape Town for the project "Biographies of Religious Engagement".

John Chesworth worked in East Africa for over twenty years, in Tanzania and Kenya, establishing the MA course in Islam and Christian-Muslim Relations at St. Paul's United Theological College (now St. Paul's University). He holds a PhD (2008) in Islamic Studies from the University of Birmingham. Currently he is Research Officer for an AHRC-funded project "Christian-Muslim Relations: A Bibliographical History 1500–1900" (CMR1900) based at the University of Birmingham. He is on secondment from the Centre for Muslim-Christian Studies in Oxford where he is an Honorary Research Fellow of St. Stephen's House. He has published articles on Islamic law in East Africa and on the use of the Bible and Qurʾān in polemical discourse.

Chikas Danfulani is a lecturer in the Religion and Philosophy Department, University of Jos, Nigeria. She recently completed her PhD on "The Re-implementation of Sharia in Northern Nigeria and the Education of Muslim Women 1999–2007" at Bayreuth International Graduate School of African Studies, University of Bayreuth, Germany.

Franz Kogelmann has been researching on Islam in Africa for more than 20 years. He is principal investigator of the Bayreuth International School of African Studies, University of Bayreuth and academic co-ordinator of the Institute of African Studies at the same University. He earned a PhD (1997) in Islamic Studies from the University of Bayreuth. He was the director of the "Sharia Debates and Their Perception by Muslims and Christians in Selected African Countries" (2006–2009) project and co-ordinated the "Sharia Debates and the Shaping of Christian and Muslim Identities in Northern Nigeria since 1999" (2002–2003) project, both funded by Volkswagen Foundation. Currently he is conducting research on *zakāt* in Northern Nigeria. He has published extensively on Islamic endowments (*waqf*) in Northern Africa and Islamic law in sub-Saharan Africa.

William A. Kopwe recently defended his PhD in Religious studies at the Open University of Tanzania. He received his Master's degree in Islam and Christian-Muslims Relations from St. Paul's United Theological College, Limuru, Kenya in 2006. He is an ordained pastor of the Evangelical Lutheran Church in Tanzania, and is currently working at the Interfaith and ecumenism desk of the Christian Council of Tanzania.

Abdul-Fatah Kola Makinde holds a Master's degree (1995) in Arabic and Islamic Studies and a PhD (2007) in Islamic Studies from the University of Ibadan, Nigeria. Since 2007, he has been a lecturer at the Department of Religious Studies of Ọbafẹmi Awolọwọ University in Ile-Ife, Nigeria.

Bernardin Mfumbusa received a PhD (2004) in Social Communication from Gregorian University, Rome. He was Senior Lecturer in Journalism and Deputy Vice-Chancellor Academic Affairs of St. Augustine University of Tanzania (SAUT), Mwanza, until 2011. A recipient of the Clement Mwila Award for excellence in journalism (2000) from the Nairobi-based Koinonia Centre, he has been on the Board of the Media Council of Tanzania since 2006. Recently he has become Bishop of the newly formed Catholic Diocese of Kondoa. He has published on journalism in Africa and Muslim-Christian Relations in Tanzania.

Esha Faki Mwinyihaji is a 2012–2013 post-doctoral fellow with the Foundation for Inter-religious and Intercultural Dialogue, University of Geneva. She received her MPhil in Islamic Studies from Moi University in 2001. She is also a lecturer at Maseno University where she completed her PhD in 2009,which has been published as *The Persistence of Divination Among the Swahili Muslims in Kenya: Beliefs and Practices*, Saarbrücken: LAP Lambert, 2010.

Rebecca Osiro received her Master's degree in Islam and Christian-Muslims Relations from St. Paul's United Theological College, Limuru, Kenya in 2006. She is a PhD candidate in Religious Studies at Maseno University, Kenya. Currently she is working for the Mennonite Church where she serves as an ordained minister.

Osman Mohamed Osman Ali received his MSc and his PhD (2004) degrees from the University of Khartoum, Sudan. Currently he is Assistant Professor at the Department of Sociology and Social Anthropology, Faculty of Economic and Social Studies, University of Khartoum. He has wide experience in teaching at diverse Sudanese institutions of higher learning and in consultancy work for NGOs.

Halkano Abdi Wario studied for his MPhil in Religious Studies at Moi University, Kenya. He was awarded his PhD in 2012 by Bayreuth International School of African Studies, University of Bayreuth, Germany, for his thesis "Networking the Nomads: A Study of Tablīghī Jamaʿāt among the Borana of Northern Kenya".

INDEX